SAVING ISRAEL

Also by Daniel Gordis

God Was Not in the Fire:
The Search for a Spiritual Judaism

Does the World Need the Jews?
Rethinking Chosenness and American Jewish Identity

Becoming a Jewish Parent:
How to Explore Spirituality and Tradition with Your Children

If a Place Can Make You Cry:
Dispatches from an Anxious State

Home to Stay:
One American Family's Chronicle
of Miracles and Struggles in Contemporary Israel

Coming Together, Coming Apart:
A Memoir of Heartbreak and Promise in Israel

SAVING ISRAEL

How the Jewish People Can
Win a War That May
Never End

DANIEL GORDIS

John Wiley & Sons, Inc.

Published by John Wiley & Sons, Inc., Hoboken, New Jersey
Published simultaneously in Canada

For general information about our other products and services, please contact our Customer Care Department within the United States at (800) 762–2974, outside the United States at (317) 572–3993 or fax (317) 572–4002.

Wiley also publishes its books in a variety of electronic formats. Some content that appears in print may not be available in electronic books. For more information about Wiley products, visit our web site at www.wiley.com.

Library of Congress Cataloging-in-Publication Data:

Gordis, Daniel.
    Saving Israel : how the Jewish people can win a war that may never end / Daniel Gordis.
        p.   cm.
    Includes bibliographical references and index.
    ISBN 978-0-471-78962-8 (cloth)
        1. Israel—Politics and government—21st century.   2. National characteristics, Israeli—Psychological aspects.   I. Title.
    DS128.2.G67   2009
    956.05'4—dc22
                                                                    2008036262

Printed in the United States of America

10 9 8 7 6 5 4 3 2

In memory of
Professor Seymour Fox, וַ"ל

Teacher, mentor, and cherished friend
who brought us here
and changed the course of our lives

בֶּן־אָדָם, הָעֲצָמוֹת הָאֵלֶּה
כָּל־בֵּית יִשְׂרָאֵל הֵמָּה;
הִנֵּה אֹמְרִים, יָבְשׁוּ עַצְמוֹתֵינוּ
וְאָבְדָה תִקְוָתֵנוּ—נִגְזַרְנוּ לָנוּ.

O mortal, these bones are
the whole House of Israel.
They say, "Our bones are dried up,
our hope is lost; we are doomed."
Ezekiel 37:11

עוֹד לֹא אָבְדָה תִּקְוָתֵנוּ,
הַתִּקְוָה בַּת שְׁנוֹת אַלְפַּיִם,
לִהְיוֹת עַם חָפְשִׁי בְּאַרְצֵנוּ

Our hope is not yet lost,
The hope of two thousand years
To be a free people in our land.
"*Hatikvah*," Israel's national anthem

Contents

ISRAEL, POST EUPHORIA

Who is wise?
The one who can foresee consequences.
—Babylonian Talmud

In the summer of 2007, Avrum Burg, scion of a distinguished Israeli political family, a former speaker of the Knesset, a former chairman of the Jewish Agency, and a man widely acknowledged in Israel as possessing both a prodigious intellect and a promising political future, published his controversial book, *Victory Over Hitler*. In it he claimed that "to define the State of Israel as a Jewish state is the key to its end. A Jewish state is explosive. It's dynamite." Burg, once seen as a possible future leader of Israel's long-dominant Labor Party, doubted that a Jewish democratic state could survive. In a postpublication interview with Israel's most elite daily newspaper, he urged Israelis to obtain foreign passports, presumably to prepare to leave.

Ironically, Burg's book appeared almost forty years to the day after the end of the Six Day War. That war had left Israelis feeling triumphant and invincible; it had seemed to set aside for once and for all the question of whether the Jewish state could survive.

In the days prior to June 1967, it was far from clear that Israel would survive. In the period now called the *hamtanah*, "the waiting," Israelis were beyond worried, preparing for the worst. Amassing its army and saber rattling, Egypt lay to the south. To the east, Israel faced Jordan, and to the north, Syria and Lebanon. All had vowed to destroy the Jewish state. As historian Michael Oren recounts in his masterful best-seller, *Six Days of War*:

> Throughout the country, thousands were hurrying to dig trenches, build shelters, and fill sandbags. In Jerusalem . . . schools were refitted as bomb shelters, and air raid drills were practiced daily. . . . An urgent request for surgeons . . . was submitted to the Red Cross, and extra units of plasma ordered from abroad. . . . Upwards of 14,000 hospital beds were readied, and antidotes stockpiled for poison gas victims, expected to arrive in waves of 200. Some 10,000 graves were dug.

But the doomsday scenarios never materialized. In a lightning preemptive strike, Israeli jets destroyed Egypt's air force just hours before it would have attacked the Jewish state, and the Israel Defense Forces captured the Sinai Peninsula and the Gaza Strip from Egyptian forces. From Syria, Israel took the strategically critical Golan Heights. From Jordan, which ignored Israel's warnings to stay out of the war and foolishly joined the fray, the IDF seized the West Bank of the Jordan River and the eastern half of Jerusalem. In six quick days, Israel tripled its size, from 8,000 to 26,000 square miles.

Finally Israel seemed to be out of danger. True, at the Khartoum conference three months after the war, Israel's Arab enemies still insisted that there would be "no peace, no recognition and no negotiations" with Israel, but neither Israelis nor American Jews paid much attention to the bluster of Khartoum. At long last, Jews worldwide felt secure. Israel seemed invincible. From America to the Soviet Union, a new pride in Israel—and in being Jewish—began to emerge. American Jews came out of the woodwork as they never had before, and Soviet Jews began what would become a relentless campaign to receive permission to emigrate.

Finally it seemed that the Shoah* and its threats had been relegated to the past. The Jews had an indestructible home; from now on, they would no longer be slaughtered at the whim of others. Everything had changed. The Jewish future appeared brighter than it had in hundreds of years.

And the reason for that bright future was the State of Israel.

But within a decade or two, a new challenge arose. Now the Palestinians insisted that they, too, deserved a state. (For our purposes, we will ignore the raging debate as to whether the Palestinians are, in fact, a nation, and why and how their "nationalism" was "created." The world accepts the argument that they are a nation, as do many Israelis, and that is the fact that Israel must reckon with.) After initial resistance, some Israelis and many American supporters of Israel began to view this nascent Palestinian nationalism as something akin to the American civil-rights movement—it was a movement representing people who had not received their due, who simply wanted to be treated fairly. African Americans wanted equal pay and social access, just like whites had. And Palestinians only wanted statehood, just like the Jews had. Despite a few high-profile Palestinians committed to terror and to Israel's destruction, Palestinian nationalism was essentially about human rights. Given a chance to realize their dreams, they would make the accommodations necessary to live beside the Jewish state.

Or so it seemed. Decades later, we know that that assessment was wildly optimistic. Rather than being a civil-rights movement with a terrorist element, Palestinian nationalism has proved itself a terror-based movement dressed in civil-rights garb. By and large, Palestinian leadership is sadly much more intent on destroying Israel than on working toward statehood and a better life for the Palestinian rank

---

*"Shoah" in Hebrew means "calamity." "Holocaust" is an English word that means "burnt offering" or "sacrifice to God." The Jews of Europe in the 1930s and 1940s were not sacrificed—they were murdered. There is a tremendous difference; this book uses the word "Shoah" in order to take that difference seriously.

and file. Those people who had believed that territorial accommodation would bring the conflict to an end were sadly proven wrong.

But Americans and Israelis refused to give up. In 2000, President Bill Clinton invited Israeli prime minister Ehud Barak and Palestinian chairman Yassir Arafat to Camp David for meetings that were designed to achieve a long-term settlement between the warring parties. According to Ambassador Dennis Ross, who served as Clinton's point man on the peace process during that period, Barak made far-reaching concessions on both territory and security. But the talks collapsed in July 2000, and two months later, war erupted.

The war didn't actually "erupt," of course. It was carefully and consciously orchestrated at least in part by Arafat, who'd had his bluff called. Still defying calls to accept Israel's existence, Arafat responded to Barak's offer by unleashing a wave of terrorism, commonly but mistakenly called the Second Intifada,* or even more cynically, the "Al Aksa Intifada." The war kept Israel miserable and fearful for four long years. Eventually, despite horrific losses on both sides, Israel's security forces managed to get the upper hand. A protective barrier was constructed along significant portions of Israel's eastern border, army intelligence successfully infiltrated much of the Palestinian terrorist network, and security inside Israel improved considerably. Gradually the violence that had kept Israel in its grip for so long began to subside.

Amazingly, Israelis decided to take yet another stab at creating peace and launching a Palestinian state. Prime Minister Ariel Sharon, long considered a right-wing hawk and nicknamed the "Bulldozer," boldly announced that he would undertake a unilateral withdrawal ("Disengagement") from Gaza in order to move Israeli troops to more defensible lines and to further the prospect of Palestinian statehood. The Disengagement meant uprooting thousands of Israelis from homes

---

*"Intifada" in Arabic means "popular uprising," which this war was not. This was not the people's uprising, and there was nothing spontaneous about it. It was executed by Arafat's security forces and other terror organizations, which he controlled and financed to various extents. For that reason, this book shies away from the term "intifada" and refers to those years as what they were—the Palestinian Terror War.

and communities that they'd built over decades. Some of these people had already been displaced once before from their homes in Yamit, an Israeli town that was evacuated in 1982 when the Sinai Desert was returned to Egypt. But still, Sharon insisted, he was going to proceed with the plan, no matter how unpopular it was in certain circles.

Despite all the prognostications to the contrary and the worry about a possible civil war, the Disengagement unfolded as scheduled in August 2005 and went smoothly. Not a shot was fired. People wept bitterly as they were led from the houses they had built, from the synagogues in which they'd celebrated and mourned. Anguished at leaving behind the communities in which their parents and their children had lived side by side, they were heartbroken, but they did not resist. The security forces, which had enormous firepower at their disposal, used none; by and large, they treated the people they were removing with extraordinary respect and compassion. It was one of Israel's more dignified moments, and it left some previously worried or despondent Israelis with a deep sense of pride, and with more than a glimmer of hope.

Israel had approached the precipice of civil war but had backed away. The Palestinians now had more land and another opportunity to begin building a state; maybe the region would witness the beginnings of a nascent Palestine with which Israel could finally reach a long-term accommodation.

But those hopes were soon dashed once again. Soon after the Disengagement was completed, Palestinians capitalized on Israel's departure and began a relentless wave of *kassam* rocket fire on Israeli civilian population centers adjoining the Gaza border. As Israelis waited to see what Sharon, "Mr. Security," would do in response, the prime minister suffered a massive stroke and fell into a permanent coma.

The *kassam* rocket fire was followed by the Palestinians' election of Hamas instead of Fatah; many Palestinians apparently preferred a terrorist organization publicly committed to Israel's destruction to the party that Yassir Arafat had started. Arafat's party had at least said publicly— even if Israelis no longer believed it—that it was ready to negotiate. Now Palestinians appeared uninterested even in the charade.

Israelis felt duped. Some were angry, most were depressed. Peace with the Palestinians—which Israelis had assumed only a few years earlier was both inevitable and just around the corner—now seemed less achievable than ever.

And then, less than a year after the Disengagement, Israel fought yet another war. Three Israeli soldiers were kidnapped from inside Israel's borders, one near Gaza and two on the northern border with Lebanon. When the latter two were kidnapped, full-scale war quickly erupted. Prime Minister Ehud Olmert, who had been elected after Sharon's incapacitation, promised a suddenly united populace that Israel would win a decisive victory, and that the war would not end until Hezbollah was disarmed and dismembered and the captured soldiers brought home.

But Israel fared poorly in the thirty-four-day war. Surprised by a Hezbollah more determined and better trained than it had expected, the IDF could not end the fire of Katyusha rockets on Israel's north. Eventually, with Hezbollah still very much intact and with the sol-diers still in captivity, their fates unknown, Israel agreed to a cease fire. It was lost on few Israelis that there was no substantive territorial dispute between Israel and Hezbollah. The issue was not borders but Israel's very existence. Short of going out of business, there was noth-ing that Israel could have done to appease Sheikh Hassan Nasrallah and his fighters. Yet unable to avert the conflict, Israel also seemed incapable of winning it.

In the forty-odd years since the lightning victory in the Six Day War, everything had changed. In 1967, Israel had won decisively; in 2006, Israel had lost. In 1967, Israel faced enemies in the form of states. Now, instead of facing nation-states such as Egypt, Jordan, and Syria, Israel faced terror organizations that could, and did, hide among a civilian population for which they felt no responsibility. And Islamic Jihad, Hezbollah, and Hamas were supported not by Egypt and Jordan, but ultimately by Iran, with its seemingly limitless petro-dollars and its looming nuclear capability.

Suddenly territorial compromise was not the issue. What was at stake was the future of the Jewish state, nothing more, nothing less. And that future seemed much less certain than it had just four decades earlier.

Israel entered a period of deep depression, compounded by a series of corruption scandals that included, by the time it reached its height, the two chief rabbis, two former justice ministers, senior officials in the Tax Authority, the police chief (as well as the man suggested as his replacement), the president (who was accused of rape), and the prime minister (implicated in six different alleged schemes) himself. Beset by enemies, Israelis began to speak about losing faith in themselves and in their ability to create a decent, civil, law-abiding society.

The euphoria was gone; once again, the looming question was whether Israel could actually survive. Even Avrum Burg, that former speaker of the Knesset, was saying that it couldn't.

A year after Burg's book appeared, a friend of ours visited us in Jerusalem. It was the summer of 2008. A prisoner exchange agreement with Hezbollah had been signed, sporadic talks with Hamas to free Gilad Shalit were still under way, and Ehud Olmert's government was exploring the possibility of serious peace negotiations with the Syrians. But very few people in Israel were optimistic. Even Israel's perennially upbeat President Shimon Peres, whose vision of a "new Middle East" had once inspired many, admitted that there was "no chance of peace with the Palestinians."

And our friend, a nationally respected leader of American Jewish life, simply couldn't bear the pessimism. With his deeply rooted sense that people at their core are decent and reasonable, he just could not understand how even our fifteen-year-old son, Micha, shared the view that he'd heard earlier in the week from General Yaakov Amidror (the former head of research in Army Intelligence). Amidror had said that no peace with the Palestinians was possible, and that none would be for at least a generation. Enormously bright, exceedingly well educated, and chronically optimistic, our friend was hearing things during his trip to Israel that simply didn't cohere with any picture he had of how American Jews ought to think about Israel.

Ultimately, as the painful conversation wore on, he focused his questions into two: "Why, really, has Israel given up hope?" he wanted to know. "And with no genuine chance for peace, why forge on?" They seemed to be reasonable questions, but as my daughter, Talia, pointed out to me a few days later, they were also wrong. "We've given up hope for *peace,*" Talia said to me, "but that doesn't mean we've given up hope." Israel had only "given up hope" if the sole hope that Israel has is for peace. But it isn't. And as for why forge on, Talia pointed out, that's only a legitimate question if Israel's only purpose is to live in peace, if it has no other reason for being. "But wanting peace isn't the same thing as being *about* peace," my daughter said. And she was right.

Yet most observers of Israel, both in Israel and outside, do not see matters that way. When they think of Israel's hopes, they think almost exclusively of peace. When asked what they want most for Israel, they respond that they want peace and security. Beyond that, they have little to say. When asked to imagine an Israel that might not ever know peace, they cannot. When asked why Israel ought to continue to exist if it will be at war well into the indefinite future, they are not certain how to respond.

That has to change. Tragically, genuine peace does not yet appear possible between Israel and its enemies. Therefore, if Israel is to survive, if Israelis are to make lives and raise their children in a country continually at war, they will need to be able to articulate to themselves why a Jewish state matters and why preserving Israel is worth the sometimes excruciating price that it exacts. Though Israel does face real threats from Iran and from terrorist groups much closer to home, those can all be dealt with—if Israelis know why their country exists and are committed to its survival. To survive, Israel needs citizens at home and supporters abroad who can articulate why the Jewish state exists in the first place and who can then take the necessary steps to preserve it. This book is designed to further that goal.

Can Israel survive? Does it deserve to? Those are the questions about Israel that are in vogue today. To be sure, some excellent books have been written to address these questions and to bolster Israel's case. Some respond point by point to the most common accusations against Israel. Others have asked *whether* Israel can survive. But the question of whether Israel can survive isn't terribly interesting. Prophecy, the Jewish tradition asserts, is a role that has now been given to fools and children. Especially in the Middle East, predicting the future is a highly risky and usually fruitless venture.

Of much greater importance than asking *whether* Israel can continue to exist is examining the question of *why* Israel's survival might matter in the first place. What has Israel done for the Jewish people? How has Israel changed Jewish life not only inside the Jewish state, but around the world? Do the Jews really need a state? And if they do, what must they do to save it?

Those are the questions this book sets out to address. In the first two chapters, I ask why the Jews *really* need a state, and how sovereignty is intended to wholly alter Jewish life. In the following five chapters, we will examine a variety of factors that now threaten the Jewish state, most of them having little to do with Israel's enemies. The final five chapters outline a variety of steps Israel must take if the dream of Jewish sovereignty is not to be lost.

Not everyone will be comfortable with what is discussed or suggested in these pages. But as is true with all of life's difficult questions, there is no avoiding them. With matters concerning Israel as with life in general, we *can* retreat, refusing to raise the painful issues. Or we can choose to think, to struggle, and to grow. This book opts for the latter choice, the pain that that choice sometimes entails notwithstanding. It does so not because there is joy in recognizing the depths of the challenges that Israel faces. Rather, we raise these issues in the hope that, convinced once again of Israel's necessity, Zionists will find the strength to stride forth with courage and vision, leading Israel to a future that is even more inspiring than its past has already been.

Chapter One

THE STATE THAT REINVENTED HOPE

O mortal, these bones are the whole House of Israel.

They say, "Our bones are dried up, *our hope is lost*; we are doomed."

—Ezekiel 37:11

Our hope is not yet lost,

The hope of two thousand years, To be a free people in our land,

—*"Hatikvah,"* Israel's national anthem

An unspoken Rorschach test is unfolding across the world today, with young Jews both in Israel and in the Diaspora. Asked to name the first thing that they associate with the word "Israel," many of these young people, and even some who are older, immediately conjure up images and words such as "Palestinians." Or "war." Conflict. Apartheid. Occupation. Checkpoints. Refugees. Intifada. Bombings. Danger. The images are increasingly negative, and for many, there is often a considerable sense of embarrassment, or shame, when they think about Israel.

This, of course, was not always the case. Not terribly long ago, among American Jews, and among many non-Jewish Americans, mention of Israel evoked images such as "democracy." The Little Engine That Could. Scrappy. Ally. Beacon of freedom. Recovery. Democracy. Miracle. Pride.

The transformation in the world's perception of Israel has been rapid, and massive. A recent study asked American Jews whether the destruction of Israel would be a personal tragedy for them. The study, we should note, asked about the *destruction* of Israel, not its gradual disappearance, or the slow withering away of the state. The study asked about a cataclysmic disappearance, and with it, presumably, a good portion of the six million Jews (itself a highly ironic number) who now dwell there. Among Jewish Americans sixty-five years of age and older, more than 80% said that Israel's destruction would, indeed, be a personal tragedy for them. But amazingly, among those aged thirty-five and younger, a full 50% said that it would not.

In many ways, this is not difficult to understand. This younger generation of Jews, both in Israel and beyond, came of age when the Shoah was no longer a recent memory, when the existence of the State of Israel seemed as natural as the rising of the sun. Like their Israeli counterparts, they have no recollection of the United Nations vote on November 29, 1947, nor any recall of the War of Independence in which survival hung in the balance for months. Today's young Americans, Jewish and not, have no memory of Israeli food rationing during the early 1950s, when there literally wasn't enough to eat in Israel. They didn't experience the *hamtanah* before the Six Day War, when Israel's very fate, and that of its population, was in question. Many of the young people unknowingly participating in this Rorschach test came of age long after the Yom Kippur War, when hundreds of Syrian tanks, virtually unopposed, were poised to slice through Israeli defenses but for some unknown reason turned around and retreated.

The first major memory that this generation has of Israel is not of 1947, 1948, 1956, 1967, or 1973, but of the emergence of organized Palestinian nationalism, and the Palestinians' extraordinarily effective use of a combination of terrorism and the international media to press their case. This generation can say very little about why the Jews might need a state, or why Jewish statehood might be legitimate. These people came of age during the Intifada, when Palestinians began to use violence to press their demands for an end to Israel's occupation and demanded the same sovereignty that the Jews had once wanted.

By the 1980s, the Palestinian demands sounded reasonable. They echoed the rhetoric of civil-rights advocates in America, of opponents of apartheid in South Africa, and of seekers of freedom across the globe. They seemed akin to the aspirations of Tibetans under Chinese domination, Chechnyans under Russia, and Basques under Spain. Indeed, many Israelis couldn't help but notice that the Palestinians were using much of the rhetoric that the Jews themselves had used prior to 1948. The Palestinians, in many ways, were the new Jews.

Young American and Israeli Jews had no idea how to respond. Jews as an "occupying power" sounded ugly and humiliating, not something of which these kids could be proud. If the Jews had a state, why couldn't the Palestinians? If Israeli soldiers were really preventing pregnant Palestinian women in labor from getting to hospitals by stopping them at roadblocks, how could these students *not* feel embarrassed?

How the occupation started, what security issues had led to the roadblocks, or what devastation Palestinian terrorism had wrought in Israeli society, this younger generation often did not know. No one told them, and they did not ask. They simply knew that the status quo had to end and that until it did, Israel would be a source of shame.

A similar development is unfolding inside Israel itself. A younger generation of Israelis, distanced not only from the Shoah but from the heady, ideologically impassioned decades of Israel's early years, has also grown tired of the occupation. They have wearied of manning those checkpoints, of being described by the international community in terms formerly reserved for Israel's enemies. They have watched generation after generation being drafted, paying a horrific cost in life and limb, all for a conflict that seems to have no solution. And when asked why Israel should exist, why things wouldn't be much simpler without the Jewish state, even many young Israelis are increasingly uncertain how to respond.

Like their American counterparts, these Israelis also know very little of their own history. But unlike the young Americans, the Israelis see Palestinian suffering from very close, and for many, there is simply no way to deny the horrific conditions, poverty, and fear of many Palestinian civilians, or Israel's role in at least part of their despondency. That fact, coupled with these young Jews' inability to say anything particularly coherent about why the Jews might need a state, means that they focus only on the evils of Israeli behavior and the suffering of the Palestinians, a conversation from which they never emerge feeling very good about who they are, or what their country is.

If Israel is to survive, this has to change. Israel's citizens and its supporters simply must be able to say something coherent about why the Jews need a state. What did the early Zionists believe that sovereignty would do for the Jewish people? What new ideas does Zionism need, now that a century has passed since Theodor Herzl convened the First Zionist Congress in Basel in 1897? If they remain unable to answer these questions, Jews will not commit to the project called Israel. Israelis will not commit to military service, or even to spending their adult lives in Israel. Without some sense that Zionism is *about* something, the State of Israel will inevitably begin to falter.

Thus questions about why Israel matters, about why the Jews want and need a state, and about what the state was supposed to do to transform the Jewish people, could not be more critical at precisely this hour.

In the neighborhood in Baltimore where I grew up, there were no streets named for dates. We had street names like Pimlico Road, Greenspring Avenue, and Woodvalley Drive, but nothing I can recall that contained a date.

Not far from our apartment in Jerusalem, though, and adjacent to the high school we chose for our sons, there's a street named "The Twenty-ninth of November." There's no year in the street name; none is needed. When the street was named, everyone in Jerusalem and throughout Israel knew what *kaf tet be-November* represented. The year was 1947, the date of the UN vote to divide British-ruled

Mandatory Palestine into two states, one Jewish and one Arab. It was
the date that made the project called Israel possible.

It was a day of voting, but of images, too. Of Jews huddled around
radios the world over, holding their breath, waiting to see if perhaps
the twentieth century might finally bear some better tidings for the
Jews. Of the cheering and the crying when the vote was over. Of
the dancing in the streets of Tel Aviv when the roll call had been completed. Of the sense that something had changed, that the tide had
shifted. Of the hope that out of the ashes of Europe something positive might still arise.

Hope. That is what the State of Israel has represented to Jews ever
since its creation. It was hope that Israel restored to the Jews; and it is
hope that would be utterly lost if Israel ever succumbed.

Amos Oz, perhaps Israel's greatest novelist and one of its most
important public intellectuals, captures that night in 1947 better than
anyone I know. He describes his family listening to the radio, following the roll call vote:

> At that the voice suddenly stopped, and an otherworldly silence
> descended and froze the scene, a terrified, panic-stricken
> silence, a silence of hundreds of people holding their breath,
> such as I have never heard in my life either before or after that
> night.

Then Oz describes the reaction after the vote:

> Our faraway street on the edge of Kerem Avraham in north-
> ern Jerusalem . . . roared all at once in a first terrifying shout
> that tore through the darkness and the buildings and trees,
> piercing itself, not a shout of joy, nothing like the shouts of
> spectators in sports grounds or excited rioting crowds, perhaps
> more like a scream of horror and bewilderment, a cataclysmic
> shout, a shout that could shift rocks, that could freeze your
> blood, as though all the dead who had ever died here and
> all those still to die had received a brief window to shout,
> and the next moment the scream of horror was replaced by

roars of joy and a medley of hoarse cries and "The Jewish People Lives."

"The Jewish People lives." Whether or not most Jews are conscious of it, this is the implicit message of the State of Israel. Many do not hear it because the mere notion that a state can have a message seems counterintuitive. But strange as the idea may sound to the contemporary ear, hope, and an insistence that "the Jewish People lives," are precisely the point of the Jewish state. Indeed, the naturalness with which contemporary Jews think about a Jewish future is due in no small measure to that message of the Jewish state. Later Oz describes how after a night of singing and celebrating, his usually reserved father, now drenched in sweat from the dancing, climbed into bed with him, as he'd never done before. And his father told him of how his own father had been tormented by Christian hooligans in Europe, and how there was nothing he could do.

> My father told me under my blanket in the early hours of November 30, 1947, "Bullies may well bother you in the street or at school someday. They may do it precisely because you are a bit like me. But from now on, from the moment we have our own state, you will never be bullied just because you are a Jew and because Jews are so- and so-s. Not that. Never again. From tonight that's finished here. Forever."

His father's tears and tenderness emerged from a sense that history was changing, that somehow, because the Jews were going to have a state, their lives would never be the same. Hope, it now seemed possible, could prevail over despair.

Though Oz's own story has nothing at all to do with the Shoah, there's no way to make sense of the euphoria in Jewish communities across the world that night without recalling that the vote at the United Nations took place just less than three years after the liberation of Auschwitz in January 1945. The cloud of the destruction of European Jewry still hung heavily over Jewish life across the globe. The creation of the Jewish state, the first major positive turn in years,

heralded, Jews hoped, an end to what had been one of the worst
centuries in all of Jewish history. They knew that virtually the entire
world had conspired either to annihilate the Jews or to permit their
annihilation, all the while pretending to be aghast. After all, FDR
had closed the shores of the United States to Jewish refugees, as had
Canada, and the United States had failed to allocate even one bombing mission to the railroad tracks leading to Auschwitz. The British,
for their own internal reasons, had also prevented Jews who were
fleeing Hitler from entering Palestine. Now the creation of a Jewish
state suggested that life might still triumph and years of encroaching
extinction might have ended.

Israel provided hope when it seemed that hope had died.

And ever since then, Israel has represented for Jews the triumph of
life over death, of hope over despair, of the possibility of a future when
a decimated past seemed to cloud every view. Indeed, *that* is the key
notion at the core of Israel's "thick" national culture (a concept I will
discuss in chapter eight), at the center of a national mythology that
is communicated in a myriad of ways. Israel—the state that restored
hope, that insisted on the possibility of a future, that audaciously
claimed that Hitler had not won.

For two thousand years prior to the creation of the State of Israel, the
complex array of holidays that had long been at the core of the Jewish
calendar had not changed. None had been removed. None had been
added. The calendar—one of the most defining characteristics of
Jewish communal life—had endured almost entirely unaltered for
twenty centuries.

Then Israel was born. Almost as soon as the country was created,
three additional holidays were added to the calendar. The first to
appear in the cycle as it now exists is Yom Ha-Shoah, established in
1959 to commemorate the six million Jews who had been murdered
in the Nazi genocide just a decade earlier. The second, which falls
a week later, is Yom Ha-Zikaron, Israel's equivalent of Memorial
Day. Set on this date in 1951 and codified into law in 1963, Yom
Ha-Zikaron is the day on which the state remembers the soldiers it lost

during the numerous military campaigns the country has endured. The third, which falls the day after Yom Ha-Zikaron, is Yom Ha-Atzma'ut, or Independence Day.

Understanding how those holidays fall, and how they are celebrated, is key to understanding how the founders of Israel, as well as many of its citizens, understood the very purpose of creating a Jewish state. Though Yom Ha-Shoah and Yom Ha-Zikaron fall a week apart and commemorate radically different memories, what is most significant for understanding how they communicate Israel's "message" is that that they are marked with astonishingly similar rituals.

On the surface, it would be difficult to imagine two days more different from each other. One is designed to remember the powerless, innocent victims of the Shoah, while the other is observed in memory of those who fell in Israel's battles. One is about Europe, the other about home. One is about passivity, the other about taking one's destiny into one's own hands. One is about powerlessness, the other about military might.

Yet despite these differences, similarities abound. On both days, air-raid sirens sound throughout the country, the moaning wail of the sirens bringing the entire country to a standstill. On the highways, cars come to a stop and drivers stand at attention outside their vehicles. In restaurants, waiters and waitresses stand immobile, food in hand, for the full two minutes of the siren, waiting for it to cease before moving on to their customers. On the streets, people stop and stand, as if cast in stone. In classes, students snap to attention and teachers cease their speaking; and even in doctors' offices and hospitals, all nonessential activity is suspended. For a moment, the country is still. Israeli life freezes, and is silent.

Silence, the country has decided, is the only appropriate way to mark the searing ache that will not heal, and that in some ways should not heal. It is, quite clearly, an intentional reflection of the biblical Aaron's reaction when his two sons were killed by God, about which the Torah remarks, with utter simplicity, "And Aaron was silent" (Leviticus 10:3). Aaron's pain was apparently so overwhelming that he could not respond. That is how Israelis mark the memory of the six million exterminated European Jews, and the approximately twenty-five thousand young Jews (and some non-Jews as well) who have since fallen in battle defending the Jewish state. Silence, both the Jewish and the Israeli traditions insist, is the only way to respond to pain so searing that no words could ever suffice.

And then, the day after Yom Ha-Zikaron, comes Yom Ha-Atzma'ut. Fireworks. Wine and beer. Music and dancing. Cultural performances throughout the country. Flags waving from car windows, and flags held aloft in the hands of children young and old. Israelis leave the cemeteries they visit on Memorial Day, and head to parties. The transition, the movement from the unspeakable pain of loss to an almost giddy celebration of independence, is agonizing, virtually impossible; but people force themselves to make it. For they understand the point of these holidays. The Jewish nation-state simply had to create them in order to proclaim the very point of its existence: Israel is about restoring hope at just the moment when it seemed that hope had perished. Somehow, not to force oneself to leave the cemetery and join the party would be to deny the very essence of what Jewish statehood has created.

The message that the Jewish state is about the triumph of possibility over devastation, of life over death, permeates Israel's national culture. Look carefully enough, and it appears virtually everywhere. It's in the architecture. It's a constant theme of Israeli literature. Israeli stamps have been created with that theme. Even the annual field trips that Israeli children take to different parts of the country are celebrations of home, of possibility and the end of landlessness. That message figures prominently in the national traditions of music and dance.

Yad Vashem, Israel's national memorial and museum to the victims of the Shoah and the heroes of the resistance, is a case in point. Adorning the cement arch at the entrance to the museum is a biblical verse. It is the promise of hope following Ezekiel's famous Vision of the Dry Bones, quoted at the beginning of this chapter, and reads: "I will put My breath into you and you shall live again, and I will set you upon your own soil" (Ezekiel 37:14). The promise of redemption. The reassurance that follows desperation. And even in this national museum and memorial, an echo of "*Hatikvah*"—("The Hope")— Israel's national anthem. Hope, the museum of the Shoah reminds the visitor, is still possible.

And then, as visitors to the site make their way to the museum itself, they find themselves almost underground. In a colossal building constructed of a grayish concrete, where the walls meet at the ceiling to form a giant triangular tunnel that twists and turns, they meander their way through the exhibit, with no choice as to where to head (an obvious message about the people whose demise they are memorializing). Gone is their sense of direction, any notion of start and finish, an architectural approximation of the total and unrelenting disorientation that the victims must have felt.

But just as it all gets too unbearable, as the horror and devastation threaten to consume the visitor, the museum ends. As the exhibit comes to a close, the walls of the museum spread apart at the top, and the visitor is ushered out onto a balcony overlooking the forest surrounding Jerusalem. Suddenly the verdant green view is what overwhelms, in a stunning, chilling contrast to the darkness from which the visitor has just emerged. Here claustrophobia gives way to space. An ominous ceiling opens up heavenward. Cement recedes and forests take its place. The once oppressive gray is now replaced by green. Death is replaced by nature. Europe is replaced by Israel. Exile is replaced by statehood, landlessness by home. And hell is replaced by hope.

Throughout Israeli culture, exhaustion and emptiness are metaphorically replaced by possibility. In the minds of Israelis, the National Water Carrier project, a vast system of pumps, aqueducts, and reservoirs that carried water from the Sea of Galilee to the rest of the country, was no ordinary system of pipes and pumps. It was, for all intents and purposes, about expanding the habitable borders of the country. "Making the desert bloom," one of the early mottos of the state, was about more than agriculture. It was about bringing water to desert, people to barrenness, vegetation to lifeless sand, life to death.

Only Israelis consumed with the message of hope that their state embodied could have fallen in love with a song about a sprinkler. When the National Water Carrier project was completed in the 1950s, Shoshana Damari, the grand dame of Israeli national folk song, wrote and recorded *"Hora Mamtera"* (The Sprinkler Dance), which became a national classic.

It's a brief song, this ode to a sprinkler, and simple. But it sounds more like a military march by John Philip Sousa than a song about water and nature. And that, of course, is no accident. For water and nature were inseparable from the military accomplishments—they were both about hope when there should have been none, life where death seemed all but omnipresent.

To be sure, today's Israeli teenagers grimace at the kitsch, at the datedness of the black-and-white grainy film showing circle upon circle of dancers bobbing to the beat of Shoshana Damari's throaty rendition of the song. Some of that is understandable; it's inevitable with the passage of time. This is the age of iPods, Internet, and a global culture of which Israeli teenagers are part no less than teenagers anywhere else; those days of completely unself-conscious national celebration are gone, and they cannot be restored.

But not everyone has given up. Despite Israel's often steamrolling modernity, there are artists and intellectuals who understand what is being lost, who attempt to remind their readers, their viewers, and their listeners how profound were the accomplishments of that former era. Dudu Elharar's 1983 recording of *"Bo Shir Ivri"* (Come, Hebrew Song) is a classic example. Long after the cynicism had begun to settle in, the song beckoned the Hebrew song to return:

> Come, Hebrew song, from the ravine, from the valley
> And bring with you the taste of the old melody.
> In the south the clod of earth has bloomed, in the north the
>   snow has melted
> Return, Hebrew song, don't be bashful.

The song goes on to note all the ways in which Israel has changed. Consciously evoking the naïveté of earlier genres of Israeli song, the lyrics point out that the country has built towns, and there are roads. And on the roads there are cars, and in the cars, everyone has a radio that "sings." The country sings "in all languages," the lyrics say. But then, on a hopeful note with a melody that is almost erotic, that sounds more like a love song than an ode to a language, the song concludes:

> But the Hebrew song, it's still here, it still persists
> It simply doesn't give up.

Israel is still about hope. There *is* some awareness of what has been lost, and many Israelis are seeking ways of recovering the innocence and the passion of the past. Numerous enduring echoes of that earlier era remain, and even many of today's Israeli children, while they may no longer dance to the beat of *"Hora Mamtera,"* seem to have intuited what the Zionist project was meant to convey. Thankfully, the sense of rebirth and of healing still pulses in portions of Israeli life, and often when it is least expected, it shapes a great deal about how Israeli youth respond to the world around them.

My daughter was about seventeen years old when she went with her high school class to Poland. It was the standard Israeli Poland trip, a combination of seeing the places in which Jewish life had thrived for centuries and visiting the unspeakably awful camps where it had all been annihilated in the space of a few years.

Like most of the students who go on these trips, she had a very powerful experience. At the assembly that the girls conducted a few weeks after their return, I heard one story that has stuck with me ever since. While they were in Poland, the girls recounted that evening, one of their teachers told them a story about a previous class that had gone from the same school fourteen years earlier. One day while in Krakow, those girls—now adult women, of course—noticed a young man selling "Jew dolls" made to look like traditional Jews. Some of the girls noticed that the "books" that these dolls were holding looked remarkably authentic. The more closely the girls looked at these books, the more convinced they became that these "books" had been cut from a real Torah scroll.

They asked the doll-maker where he'd gotten the calligraphed parchment, and he told them that his uncle had a big scroll of it in the nearby town, Limanova. Asked where the uncle had gotten the scroll, he told them that during the war, it had been in the house of a Jew, and his uncle had taken it after the Jew disappeared. "Could they see it?" they wanted to know. He agreed to bring it back the next day.

The next day, he showed them what was left: Genesis, Exodus, and Leviticus. The two other books, apparently, had been cut up for the dolls. The girls instinctively knew what they had to do. They pooled their relatively limited pocket money and bought the Torah from the man for whatever they had managed to scrounge together.

They carried the now destroyed and unusable Torah with them for the remainder of their trip. As the time to depart Poland grew closer, however, they were faced with a dilemma. All Jewish property from before the war now belonged to the state, and removing the Torah from Poland was against the law. If Israeli teenagers were caught smuggling Polish government property, matters would be most unpleasant.

They talked it over, the teacher reported now many years later, and decided to smuggle the Torah out of Poland and to bring it home to Jerusalem.

At the airport, however, each girl was required to pass her bags through the X-ray machine. The first girl in line, when she was told to put her bags on the belt, passed the Torah to the next girl in line. When that girl was told to do the same thing, she surreptitiously passed it to the girl behind her, and so forth. For the next few minutes, the Torah silently made its way back down the line, until it seemed that they were not going to get it out.

And then the belt broke. The machine simply quit. The Polish authorities, too concerned with fixing the belt to inspect all the bags being brought through, just ushered the remaining girls by, the Torah included. The girls brought the Torah to a place in Jerusalem where such scrolls are repaired, but because this work is exceedingly expensive, there was no money to fix the scroll. With time, the girls graduated. They went on to the army or National Service, and then to university. Then followed marriage, children, and careers. The Torah languished unrepaired.

Fourteen years later, my daughter's senior class went to Poland. And when they heard the story of the Torah, they resolved to raise the money to restore it. Upon their return, they got to work. They raised the money, and the Torah was fixed over many months. A short time later, it was danced into its new home in the school's auditorium/synagogue. During the ceremony that these young women created to mark the homecoming of this Torah scroll, as I listened to the story, I asked myself what it was that had gotten those girls to smuggle the Torah back to Israel. What possessed them to violate Polish law, perhaps at considerable personal risk, to try to bring that Torah home? Why would the teachers accompanying them on the trip allow them to do it? Why did they all, teachers and students alike, understand that the Torah simply had to be brought home? And why did my daughter's class understand that now that the Torah was in Israel, it simply *had* to be repaired and used, that it could no longer languish in storage?

It was, I believe, because on some level they've intuited that Israel is about life, about recovery. Leaving a Torah in Poland, to be cut up by a doll-maker, would have been to deny the possibility of the redemption of the Jewish life that had once existed there. The Torah, for these religious girls, represented that life, now mostly extinguished. And the Torah, eaten away by the doll-maker so that only two-thirds of it remained, simply needed to be repaired. These girls, raised and educated in Israel, understood the message of repair, of recovery, of healing. The Torah had to come home. It needed to be brought back to life.

I watched my daughter, Talia, watching the speakers. I couldn't get a seat anywhere near her, but I could see her—listening intently, her eyes, at certain moments, brimming with tears. As we left the ceremony, I got a close look at the *parochet* (the cloth covering at the front of the ark where the Torah was to be kept) and saw that there were some verses embroidered on it. In exquisite lettering, embroidered with a love that was palpable, were the famous verses from Jeremiah 31:15–16 that had been chosen to welcome the Torah home:

> Ki yesh sachar li-fe'ulateikh,
> Ve-yesh tikvah la-acharitekh
> Ve-shavu vanim li-gvulam
>
> There is reward for your labor
> And there is hope for your future
> Your children shall return to their country.

Here it was again: the reminder that "reward for your labor," and more important, that "hope for your future" is what Israel is all about. Israel has done for the Jewish people what these girls did for the Torah scroll. Like that Torah, the Jewish people was brought home, broken and tattered, but at least now protected. And then, also like that Torah, the Jewish people could be healed. It would take time and it would not be easy, but the Torah would be danced back into a sanctuary, and the Jews, now ensconced in their own national sanctuary, would begin to thrive once again.

These young women understood that. Though they are in many ways just like American or European girls their age, Zionism's essential message still resonates with them. Even this generation, or at least parts of it, understands that at its core, Israel is about Jewish recovery, Jewish flourishing, and the possibility of a vital Jewish future.

When Avi, our next child, went to Poland three years later with his high school class, he saw similar places. And he came back equally moved. A few days after his return, he and I were sitting in his room, where he'd just transferred the pictures from his digital camera onto his computer. I sat at his side, and we went through the pictures, one by one, as he told me about the places he'd seen. Soon we came to a picture of someone I didn't recognize. "Where was this taken?" I asked.

"Majdanek," he said, referring to the concentration camp near Lublin, in eastern Poland.

"And who's that?" I asked him, pointing to the one person in the picture.

He laughed. "Funny," he said. But when he realized that I really didn't know who it was, he looked at me strangely and said, "That's me, Abba."

It was, I realized, my son. Part of the reason I didn't recognize him was that it was cold when they were in Poland, and he was wearing a black knitted ski cap pulled down almost to his eyebrows. But it was more than that. The usual glimmer of his eyes and his almost always shining visage were completely gone. Coming out of the concentration camp, his eyes were hollow, his stare vacant, his mind obviously still trying to make sense of that which is, ultimately, utterly incomprehensible.

And in his parka, bundled against the cold, he stared not at the camera but beyond it, hugging an Israeli flag to his chest. It reminded me of him as a toddler, hugging his stuffed animals to his shoulder as he went to sleep at night, the need for some comfort and reassurance paramount as the day was ending.

He was much older in this picture, almost an adult, and there he was, hugging something to himself, still needing reassurance. This time, it wasn't his stuffed tiger but an Israeli flag on a pole, held tightly against his chest as he struggled forward, even in the face of what he'd seen. He was going to return home in a few days, that flag seemed to remind him—to a place created in large measure because of this, to a place designed to guarantee that it couldn't happen again, to a place that insisted that there had to be a future even after that darkness.

I realized, looking at that photo, that he, too, had come to understand very well what Israel's founders had once hoped the mere existence of their new state would convey. Here was a young Israeli, "ingathered from the Diaspora," staring out of a place of darkness and utter despair, grasping his adopted flag, knowing that in a matter of days he'd head back home to the one place that had been created to ensure that Majdanek would be part of the Jewish past and never of its future.

It is not only Israelis who are touched by the power of this message. Each visit of the now more than one hundred thousand students who have been brought to Israel on a program called "Taglit-Birthright Israel" is testimony to the way in which Israel's vitality speaks even to those who are not its citizens. In 2000, two major American Jewish philanthropists, in cooperation with other donors and the State of Israel, inaugurated "Birthright Israel" in the hopes of bringing thousands of Jewish college students and young adults to Israel for a free ten-day trip. The purpose of the trip, which was inspired by an idea initially proposed by Israeli politician Yossi Beilin, was to counteract the declining indicators of Jewish identity among young adults in the Diaspora. Bring them to Israel, the argument went, show them the vitality of Jewish life in the Jewish state, and they'll feel something that they won't ever want to abandon.

Though Birthright broke almost every rule in the book for what constituted serious educational planning, it worked. Apathy did evaporate. Decades of disengagement did disappear. Jewish college students suddenly pledged themselves to giving Jewish commitment priority in their lives, and spoke openly and unabashedly about how the experience had changed much of who they wanted to be. They encouraged their friends to go to Israel. In time, some of them married each other. By 2007 more than 120,000 students had participated, and a new philanthropist had entered the picture, contributing an additional $60 million to ensure the program's future.

Many leading educators were dumbfounded. Why did Birthright work? What *happened* to these people, they wanted to know. How could one explain the impact of ten days of simply touring a country?

Part of the power of the experience stemmed from the fact that their Jewishness no longer set them apart. When they landed at Ben-Gurion Airport, it was the very first time they experienced that being Jewish was the norm, that the majority of the people they were encountering were Jews. There were soldiers, but they, too, were Jewish. Some wore kippot, some didn't. Some had white skin, and others were dark, of Ethiopian descent. Some were men, while others were women. And suddenly, these visiting students intuited two profoundly important lessons: there is no one model of what it means to be a Jew, and being Jewish does not have to mean being peripheral or "other."

The kippah was no longer that thing that you had to wear in Temple on the High Holidays but had to remember to take off before you left the building so you didn't stick out as "different" on the streets of American suburbia. Hebrew, no longer the arcane language that they scarcely learned in Hebrew school and didn't understand at the Passover seder, was everywhere. The signs for "Customs" and "Police" and "Rest Rooms" were all in Hebrew (and in English, of course, as in any major international airport).

But what worked about Birthright was more than not being different. The students would gather their bags, get on a bus, and head for Jerusalem. If the guide on the bus was good, she or he would point out the caves where the Maccabees had fought off the Greeks thousands of years earlier, and the hills, right along the highway, where Jewish troops battled Arab soldiers for control of the road leading to Jerusalem in the 1948 War of Independence. They'd be shown the burnt-out but still carefully preserved carcasses of the convoy trucks that had not made it through. And these students would suddenly feel something that they couldn't articulate. It was just a road, that highway, but it was a road that told a story. It told *their* story.

Roads that evoke *feeling* and a sense of belonging—that, too, was something that most of these Birthright participants had never experienced before.

They'd be taken to the Old City, and instead of a seeing a site discussed incessantly in the *Washington Post* or the *New York Times* as the focus of a bitter international dispute, they would see the remnants of an ancient home. They would stand at the very site to which thousands upon thousands of Jews, millennia ago, had walked and hiked in order to worship at the Temple in Jerusalem. In the north, hiking the Golan Heights, they would encounter both natural beauty and the burnt-out tanks that are abiding testimony to what people like them—Jews, like them, and people exactly their age—gave up so that the little country in which they now found themselves could survive.

If in the minds of the Birthright college students "Jewish" had too often been associated with the Shoah, with their being told that they had an obligation to commit to Jewish life so as not to give Hitler a posthumous victory, "Jewish" suddenly meant something very different. In Israel, they intuited, "Jewish" meant "alive," "thriving," "reborn." In Israel, they suddenly discovered that being Jewish meant that they were part of a narrative, a history, a national struggle, much larger and much more profound than their own lives.

And implicitly, many of them asked themselves, "What would *I* give everything for? Is there anything *I* believe in that is more important than I am?" They were part of something grand, panoramic, and multifaceted, these young Jews discovered. And in thousands of cases, they decided that no matter what else they did, they weren't going to walk away from it all.

This commitment to rebirth and to regeneration is key to understanding Israel's almost inexplicable drive to settle every Jew who came to its borders.

More than 500,000 Jews fled the Nazis and came to Jewish Palestine, and then Israel. In the early years of the state, some 750,000 Jews were expelled from Muslim countries in North Africa and were absorbed by Israel (unlike a similar number of Palestinian refugees, by the way, who were never integrated by Lebanon, Syria, Jordan, or Egypt; those countries decided to keep them as refugees so that they could be pawns in future negotiations with Israel). Still later, Israel took in approximately 1,000,000 Jews (and non-Jews) from the Soviet Union. Throughout, this commitment to welcoming immigrants was another reflection of the desire to create something from nothing, to build a future with those who seemingly had none.

It goes without saying that Israel was clearly also seeking to increase its population. But Israel's strategy was always about more than mere demography. These immigrants, many of whom were poor and illiterate, were not exactly the ideal profile of population that a young, struggling country might want; yet they were, despite their poverty and illiteracy, critical to the country's attempt to stand for a commitment to Jewish life, above and beyond all else, after what had happened in the twentieth century.

Even with all the inadequacies (in addition to many extraordinary successes) of how Israelis dealt with these immigrants once they arrived, Israelis have always intuited the relationship between immigrant absorption and their country's purpose. There is no other way to explain the excitement that Israelis felt when hearing the stories of how Caucasian Israeli pilots had landed lumbering, converted C-130 jets on narrow airstrips in the midst of a civil war that was none of Israel's business, just to get Ethiopian Jews to Israel in Operation Solomon.

Operation Solomon brought to Israel people of a different race, a different language, no meaningful exposure to the modern world, and even religious practices that were almost unrecognizable to other Jews. Yet Israelis were beyond proud, giddily excited. Why? Because the effort bespoke the infatuation with saving Jewish life that still pulses through the veins of the Jewish state.

While it is true (though difficult to fathom) that two-thirds of American Jews have not visited Israel, the existence of a Jewish state touches their lives in ways they can hardly begin to appreciate. In the field of Jewish education, there are scarcely any educational leaders who have not spent a significant amount of time in Israel, and those who do visit Israel return to the United States with much of the message of the triumph over despair fully internalized. That message is then transmitted in a variety of ways in educational programs across America. Israel Independence Day parades, Israel programming on college campuses, cultural events, and more all use the foundation of Israel's success as a means of injecting a profound sense of optimism into American Jewish life.

Nor is it an accident that virtually every rabbinic and cantorial training program in the United States requires of its students a year of study in Israel. To be sure, part of that requirement stems from a desire to advance the students' Hebrew fluency and their familiarity with some of the critical issues facing the Jewish world. But the commitment goes deeper than that. Rabbi David Ellenson, president of the Reform movement's Hebrew Union College and widely regarded as one of American Judaism's most visionary leaders, refused to scale back his school's Israel-year requirement, even when the Palestinian Terror War raged. Despite criticism of his position, Ellenson was unfazed and unrepentant. The nature of "Jewish national rebirth in *Eretz Yisrael*," he consistently argues, is the reason that those students need to spend significant time in Israel. The image of the Jew as actor, determiner of his or her own destiny, is derivative of Jewish sovereignty.

To all this, we should add the obvious note that were Israel to be destroyed and another six million Jews lost in that process, it is highly unlikely that American Jews could recover. The loss of a *second* round of six million Jews would undoubtedly set American Jews back significantly. The loss of inspiration that Israel's regeneration provides, the sense of guilt that would inevitably accompany Israel's demise, and the impact of a second loss of millions of Jews in the space of a century would almost certainly prove overwhelming and insurmountable. It is highly likely that the American Judaism that remained a generation or two after that loss would be but a faint reflection of what American Jews have created and now enjoy.

Outside Israel and the United States, no statistically significant Jewish communities remain. There is a middle-sized community in France (which is itself very threatened), and all the rest are much smaller. The loss of the Israel and American Jewish communities would thus spell the end for Jewish life as we know it, not only in Israel and North America, but across the globe.

At stake in Israel's survival, then, is the Jewish belief in the possibility of the future. When Israelis, or American Jews, wonder aloud in the face of a world no longer supportive of Israel whether the continued battle to preserve Israel is still worthwhile, there is but one clear question, and one clear answer.

Could the Jewish people survive without the anchor that Israel represents? There's almost no chance.

Yet that's precisely the scenario that may be tested. For despite the hope that Israel has restored, the optimism of yesteryear has begun to fade. We've mentioned the causes briefly, and we'll return to them— the wars that will not cease, the fact that peace seems unattainable, Israel's loss of the Second Lebanon War, successive governments rife with corrupt officials, and what perhaps is most ominous, a generation of young Israelis who are no longer so certain what it is that they're fighting for, or why the Jewish state might matter enough to be worth sacrificing for. It's an era of increased rates of able-bodied young men avoiding the draft (a 2008 report suggested that seven thousand able-bodied men had avoided the draft in the previous year, and that the annual rate was rising steadily), of Israelis feeling guilty for an occupation that began in a war for their survival that they did not choose. It was easier to be the victims than the oppressors, Israelis lament, forgetting that they only became "occupiers" when they successfully repelled aggression. Wave after wave of disappointment and self-doubt has drained Israel of hope.

In many ways, the loss of Israeli optimism is understandable. Israelis are battle weary, and they feel abandoned. They crave normalcy but see none forthcoming, even on the horizon. They vanquish enemies only to have new ones replace the old. It would be astonishing if all this did not take a toll.

But at the same time, ironically, some of the loss of passion and vision stems from the great success that Israel has been. The unpredictable success of what was a fledgling state only decades ago has so totally erased the collective memory of what Jewish life was like without sovereignty, that many Jews can no longer imagine the Jewish world without a country, without a stage for Jewish peoplehood as we know it today.

There is a danger to this loss of collective memory, for with no memory of what the world was like without Israel, it is all the more difficult for young Jews today to remember how dramatically the Jewish state has transformed Jewish life. Israel has to work to recreate that awareness of how dramatically Jewish sovereignty has altered the Jewish condition, and it must find a way to restore to its citizens the hope and the passion that it once evoked, leading them to defend their state and to see to its thriving.

Otherwise, it is more than hope or passion that will be lost. For what is at stake is not only a country, but the people it was meant to save.

Chapter Two

JEWS MAKING
JEWISH DECISIONS

Did there really exist a Jewish people for thousands of
years while all the other peoples of the world melted away and
disappeared? Was there really an exile of the citizens of Judah
after the destruction of the Second Temple? . . . And if there
never was an exile, what happened to the locals, and who were
those millions of Jews who appeared on the stage of history in
such unexpected distant places?
                                     —Shlomo Sand, *When and How Was the*
                                                 Jewish People Invented?

British General Sir Edmund Allenby hadn't even captured
Jerusalem yet. His famed entry, which despite his status as a great
horseman he made on foot out of respect for the sacred city, would
not take place until December 11, 1917. But the fact that they did not
yet have full control over Palestine did not stop the British, who were
confident of their ability to take Jerusalem, from declaring more than
a month earlier in the famed Balfour Declaration that "His Majesty's
Government view with favour the establishment in Palestine of a

national home for the Jewish people, and will use their best endeavours to facilitate the achievement of this object."

Interestingly, the British did not use the word "state" but instead chose to speak of a "national home." It's an interesting choice, this word "home." For while the Jews often speak of Israel as their "state," or as the "Jewish state," the problem with that nomenclature is that it suggests that the ultimate goal was statehood, or national sovereignty. But focusing on Israel exclusively as the locus of Jewish national sovereignty, of political independence, invites the more critical question that contemporary Jews need to address once again: Statehood as a means to what? *Why* did the Jews want, or need, a state? What, even beyond hope and the possibility of a Jewish future, does statehood do for the Jews today?

"State" and "home" have different connotations. Perhaps it might be useful for a moment to think about "home" in the lives of individual people or families, before taking on the notion of a national home. What is home?

Home, quite simply, is where we go to be ourselves.

Home is where we go in order to heal, to recover. Home is where we define a world in which we believe we can thrive, in which *we,* and not others, are the determinants of how we will live. People with no place to call their own, to which they can "retreat" at nightfall, can do nothing but eke out a meager survival from day to day, hoping to sleep for a few hours before the daily struggle to stay alive continues. There is no place for them to thrive, to define the contours of their life, to set the tone of their existence. It is more or less the same for an entire people.

For all of us, homes are not simply a refuge, but an opportunity to create a world with ourselves at the center. It is in the privacy and comfort of our homes that we dress how we like to, and we talk as we wish. We are surrounded by the art and the books that speak to us; we set up the space in a way that works for us, that enables us to relax, to be ourselves. We listen to the music that *we* want to hear, we celebrate the holidays that are important to *us* in the way that *we* choose to mark them. Home is the place where we set the standards of how people speak and interact; home is where we decide on our financial priorities and how to raise our children. Home is the place where *we* are the center, the place that actually exists in order to be *about* us and *for* us.

The same is true of peoples, and for nations. A "national home," as the British called it, would do similar things for the Jews. Isaiah Berlin, the famed British philosopher, once said that Israel's greatest accomplishment is that Jews felt comfortable with themselves there, for they no longer had to be "sophisticated, chess playing, café-intellectuals." They had earned the right to "normality" there, he said. Berlin was right. Homes, for individuals as well as for nations, are also the places where they can act out, where they can "lose their cool" with less vulnerability than if they did so at work—or in the case of a nation, while dependent on another country to act as their hosts. That, too, Israel has provided; the results may not always make Jews around the world terribly proud, but they point nonetheless to the sense of psychic security that comes from being at home.

But this amorphous notion of Israel as home is not sufficient if we are to understand further the ways in which statehood has shaped the Jewish present. What has actually transpired in this Jewish national home? What precisely have the Jews recovered there? Much has happened, some of it even beyond adequate expression. But there are three elements of Jewish life to which we must point if we are to more fully gauge how statehood has fundamentally altered the Jewish condition. They are the notion of Jewish peoplehood, the Hebrew language, and the return of the Jews to the stage of history.

"We are a people—one people," Theodor Herzl wrote in *The Jewish State*. Today, because of Herzl's work and that of the American Jewish philosopher and rabbi Mordecai Kaplan (among others, of course), for whom peoplehood was a central pillar of their thought, the phrase "Jewish people" or "Jewish peoplehood" has become so ubiquitous that it sounds patently obvious. (That is why some post-Zionist historians, such as Shlomo Sand, quoted at the outset of this chapter, delegitimize the very notion of a Jewish state by suggesting that Zionists "invented" the notion of a Jewish people.)

What was revolutionary about Herzl's notion toward the end of the nineteenth century was his claim that the Jewish people would never be at home anywhere other than in a Jewish state. Even when they shed all the trappings of Jewishness other than religion, he said, thus seeking to eviscerate any accusation of dual loyalty or of not belonging, they would forever be unsuccessful:

> We have honestly endeavored, everywhere, to submerge our-
> selves in the surrounding community and to preserve only
> the faith of our fathers. We are not permitted to do so. In vain
> are we loyal patriots . . . in countries where we may already
> have lived for centuries we are still proclaimed strangers. . . .
> I believe we shall not be left in peace.

They could impoverish themselves culturally, Herzl insisted, but the Jews would never find a genuine home in Europe. Jews were a people, he wrote, no less than any of the peoples who intermittently welcomed them and shunned them. There was something unnatural about shedding so much of their selves that they reduced themselves to simply a faith-based community, which Jews knew was a faint remnant of what they genuinely were.

In his complaint that the Jews were being forced to "preserve only the faith of our fathers," Herzl was expressing what Jews deeply immersed in the Jewish experience already knew: there was a *je ne sais quoi* that made the Jews who they were. And in insisting that the Jews were a people, Herzl demanded that they not give that up. Relinquishing it would emaciate them, and it would never suffice to gain them the long-term acceptance that they craved.

We are often frustrated that there is something simply ineffable at the core of Jewish life. Contemporary culture and intellectual dispositions seek measurement, proofs. And when there are dimensions of peoplehood that we cannot explain, we tend to scoff, to assume that there's a sleight of hand being performed, that this people isn't real (a fact on which Shlomo Sand's book, *When and How Was the Jewish People Invented,* seizes).

Admittedly, it is difficult to explain how European Jews—who tell a national narrative that begins with exile to Babylon, eventually heads to Europe, knows glory years in the Middle Ages but is later destroyed in the Shoah, and finally heads to Israel—feel a visceral connection to other Jews from North Africa or Yemen, whose narrative is entirely different. Why did young Orthodox U.S. college students campaign so energetically for Soviet Jews who did not speak the same language, did not share their theological assumptions or religious way of life? Why did Israeli pilots risk everything in Operation Solomon to land C-130 cargo planes in Ethiopia to extract people of a different race, who spoke a different language, had a different history, shared virtually none of the canon that had long defined Jewish conversations, and had scarcely encountered modernity? What did they have in common with them? By virtue of what measurable quality could these two groups have been said to be part of any coherent whole?

Peoplehood, Herzl clearly would have said, was the answer.

Herzl, of course, did not invent the notion of Jews as a people. As far back as the biblical era, God speaks to the Israelites through Moses and commands, "And you will be for Me a kingdom of priests and a holy nation" (Exodus 19:5). Later, still in the desert, when the Moabite king Balak sends his prophet, Balaam, to curse the Israelites, Balaam is overwhelmed by the community he witnesses and utters, "There is a people that dwells apart, not reckoned among the nations" (Numbers 23:9). And in much more pernicious circumstances, when Haman seeks to convince the king of Persia that the Jews are a menace who ought to be destroyed, he says, "There is a certain people, scattered and dispersed among the other peoples in all the provinces of your realm, whose laws are different from those of any other people . . . and it is not in Your Majesty's interest to tolerate them" (Esther 3:8). Other examples abound. The Jews, their admirers, and their enemies all understood that that the Jews were, first and foremost, a people.

Yet, while a certain sense of peoplehood precedes statehood, statehood has given expression to Jewish peoplehood in ways that Israel's founders might not have anticipated. If prior to statehood, American Jews and Yemenite Jews each had a conception of what

Jews looked like or *were* like, those who have come to Israel have had those assumptions completely upended. There are Jews who are light and Jews who are dark. Jews speak Hebrew, French, Russian, Amharic, and English. They are of all different builds. Some grew up in democracies and others under repressive totalitarian regimes. They are deeply religious, a bit religious, and not religious at all. They are highly literate, and almost completely illiterate (in a very few remaining cases). The communities of their countries of origin had virtually nothing in common, except for some inexplicable sense that they were all part of a larger whole. And statehood has transformed that sense from a mere notion to a complex reality.

On even casual visits to Jerusalem, one can often see groups of new army recruits ambling down the street. Their officers are usually lecturing them, pointing to significant locations as markers in the history they all share. The shared lecture notwithstanding, it is difficult not to be struck by their diversity. But somehow, inexplicably, they all coexist in the same unit, not simply because a larger entity such as the army has grouped them together, but because on a much more significant level, each is the heir of a narrative that describes him or her as part of the same whole.

Israel's social critics—and they are many, for there is, indeed, much to critique—point out that Israel is a highly segregated society. By and large, they remind us, the Russians live in their own enclaves, as do the French, the Yemenites, the Iraqis, and the Americans. Too often, the children of one group are not educated alongside the children of the next. If that is the case, the critics ask, if people are all citizens of the same entity but they don't really interact in any meaningful way, to what extent can one legitimately claim that Jewish peoplehood genuinely comes to life in Israel?

The truth is, Israel *is* segregated, and too much so. (So, too, were the New York and Los Angeles communities in which I lived for decades.) The economic gap between rich and poor is wider in Israel than in any other developed country. The neighborhoods of all these groups are largely separate, and some groups, such as the Ethiopians, are still having considerable difficulty with upward social mobility.

The critics are absolutely correct in pointing to the sorts of social problems with which most capitalist societies must wrestle, problems that are only compounded by the weight of immigrants Israel has had to absorb. But Israeli life is replete with moments when one realizes that despite all the shortcomings, sovereignty has breathed new life into Jewish peoplehood.

Each Election Day, as I wait on line to vote at the local public school (to which people from many different neighborhoods are assigned), it becomes undeniably clear that something unique is transpiring, that an extraordinary resuscitation of peoplehood has unfolded in the Jewish state. The people waiting their turn to choose the next government don't all speak the same language. They are dressed differently. Their histories are radically different, as are their religious worldviews and their political ideologies. Even after generations in Israel, their cultures each entail practices that the others would find foreign, perhaps even objectionable.

But all these people are nonetheless linked by a sense of shared destiny. In some ironic and unfathomable way, they may not all agree on the goals of their society, but they are nonetheless committed to realizing those goals as part of a shared venture that none of them could have imagined just decades ago. Only in the country that brought them all to live together could the notion of Jewish peoplehood have been reborn.

Israeli life is replete with moments such as these. The fact that peoplehood is somewhat ineffable does not lessen its impact on the Jews who make Israel their home. The state that has made possible the "ingathering of the exiles" has done more than bring people together. It has wholly altered their sense of the larger whole—the People—of which they are a part.

Yet having a "national home," in the words of the Balfour Declaration, has done much more than restore a sense of peoplehood to the Jews. It has also afforded the Jews an opportunity to revitalize other dimensions of their national character that life in the Diaspora would have not permitted.

Consider once again that line of voters, waiting to cast their ballots. Listening carefully, one discovers another dimension of Jewish life that statehood has permitted to flourish. Often, many of these adults can't converse with each other (or if they must, they make do with a rudimentary Hebrew that precludes any nuance). But their children, standing on line with them, chatter away with each other easily, conversing in a language that a century ago very few people spoke. This too, seems entirely natural, but we ought not take it for granted; in addition to the revival of peoplehood in its current form, the Jewish state has also made possible the revival of the language of the Jews.

It would be a mistake to see the revival of Hebrew as purely instrumental, as a mere tool that people needed in order to build a society together. Yes, the Jews gathering in what was then Palestine needed a language in which to converse. But Palestine was part of a British Mandate, and English could easily have been adopted. India is a perfect example of how deeply English rooted itself in cultures in which it was an import. Given the surrounding culture, one could also have imagined a decision—unlikely, of course, but still possible—to make Arabic the lingua franca of the emerging state.

But it was clear to Zionists everywhere—in Europe, in Palestine, and beyond—that anything other than Hebrew was a nonstarter. Hebrew, after all, was the only language to which all the Jews who they hoped would soon be gathering in Palestine had some shared connection. More than that, Hebrew was the language of the one book to which they all owed their sense of self. And Hebrew had been the language of the Jews when they were sovereign, when the nation-state under kings David and Solomon was in its glory days. Hebrew, for these Zionists, was the language of the Jews prior to exile, situated on their own land. Hebrew was the language the Jews spoke when they had determined their own destiny, and it would be the language they would speak once again. Therefore, it is noteworthy but not surprising that just three years after the founding of the state, the Department for Cultural Absorption in the Ministry of Education and Culture was renamed the Department for Bequeathing the Language. The Hebrew word for "bequeathing" is a biblical one, thus implicitly reminding all listeners that this was not the creation of something new but the *re*-creation of days of glory long past. Renewing that language, bequeathing it to newcomers, and restoring the Jewish autonomy of which the Bible spoke would all be prime functions of the newly emerging state.

A language, Zionism's leaders understood, is part of what it takes to be a people. There would have been no Verdi without an Italian-speaking culture for which he could write, in whose language he could express his genius. Without a community in which German was the dominant culture, in which German history, language, and cultural literacy blended, there would have been no Thomas Mann. Read Albert Camus in French and then in any great translation, and it's clear: the gist gets conveyed, but something is missing. What Camus has to say in French can only be said in French.

Eliezer Ben-Yehudah, who raised his children in Hebrew at a time when no one else on earth used Hebrew as a daily language, and who, as a result, spent a great deal of his life creating Hebrew words for items that did not yet figure in Hebrew's vocabulary, understood that. So, too, did the great Jewish poet Hayim Nahman Bialik (once referred to as the "poet of the national renaissance"), whose Hebrew writing played a central role in the revitalization of Hebrew. (Ze'ev Jabotinsky, the leader of revisionist Zionism that would later spawn Menachem Begin and the Likkud party, said of Bialik that he was "the one poet in all of modern literature whose poetry directly molded the soul of a generation.") In a much-quoted aphorism, Bialik is said to have remarked that reading the great works of the Jewish canon in any language other than Hebrew is like kissing a bride through the veil. It is a kiss, perhaps, but it is hardly the stuff, to paraphrase Shakespeare, on which dreams are made.

Contemporary Israeli discourse is filled, often unknowingly on the parts of those who speak it, with biblical and Talmudic aphorisms. As Israeli students encounter the book of Isaiah, be they in high school or beyond, they cannot help but be struck by the hundreds of biblical phrases that now make up their daily vocabulary. Thousands of years have gone by, and often the usages have changed. But a Jewish conversation has continued, they discover, and they are part of it.

The richness of a people's ability to communicate what is unique to it is very often dependent on its having its own language; but having that language is often dependent, in turn, on that people having a place for that language to flourish. For the Jews, language could not have flourished without their state. Without their state, the culture of the Jews, as only a language can create and transmit it, would have been impossible. That, too, is a dimension of home, of what Balfour's "national home" afforded the Jews.

Consider how different has been the fate of Hebrew in the United States from what it has been in Israel. At this writing, there are just as many Jews in the United States as there are in Israel. Their standard of living is higher, and they are probably, on the whole, better educated.

Yet interestingly, those millions of American Jews produce virtually no publications in Hebrew. Yes, there are prayer books, Bibles, some new editions of classic Jewish works such as the Mishnah and the Talmud, usually accompanied by new translations. But other than religious works, most of which are essentially reprints, almost nothing of great note gets produced in Hebrew.

True, a rich American Jewish literature has emerged, and it has included extraordinary talents such as Emma Lazarus, Bernard Malamud, Saul Bellow, Philip Roth, and Cynthia Ozick, among many others. Jonathan Safran Foer and Nicole Krauss are among the more recent additions to this rich tradition, and their work, too, is ingenious. And it is Jewish, deeply so.

It is Jewish, but it has a different Jewish valence than it would have had if it were written in Hebrew. It is of a different tenor than it would have been, had it been written in a setting in which the majority culture was Jewish, in which "acceptance" was not both simultaneously miraculous and tenuous. What happens in Israeli literature is the product of a unique set of characteristics—an almost erotic (if troubled) relationship with the land, a sense of miraculous homecoming (often coupled with guilt at what happened to an indigenous population), a sense of rebirth both historic and linguistic and the knowledge that in writing in Hebrew, one is writing for a very small segment of the world's readership—all these contribute to the sense that writing like that is part and parcel of the restoration and flourishing of a certain people.

Just as Israel's creation has afforded the Jews the sense that they now live on land that is genuinely their own (even if many believe that they will ultimately have to cede some of that land in order to settle their conflict with the Palestinians), the re-creation of their language creates for them the sense that every dimension of life can be lived as Jews, without depending on German, or French, or English. University lectures and elementary school classes take place in Hebrew. Surgeries are performed with Hebrew as the language of discourse, and pilots use the language during maneuvers. Little children play—and fight—in Hebrew in sandboxes across the country. Their parents make love speaking Hebrew. Children's literature, romance novels, and serious literature appear in Hebrew. So do weekly magazines, Web sites, and even pornography.

There undoubtedly are those who find the use of Hebrew, the "sacred language" of the Jews, for pornographic purposes or even for children's literature thoroughly scandalous. But the fact remains that that, too, is an indication of the "normalcy" of the Jewish condition that Hebrew marks, a dimension of Jewish revival post-Shoah that only a national center, with a majority of Jews, speaking a language all its own, could ever hope to make possible.

Yet the extraordinary accomplishment of the revitalization of Hebrew ought not delude anyone into believing that that accomplishment alone can safeguard the substance of Israeli discourse long into the future. Hillel Halkin, the Israeli literary critic, writer, and translator, is correct when he asserts that the secularization of Zionism has been so successful that it has rendered a generation of Israelis so ignorant of their heritage that they could well be called "Hebrew speaking gentiles." "I do not believe," he wrote, "that a polity of Israelis who are not culturally Jews, whose roots in this land go no deeper than thirty years and no wider than the boundaries of an arid nation-state, has a future in the Middle East for very long. In one way or another . . . it will be blown away like chaff as though it never were, leaving neither Jews nor Israelis behind it."

Hebrew is not enough; it needs to be coupled with cultural and historical nuance and content, and on that front, Israel is surely struggling. We'll return to that problem. But the legitimacy of Halkin's critique (shared by many others) should in no way diminish the magnitude of the accomplishment of the fact that an entire nation now speaks a language that just a century ago was mostly forgotten. Israel may not be about "normalcy." Indeed, we will argue that it is not. But to the extent that the Jews sought to be a people like any other, they needed to revive their language. And without Israel, that simply could never have happened.

Beyond peoplehood and beyond language, statehood has changed the Jewish condition in yet another way. It has enabled what the philosopher Emil Fackenheim called (in a different context) the "Jewish return to history." To be sure, Benjamin Disraeli, Henry Kissinger, Ruth Bader Ginsburg, Joseph Lieberman, and countless others did not need statehood to become statesmen. But Disraeli acted first and foremost in his role as a British citizen. And as Kissinger reminded the Jewish world during the Yom Kippur War, he would not let his Jewish commitments shape his policy or his recommendations to his president. In Israel, what has changed is that it is not individual Jews who have come to power, but Jews acting and thinking as Jews and representing Jews who have an opportunity to take Jewish ideas and to unself-consciously weave them into the tapestry of Israeli policy. To paraphrase Fackenheim again, Jews have returned to the stage of history not simply as citizens of their adopted countries, but as Jews qua Jews.

There's a wonderful comment toward the beginning of Saul Bellow's novel *Humboldt's Gift* in which the narrator says of Humboldt, "He said that history was a nightmare during which he was trying to get a good night's sleep." It is easy to understand why Bellow's character, a Jew who'd made his way to America, particularly after the horrors of Europe in the mid-twentieth century, might think of history as a nightmare, and might want nothing more than in the midst of that nightmare to get a good night's sleep.

But Israel, one might say, was created, in part, for precisely the opposite purpose. Instead of being about getting a good night's sleep, it was actually about consciously returning to the complexities of history. Being actors in history is critical not only for the purpose of making sure that Jews do not forever live subject to the whim of others (something that after the twentieth century and its horrors most Zionists considered to be simply unthinkable). Rather, it is essential because it is through living in history, in being a player on the stage of history, that Jews can give expression to the ideas that they have long cultivated but have never been able to express in action. Now the choices—and the consequences of those choices—would be theirs to make and to bear. That, too, is a critical dimension of peoplehood.

Jean Jacques Rousseau, writing in *Émile* in 1762, clearly understood this well. "I shall never believe I have heard the arguments of the Jews until they have a free state," Rousseau said. "Only then will we know what they have to say."

More than a century before Theodor Herzl "invented" political Zionism, Rousseau articulated a notion that would eventually become a major motivating force for the creators of the State of Israel: a people becomes "real" when it has the capacity to take the ideas it has nurtured in theory and apply them to the world. It becomes real because the world can finally hear what that people has to say, and it becomes real because that people itself can finally test the degree to which its ideas actually make any difference in the world.

Two cases in point from 2004 come to mind. As January 2004 approached, and as it became clear that Israel was getting ready to trade a large number of terrorists for the bodies of three Israel soldiers and Elhanan Tenenbaum, a businessman kidnapped while abroad, public debate in Israel raged about the deal. The three soldiers, Israelis knew, were dead. Though everyone understood their families' desperate desire to have their sons brought home for a decent burial, the question remained whether the release of so many captured terrorists (or the release of any at all) was a wise move. Would it not motivate Hezbollah, Hamas, and others to try to capture more Israelis, or even to keep the bodies of dead Israelis, for future trades? And what would Israel's leaders say to the families of those soldiers who had been killed while arresting these people who would now be returned in exchange for three corpses and a reputed criminal?

Those in favor of the trade pointed out that Elhanan Tenenbaum was still alive. Even if he'd been up to no good (which was widely suspected, though not yet proven) when he was kidnapped, he was Israeli. He'd been an officer in the army and might divulge information if he were tortured. He had children. Many of those who supported the trade, and who called in to Israel's ubiquitous radio talk shows, pointed to the high priority that Jewish law and Jewish tradition place on the commandment of *pidyon shevuyim,* the redemption of captives.

But the citation of Jewish legal sources about the importance of redeeming captives was no trump card in these radio-disseminated conversations, for other callers—including many who made a point of noting that they were not personally religious—raised an entirely different perspective. They made reference to the case of Rabbi Meir of Rotenburg (1222–1293), one of the leading Jewish scholars of his time, who was captured trying to evade the edicts of Emperor Rudolf I of Hapsburg. The emperor had him imprisoned, demanding an exorbitant ransom from the Jewish community for his release.

Interestingly, however, the Maharam, as Rabbi Meir of Rottenburg is known today, was not willing to be freed under these conditions. He feared that this precedent would lead other rulers to capture high-profile Jews, demand high sums for their release, and thus slowly but surely bankrupt and destroy the very Jewish community to which he had devoted his life. Despite widespread appeals that he relent, Rabbi Meir languished in prison for seven years until his death, and indeed, it was not until fourteen years later that his body was released, when a wealthy Jew paid a much-reduced ransom for the remains.

What ought a society to do when it seeks to place Jewish values front and center in both its discourse and its actions? The Talmud argues that the redemption of captives is a command of supreme importance, because of the horror that captivity must be for the person who has been seized. But Rabbi Meir of Rotenburg suggested that any trade would inevitably lead to more kidnappings, to higher ransoms and to a situation that would bankrupt or endanger the society doing the trading? How can a society committed to Jewish values balance both of these? What would be the moral thing for Israel to do? What would be the act most deeply informed by Jewish sensibilities? Is there something unique about the way that a *Jewish* state ought to respond to this challenge?

As if this conundrum were not sufficiently daunting, a few months later, in May 2004, another tragic debate erupted on the airwaves of Israeli radio. In rapid succession, two bombs in the Gaza Strip destroyed Israeli military vehicles, the second incident unfolding at the Philadelphi corridor at the southern tip of the Strip on the Egyptian border. Not only were all the occupants of the vehicle killed, but the armaments inside their vehicle had exploded, pulverizing their bodies and scattering small pieces of flesh over a wide radius. Once again, Israel was thrust into an agonizing debate. How could Israeli commanders reasonably endanger more troops by having them go to Philadelphi and, on their hands and knees, sift through the sand and the rocks seeking something to bring home so that the parents of the dead soldiers would have something to bury? On the one hand, the desire to have a burial was deep, and thoroughly understandable. Giving those soldiers some form of a burial reflected a deeply held Jewish value. It is a commitment expressed perhaps most notably by the Zaka workers in Israel, the ultra-Orthodox men clad in white shirts and yellow emergency vests, *tzitzit* fringes hanging off to the sides of their pants, razor blades and plastic bags in hand. These men arrive at scenes of carnage and scrape blood and flesh off the sidewalk, putting whatever they can into the bags, so that in keeping with Jewish tradition, all of the victims' body parts, shredded flesh and splattered blood included, can receive a proper burial.

Given this pervasive Jewish attitude to burial, how could Israel choose not to do everything conceivable or possible to bring something back? But that value conflicted with another Jewish value, the desire to protect life at all cost, and to reduce risk to human life to an absolute minimum. What should Israel do here? Send more soldiers in, only to have them risk their lives with Palestinian snipers still in the area? Or tell the parents that sadly, nothing could be done?

In the first case, the trade was made, and Tenenbaum and the three soldiers were brought home. In the second, soldiers were sent in, pieces of the bodies were recovered, and no one else was injured. But the outcomes of the debates struck me even then as less significant than the fact that the debate was taking place. Listening to these radio programs during those weeks, I had the sense that we were witnessing precisely what a Jewish state afforded that no other place could.

These conversations were but a small reflection of the great triumph of Jewish statehood: Jews, making Jewish decisions, with reference to the complexity and even internal tensions in the Jewish tradition. These moments, though likely to be forgotten with time, were perfect examples of the rebirth of the Jewish people. They offered us a glimpse of what the Jewish return to history could mean.

Nor should we assume that this return to Jewish history manifests itself only in military matters, or only in matters pertaining to Jews. In 2007, as Sudanese refugees began to flow into Israel, some fleeing the horrific genocide of Darfur but many more simply seeking a better standard of living, Israel was embroiled in a discussion of what to do. How, some wondered, could a country founded on the backs of refugees not do everything in its power to harbor victims of genocide? At the same time, others asked, with Israel's Jewish majority already threatened, given that that majority is critical to Israel remaining both Jewish and democratic, how could Israel possibly endanger its survival as a Jewish state by opening its borders to a potential flood of such refugees? Rabbi Dov Lior, the rabbi of Hebron and Quiryat Arba, entered the fray, citing the Talmudic stipulation that the "poor of your city take precedence" over others who may need assistance. Given that too many Israeli children already live under the poverty line, he said (a claim that is tragically true), and given that there was virtually no limit to the number of refugees who might seek asylum in Israel were word to get out that the borders were open (also probably true), Israel had no choice but to deny entry and refuge to these people, as tragic as their situation was.

But Rabbi Lior's declaration did nothing to settle the issue. Daniel Friedmann, Israel's minister of justice (and once a candidate for the Knesset with the Shinnui party, known for its radically secular positions), vehemently disagreed. How, Friedmann wanted to know, can Israel claim to reflect the biblical demand for compassion while it turns such refugees away? Is there not a direct parallel to the Jewish experience of the Israelites crossing the desert from Egypt to the Promised Land, fleeing slavery and seeking freedom? Is the Sudanese experience not harrowingly similar to the story that Jews tell about themselves each Passover? A Jewish state, Friedmann argued, had no choice. The refugees must be admitted.

Ehud Olmert's government, struggling with corruption scandals, the fallout of the Second Lebanon War, the challenges of the Annapolis peace initiative, and other problems, never articulated a clear policy on the issue, and the status of the Sudanese refugees languished, insufficiently addressed and inadequately clarified. But the debate between Lior and Friedmann echoed across the country. It was yet another example of how having both a history and a border forced Jews to confront issues that they did not and do not face in the United States, in England, or in France, and returned them, however painfully, to the stage of history. It meant that Jews had to make decisions as Jews, asking themselves how Jewish tradition and Jewish experience would color the choices that sovereignty both enabled and forced them to make.

This return to history also forces Israelis to confront the enormously complex question of what should constitute Jewishness. Jewish law states explicitly that to be a Jew, one has to be born of a Jewish mother, or convert to Judaism. Jewish law also states that only Jews can be buried in Jewish cemeteries. What then should Israel do when a Russian young man who is admitted to Israel by the Law of Return (which requires only one Jewish grandparent in order to be considered Jewish) but is not technically Jewish (according to traditional Jewish law) dies on the battlefield defending the Jewish state? The Rabbinate, understandably from its perspective, insists that the young man cannot be buried in a Jewish cemetery, for he is not Jewish according to the dictates of Jewish law. The parents, equally understandably, are distraught, and want to know how the Jewish state can deny that the soldier was Jewish, when he came to Israel under the Law of Return and died defending the Jewish state. The issue, sadly, has arisen more than once in the past decades, since the massive wave of Russian immigration.

What, at the end of the day, does it mean to be a Jew? Is this simply a matter of legal technicality, or of the mother's religious affiliation? Or does statehood somehow require rethinking what Jewishness is?

Given the opportunity, for the first time in two thousand years, to shape and guide a society in which it has genuine control, what will the Jewish people do? Now that the Jews are both blessed and burdened with sovereignty, the question is not what Jews say in the pages of Talmudic arguments about what they *would* do if they could. Now they *can* do. And that test of Jews' moral fiber, sophistication, creativity, and nuance is both an enormous burden and, at the same time, a gift that allows Jewish life and dialogue to thrive as they could nowhere else.

Many Israelis have very strongly held views on these issues. And they differ, often vigorously. But that is to be expected, and it is fine. What is not fine is when Israelis fail to understand that one of Israel's greatest contributions to Jewish life— and to the world, for that matter —is that it provides a stage on which these questions can be eagerly, knowledgably, and lovingly debated. As Rousseau understood, that possibility makes a people into a nation; it makes that nation real.

Israel has dramatically transformed the contemporary Jewish condition. By creating a "national home for the Jewish people," to quote the Balfour Declaration once again, it has allowed the Jews to re-create peoplehood in a way that Diaspora dispersion did not permit. It has required, but also fostered, the resuscitation of Hebrew as the Jewish language, and it has restored Jews to the stage of history—as Jews.

The transformations we've seen here, though, are best appreciated by those who knew a different era. For Israeli children growing up today, none of these accomplishments seems terribly impressive. Today's Israeli children take for granted that Jews come in all shapes and sizes, colors and builds. They understand that Jews have different backgrounds and cultural heritages. But what strikes today's younger generation, more often than not, is not the renewed sense of peoplehood that Israel has made possible, but the enduring discrimination against Ethiopian Jews, or the stereotypes that Russians are responsible for more than their share of crime, that American immigrants are wealthy and aloof, and so on. The extraordinary diversity of Israel's society today is often seen not as an accomplishment but as a series of major social and economic challenges that Israel has yet to face. The notion of revolutionary shift in the Jewish condition is something that few of these young Israelis think about any longer.

The same could be said of the revival of Hebrew. Today's Israeli children and young adults never knew a world in which Hebrew was not a flourishing language. They take the existence of bookstores filled with Hebrew books as a matter of course. If anything, rather than see the revival of Hebrew as an extraordinary feat, they see their incomplete mastery of English as a drawback. In an Internet-driven age, in which they are on the very same Web sites as teenagers and university students in the United States or in England, it is English that strikes them as the language to know, while Hebrew seems stifling, limiting, and parochial.

As for the return of Jews to the stage of history, the relentlessness of the Israeli-Palestinian conflict simply makes history seem like the nightmare that Saul Bellow's character wanted to avoid. To a generation that is not schooled in the canonical texts of Jewish life, and that therefore can't articulate specifically Jewish positions on the issues we pointed to (or countless others that could have been raised), the myriad issues that Israel faces seem an unnecessary burden, not a privilege. To a generation that never knew Jewish powerlessness, Jewish power seems a curse, an opportunity to make mistakes, a reason to be despised and reviled.

It is precisely for this reason that some, both in Israel and abroad, suggest that perhaps the Jews would be better off with a "national home" that was not a state. Why not create a single country between the Jordan and the Mediterranean, home to both Jews and Palestinians? Yes, Jews would technically be a minority, but they would be a very large minority, at least for a while. Couldn't Hebrew thrive and Jewish culture flourish with the kind of concentration of Jews that Israel now has, just without the army and the borders and the conflict?

It would never work. It wouldn't work because a "national home" without sovereignty does not make Jews decision makers, and does not restore the Jewish people to the stage of history. And it wouldn't work because it is patently naive to assume that they would be physically safe without being a majority. Does any observer of what has transpired in the Middle East in the last three-quarters of a century really dare suggest that Jews as a significant minority in an Arab country would have any protections, or in the long run any possibility of maintaining the advancements that Israel has made possible? Sovereignty, for better or for worse, needs to remain part of the package.

Amazingly, though, there are many Israelis who are tempted by precisely that vision of a single state for the two peoples, a sadly clear indication that Israel's successes in transforming the Jewish condition have been so profound that they are lost on a generation of Israelis that sees no vestiges of what the Jewish condition once had been. Would Israel have been better off had the successes been less complete, if the ingathering of the exiles were still a dream devoutly to be wished, if Hebrew were still a struggling language, or if the Jews were still dreaming of reentering the stage of history?

Perhaps. But that is the nature of all successful revolutions. U.S. college students give little thought, for the most part, to the meaning of "life, liberty and the pursuit of happiness." Fifty-something years after Hungary's revolution, the zeal that motivated young Hungarian students in 1956 is long gone, and their campuses are much like the campuses of any other country.

One of the great ironies of Jewish life today is that Israelis and Jews take the State of Israel and its accomplishments for granted. They can scarcely articulate how statehood has transformed the very nature of being a Jew, while Israel's enemies seem keenly aware of what has been created and the impact it has had. What needs to be restored to the center of Jewish discourse today is an awareness of how Israel has transformed Jewish life, what statehood has done to alter the Jewish condition, and how those accomplishments can be preserved before they are lost once again, perhaps forever.

Chapter Three

THE FIRST WAR,
ALL OVER AGAIN

Even if the blockade [of Gaza] continues indefinitely, we
will not recognize the State of Israel.
—Ismail Haniyyeh, head of the Hamas government,
on June 12, 2008, a day on which 50 mortars and
25 rockets were fired at Israeli cities from Gaza

If we do not take advantage of this calm in order to further
negotiations with the PA and with Syria, we will play into the
hands of Hamas.
—Knesset member Yossi Beilin, on the same day,
quoted on the same Web site at the same time

To regular readers of Israeli Web sites and newspapers, the coin-
cidence of the two quotations above, from the same site, on
the same day, online at the very same moment, is no longer terribly
surprising. One of the things that is most amazing about Israeli life,
particularly after the Palestinian Terror War of 2000, is that some
very intelligent people remain unwilling to admit what is sadly
undeniable: there is no peace to be had. Some American politicians

and journalists still urge the United States to take a more active role in the Middle East because they assume that peace can still be achieved. But with each passing year, fewer and fewer Israelis believe that.

Most Israelis wish matters were otherwise, for they desperately want to end their control of millions of Palestinians. They understand that in the long term, if the Palestinians do not achieve some degree of sovereignty, accusations that Israel is not a genuine democracy will gain credence. But they also know that, sadly, there is at present no alternative. Every Israeli attempt to cede land to the Palestinians has been interpreted as weakness, and has resulted in escalated attacks on the Jewish state.

True, there are also, as the quotes at the beginning of this chapter make clear, intelligent Israelis who believe that peace is possible, and that Israel must do even more to pursue it. But part of the reason for the collapse of the power of Israel's Labor Party is the fact that increasingly, Israel's electorate doubts that that is true. Even those who once prided themselves as being on the political left now find themselves despairing, convinced that the optimism that once defined them was tragically misplaced. For what the Palestinians want, they have now come to understand, is not the creation of a Palestinian state. The Palestinians' real goal is the destruction of the Jewish one.

In the very first days after the Second Lebanon War erupted in the summer of 2006, a rocket hit Haifa, one of Israel's largest cities, deep inside the country and far from the northern border. The explosion killed no one, but it injured a number of people. It also tore the face off an apartment complex, leaving the apartments inside eerily exposed, naked, for all to gaze into. That small block of Haifa, with its shattered shell of a building, rubble all along the street, citizens dazed as they wandered about looking at it all, appeared to be exactly what it was: a war zone. The war had come to the heart of Israel.

Yet amazingly, the people in the street stayed near their homes, going nowhere. The newscaster asked them why they didn't go someplace else where it might be safer. One man answered with a strange sort of logic. "Why leave now? We've already been hit. The chances of us being hit again are one in a million." To which another man responded almost with outrage. "What do numbers have to do with it?" he asked. Then he turned to the camera, almost screaming, pointed to the broken building, and said, "This is our home. *Mi-po ani lo zaz*. From here, I am not budging." And he repeated his refrain over and over again. "This is my home. From here, I am not budging." "*Mi-po ani lo zaz*."

He articulated what many Israelis felt, at least during the war itself. Reluctantly but ineluctably, Israelis had come to understand that the war was not about terrorists. It was not about borders. Nor was it about one United Nations resolution or another, or Israeli policies in the West Bank and Gaza Strip. It was a war being conducted by a terrorist organization that had no territorial dispute with Israel anymore (with the tiny exception of Shebaa Farms, which even Hezbollah did not claim was the reason for the war). It was a war over their homes, over the possibility of any home in that region. That summer, it was a war over their homes in the north. But eventually, Israelis all realized in some unspoken but deeply unsettling way, it would be war over all of their homes.

It was the War of Independence, still unresolved. It was the first war, all over again.

It was the first war all over again, but this time, that war was being fought with Israeli faith in the power of their vaunted military establishment more than slightly shaken. Osama bin Laden, who did not have cruise missiles, had used jetliners to effectively create cruise missiles in September 2001; the Palestinians, who did not have tanks, used human sacrifices to explode Israel's cities, restaurants, and public buses. And now Hezbollah did not need an air force to attack Israel's cities. Its rockets had become both so mobile and so reasonably accurate that the Israeli Air Force could not put a stop to the attacks. True, these were not the powerful weapons that Israel had, but that made little difference. Even these low-tech rockets would, and did, kill. They were more than sufficient to keep the northern third of Israel cowering in long-neglected, stifling bomb shelters for week after week in the middle of an arid summer.

A crude balance of terror had settled on the region, restoring Israelis to a mind-set that predated the 1967 war, to the mind-set of the very earliest days of the state.

Though Israel is normally a fractious society, Israelis bonded together in a moving way during the Second Lebanon War. Even as air-raid sirens went off across the country in the weeks that followed, as people dashed across streets, panicked, running desperately to find the nearest bomb shelter, no one complained about the government. Unlike conflicts in the territories, regarding which Israelis were divided into left and right, religious and nonreligious, hawks and doves, during the Second Lebanon War no one complained—at least while the war was still raging—about the amount of time it was taking the air force to put a stop to the shelling.

All over Jerusalem, advertisements on bus stops were replaced with a photo of an Israeli flag and the phrase *Chazak Ve-ematz*—"Be strong and resolute" (Moses's words to Joshua in Deuteronomy 31:7). Even the people who'd lost family members, who were interviewed while still overwrought with grief, had no complaints about the government or the army. "*Finish this job,*" they effectively said. "*We'll stick it out.*" They'd stick it out, they said to themselves, because they understood what this was: it was the first war, all over again. This was the first war, still unfolding; it was still a war over their homes, and their right to have those homes.

That was why, when Prime Minister Ehud Olmert—not terribly popular prior to the outbreak of the war, to put it mildly—declared before the Knesset, in the opening days of the conflict, that the war would not end until Hezbollah was disarmed and the two kidnapped soldiers were returned, Israelis were almost euphoric, at least given the circumstances. Finally, they said to themselves and to each other, someone gets it. And that was why, when the war ended with the two soldiers still in captivity, with Hezbollah wounded but by no means eradicated, and thus with the specter of having to fight those battles again already over the horizon, the malaise proved so deep.

It was lost on virtually no Israelis that the two primary fronts on which Israel was fighting that summer were precisely the two fronts from which Israel had withdrawn to internationally recognized borders. Israel had withdrawn from Gaza, despite all the internal objections prior to the Disengagement of 2005, hoping to move Palestinian statehood—and peace—one step closer. But in response, the Palestinians elected Hamas, and Hamas and Islamic Jihad unleashed a barrage of more than 800 *kassam*s that they refused to end.

And then Corporal Gilad Shalit was kidnapped. He was stolen not from Gaza, which Israel had already exited, and not from some contested no-man's-land, but from inside Israel's internationally recognized borders. Israelis understood quite well the point that Hamas was trying to make: *There is no place that you're safe. There is no place to which we won't take this war. You can't stay here, not now, not ever.* It was the first war, all over again.

Ever increasing numbers of Israelis found themselves believing what they had previously assumed was nothing more than a right-wing canard. Now they understood: the Palestinians had no interest in building their own homeland. The Palestinians were interested only in destroying Israel. The classic notion that all human beings really want the same things—a solid economy, opportunity for their children, improved education—and that they would give up war the minute that they had those possibilities, had sadly proved irrelevant to the Middle East. Israelis had to admit to themselves that while the peaceniks among them had assumed that the Palestinians wanted exactly the sort of future that they did, that assumption was tragically incorrect.

Nor was Gaza the only front on which Israel had taken major steps to secure peace but on which it was now at war. Six years prior to the Second Lebanon War, Israel had also pulled out of Lebanon. And as in Gaza, this time in defiance of UN resolution 1559, Hezbollah armed itself to the teeth. And as it did so, Israel—under Prime Minister Ariel Sharon, who as a survivor of the Lebanon debacle of 1982 was probably the one Israeli leader who could not risk going into Lebanon again—watched and did nothing. Hezbollah accumulated more than 10,000 rockets. It dug itself into the mountains. It established itself in Beirut, effectively using the civilian population of the Lebanese capital as human shields. And then, assuming that there was little that Israel could or would do, Hezbollah attacked on June 12; eight soldiers were killed, and reservists Ehud Goldwasser and Eldad Regev were taken into captivity from inside Israel's borders.

No one could ignore the fact that the site of the kidnapping was not southern Lebanon. Nor was it Shebaa Farms, that tiny, still-contested hilltop. This kidnapping, too, like that of Gilad Shalit, took place inside Israel, inside a line that no one contested—unless, of course, they contested the idea of the whole enterprise. Which Hezbollah did, and which was precisely the point that was not lost on Israelis.

It was really not the horrific casualties that caused the malaise, or the failure to rout Hezbollah. Or the inability to get the kidnapped soldiers back. It was ultimately the fact that Israel was no closer to being given a chance simply to live than it had ever been. That first war, all over again.

On TV one night during the war, one of Israel's nightly news shows started off with a brief comedic episode. It showed two guys, looking and acting Israeli to the hilt. One of them was speaking in a heavily caricatured Sephardic North African accent, spitting toothpicks as he carried on, telling his friend, over and over and over (referring to the news clip mentioned earlier), "*Mi-po ani lo zaz*. This is the only place where Jews can be safe," he insisted. "This is the place we must stay. From here, I'm not moving." Then the camera panned back, until gradually you realized that the background you were staring at was the London Bridge and the Tower of London.

It was meant to be funny, but for most of the Israelis with whom I spoke about it, it felt mostly sad.

It was sad, because not terribly far below the surface, people couldn't help but begin to wonder. Would going to London, or New York, be the only way to get beyond the hate that threatened to consume them, their families, and their homes? Just over a century after Theodor Herzl had written *The Jewish State* urging the creation of a Jewish home outside of Europe because Jews would not survive there, were the Jews now on the verge of having to flee *back* to Europe?

It seemed that wherever they went, the Jews weren't welcome. Europe had destroyed them. The world voted to give them a state. Israel's enemies attacked, but Israel won, tripling her size. Then, in response to both internal and international pressure, Israel began to retract back toward the 1967 borders, now in an attempt to facilitate the creation of a *Palestinian* state. But it didn't seem to help. *We got out of Lebanon,* Israelis said. *We left Gaza. Olmert was elected after he openly declared his intention to give back the majority of the West Bank. But without intending to, we called their bluff. And then, in the summer of 2006, we learned: the issue isn't their statehood. It's ours.*

The sadness came from the sudden clarity. Israelis could sign peace treaties. They could withdraw. They could create, at tremendous financial and human cost, the region's most powerful military force. But none of that would give them quiet.

For many, the specter of having to endure this for another generation was simply too much to bear. The situation seemed insurmountable, insoluble. You sign a treaty with Egypt, but then Syria takes over Lebanon and uses Hezbollah as its proxy. You get peace with Jordan, but Iran joins the fray. You learn to defend your border, so they attack you from well within their countries.

Peace, even quiet, seemed as far away as they had ever been.

The Second Lebanon War didn't feel like the seventh war. It felt like a continuation of the first. *Could it be,* Israelis asked themselves, *that we're right back where we started?*

Maybe that's why nobody I know actually laughed at the Tower of London skit. For the questions weren't really funny. Would bomb shelters once again be part of the reality of Israeli kids' daily lives? Had we returned to the late 1940s and 1950s, when border towns had to live with the ongoing dread that Fedayeen would sneak across the border and kill people? What made matters even worse, Israelis understood, was the fact that now, in the era of missiles, most of the country is a border town.

And no one laughed because those who know anything about Jewish history know far too well that even going to England, or to the United States, or anywhere else, would do nothing to make the Jews safe. Israel was created precisely *because* Jews have learned that lesson; they know that if they flee Israel because of its dangers, those dangers will follow them wherever they go.

This was an old story, because there was nowhere to flee to, even outside of Israel, and because the new war was like the old wars. The Second Lebanon War was like the old wars because the war was fought inside Israel's own cities. It was like the old wars because the casualties mounted far beyond what anyone had dared imagine. It was like the old wars because it wasn't just the regular conscripts who fought it. It was thousands of soldiers, in a war that the IDF had first assured Israelis could be won from the air. They were regular infantry, and elite units. They were young soldiers in the midst of their military service, and reservists—fathers, husbands, men long past their physical prime being called upon to give it their all—and not all of them made it home. Israel had been there before, too. But Israelis had allowed themselves to believe that they were done with that.

And the Second Lebanon War was like the first war because of the television news that broadcast lines of Arab refugees fleeing the fighting in Beirut, heading north, or fleeing to Syria. Israeli TV showed footage of the Hezbollah stronghold in Beirut that looked much more like Dresden than like Beirut. (Did Arab stations show the misery on the Israeli side? Most Israelis doubted it.) There were probably some Israelis who couldn't care less, but the ones that I talked to, worked with, and shared a neighborhood with did care. They understood that we probably had no choice, for Hezbollah had decided to use those neighborhoods of Beirut as its human shield, and for years and years Lebanon did not stop them. And we had no choice but to survive.

But the Israelis I spoke with during the war were still saddened, even distraught, by the miles-long lines of thousands upon thousands upon thousands of Lebanese refugees, fleeing their homes and rubble-filled neighborhoods with white flags hanging outside their cars even as Israeli war planes roared overhead. Simply on a human level, we knew that the suffering was incalculable. We couldn't help but remember the old black-and-white footage from the War of Independence. We were saddened for them, and worried for ourselves. We were saddened for them because the sight of people leaving their homes, with nowhere to go as their neighborhoods were reduced to rubble, is horrifying no matter who the victims are.

Yet we were also worried for ourselves, because as a problem for Israel, we knew, Arab refugees don't disappear. They attack, we respond, they flee. When 500,000 Jewish refugees from Europe arrived on the shores of Palestine in the late 1940s and early 1950s, the Jewish community absorbed them. When 750,000 Jewish refugees arrived from Arab lands (evicted from those countries for the crime of belonging to a people that had decided not to die), Israel took them in, too, even though it could hardly afford to. But Arab countries by and large make no attempt to settle Arab refugees. Those people are kept homeless and indigent by governments who want more pawns in their chess match against Israel. That's what had happened with the Palestinian refugees from 1948, and it might well be what would happen here, too. As a problem for Israel, Arab refugees don't just go away.

That, too, we'd learned from the War of Independence. And that, too, we were reliving. That first war just didn't seem to end.

So it was the seventh war. (Or the eighth, if you count the War of Attrition of 1967–1970. Or the ninth, if you count the Intifada of 1987–1992.) And the first war. It was all the wars. They're all the same, in the end, because Israel can't afford to lose. Because the whole enterprise is at stake. Because nothing much has changed.

For people who do not live in Israel, it's difficult to fully internalize the extent of this emotional exhaustion, but to understand the conflict, and the depression that has set into Israel, it is important to try. It's one thing—and a horrific one—to have to go to war. When you live in a country in which your neighbors and their children, your colleagues at the office and the guys who work behind the counter at the supermarket, your doctor and your lawyer and your computer technicians—and everyone else—have all gone off to war, the subject of their experiences inevitably comes up, sometimes when you least expect it.

And when it does, you see their eyes change—the glazed-over vacant stare at something far beyond you, the faces of people recalling things that often they have chosen never to discuss. They're thinking of the friends they lost, the friends who came back without limbs, the terror that many of them felt when the roar and chaos of battle raged around them, the fear that probably still stalks them occasionally in the middle of the night.

For generations now, Israelis have trudged off to war, telling themselves that this war, perhaps, would be the last one. They would head into the hell of battle in order to ensure that their children would not have to, in order to make it possible for their grandchildren to inherit a radically different world.

When the 1973 Yom Kippur War was at its height, Yehoram Gaon, one of Israel's foremost pop singers, went to the front and sang the now famous lyrics, *Ani mavti'ach lach*—"I promise you, my little girl, that this will be the last war." It was an enormously popular song in Israel for decades. It evoked the spoken and unspoken ethos of Israeli life: *Yes, it's difficult, and yes, the pain is unbearable. But it doesn't have to always be this way. One more war and they'll understand. One more war, and they'll let us be. One more war, and this will be over.*

But Israeli radio never plays that song anymore. I haven't heard it since the Palestinian Terror War, the first war that Israel fought after Oslo, the first war after Camp David, the first war after Israel unwittingly called the Palestinians' bluff by coming too close to an agreement. Today, after that war, no one in Israel believes that we've fought the last war. And that, perhaps more than anything else, is the cause of the pain. That was the source of the emptiness, the exhaustion. That was the reason that some people began to wonder, even aloud, how much longer they could still go on.

What the Second Lebanon War did to Israel was to erode any real hope the Israelis who had children in the army might have had that they would not have to watch their grandchildren go off to war. Today's Israelis are the first generation of Israelis that, when it speaks about "peace," feels self-conscious, as if they're speaking to other adults about the tooth fairy, about things that are more figures of speech than they are matters that exist—or even might come to exist.

Half a year after the war was over, Yonatan Bassi, the man whom Ariel Sharon had appointed to oversee the relocation and long-term welfare of Israeli citizens who would be removed from Gaza, wrote a short piece on that week's Torah reading. (Such commentaries are widely distributed in synagogues throughout Israel.) It had been months since the war, and the country was quiet (except for the occasional *kassam* from Gaza). On the verses dealing with blessing children, Bassi mused:

> In the midst of the battles of the War of Independence, my father—a soldier in Battalion 13 of the Golani Brigades— received a brief leave so that he could participate in the *brit* [ritual circumcision] of his first-born son. The blessing which I received from him, an intuitive blessing that flowed from his wellspring of emotions, was, "May it be God's will that in the merit of my participating in this war, my son might know what war is only from the stories that I will tell him when he is older."
>
> My father died forty years ago this week, a week before I was drafted into the IDF. . . . In the meantime, all my sons have fought in Israel's wars, and in five years, my eldest grandson will don his uniform. And the eternal vision of peace seems more unattainable than ever. Thus, how is it possible to bless my grandson, and those of his generation, without sounding pathetic?

Bassi's question, of how parents can bless their children with peace without sounding absurd, is the challenge that Israelis now face. When the mere act of blessing your children seems pathetic, it can become difficult, indeed, to soldier on.

In truth, though, the Second Lebanon War wasn't quite identical to the War of Independence, and the differences between those wars actually contributed to Israel's despondency.

First, Israel was no longer fighting a standing army representing a nation like Egypt, Jordan, or Syria. Israel was fighting a terrorist organization that felt no responsibility for its civilian population, that, like a cancerous growth on the country it inhabited, was exclusively parasitic. It used the civilian population as cover, without concern. Fighting a terrorist organization, as the United States was learning at the same time in Iraq, is an entirely different matter from fighting a standing army. Israel would have to learn to fight all over again.

Second, Israel was no longer fighting just its enemies. It was now fighting proxies. Iran, which has no border or territorial dispute with Israel, was supplying and training the people Israel was fighting. The list of potential enemies, therefore, was longer than it had ever been. It was close to endless.

And finally, technology was changing the balance of power in the Middle East. With Iran threatening to acquire nuclear weapons, and with a messianic madman at the helm of that government, Israeli parents had to face the fact that even if Israel *could* force the Palestinians into submission (which it couldn't), they still couldn't keep their children safe. A century after Zionists had decided to leave Europe for safer harbors, Israel had become the most dangerous place in the world to be a Jew. *That is what decades of building and dreaming have wrought?* they wondered. For the first time, Israeli parents had to ask themselves if raising their children in Israel was possibly an immoral thing to do. Who, if they had a choice, would rightly raise their children in the crosshairs of a nuclear-armed maniac?

So it was the first war, all over again. But it wasn't. The threat was spreading. The War of Independence had seemed devastating because Israel lost one percent of its civilian population in that conflict; that level of loss, though, could be child's play if Mahmoud Ahmadinejad got his way.

It was in the face of the loss of that hope, in the face of the sense that they'd suddenly found themselves back in 1950, or even earlier, that many Israelis began to wonder how much longer they could hang on. How much longer, they began to ask themselves in hushed whispers over the dinner table and in cafés, and sometimes more explicitly on radio talk shows, could they expect their society to survive when they, their children, and their grandchildren had to worry about their very existence? Was this perhaps the time to escape?

As if this were not enough, as if the relentlessness of war and conflict were not sufficient to undermine Israelis' faith in the possibility of a future (the very faith that a Jewish state had been meant to restore), yet another cloud began to roll over the horizon. In addition to all its armed enemies and their relentless refusal to accept the mere fact of Israel's resistance, Israelis now had to acknowledge that they also faced a hostile and infinitely more critical international community. More and more, Israelis saw, even as they struggled to defend themselves and their children, they were alone, pariahs in a world that had once celebrated them, abandoned and disdained by the very world that had voted just decades earlier to create their now besieged state.

In the face of this new abandonment, their despair only deepened.

Chapter Four

A NATION THAT DWELLS ALONE

The United States has a terrorism problem in good part because it is so closely allied with Israel. . . . U.S. support for Israel makes it easier for extremists like bin Laden to rally popular support. . . . Washington would not be nearly as worried about Iran, Ba'thist Iraq or Syria were it not so closely tied to Israel. . . . Treating Israel as America's most important ally in the campaign against terrorism . . . ignores the ways that Israel's policies make U.S. efforts more difficult.

—U.S. professors John Mearsheimer and Stephen M. Walt

[I]f one day . . . the Islamic world will also be equipped with the weapons available to Israel now, the imperialist strategy will reach an impasse, because the employment of even one atomic bomb inside Israel will wipe it off the face of the earth, but would only do damage to the Islamic world.

—Former Iranian president Rafsanjani

In March 2006, two well known and highly regarded professors, Stephen Walt of Harvard University's Kennedy School of Government and John Mearsheimer of the University of Chicago, published a working paper entitled "The Israel Lobby and U.S. Foreign Policy" on the Kennedy School Web site. The authors suggested that the American Israel "lobby" had a "stranglehold" on the U.S. media and government. They claimed that U.S. support of Israel was morally unjustified, since Israel was guilty of "massacres" and "rapes by Jews" (when most authorities agree that rapes by Israeli soldiers are exceedingly rare, and when charges of "massacres," such as those that emerged after the battle of Jenin, have been proven false). Referring to Israel's Law of Return, which automatically grants Jews citizenship, Walt and Mearsheimer concluded that Israel has "racial" citizenship laws, an incendiary term in America, and a surprising claim in light of the fact that Israel's Jews are Ashkenani, Sephardi, Ethiopian, and more—and they have been granted citizenship without any regard to race. But for two academics determined to portray Israel in the worst possible light, the racism card was too tempting to ignore.

As to why their working paper eventually was published in the *London Review of Books* and not in a U.S. journal, Walt and Mearsheimer claimed that that, too, was a function of Jewish power. "John Mearsheimer says that the pro-Israel lobby is so powerful that he and coauthor Stephen Walt would never have been able to place their report in an American-based scientific publication," the *Forward* reported.

A flood of critique followed the publication of their paper. Yet despite the highly critical responses to their work, Walt and Mearsheimer were able to publish the article as a book in the fall of 2007 under the same title. Response to the book was no less critical, often accusing the authors of blatant unfairness. Precisely because some of the critique captures so eloquently not only what was wrong with the Walt and Mearhsheimer book, but what had begun to characterize international discussions of Israel in general, it's worth quoting at some length.

William Grimes, writing in the *New York Times*, said:

The general tone of hostility to Israel grates on the nerves, however, along with an unignorable impression that hard-headed political realism can be subject to its own peculiar fantasies. . . . They also seem to feel that, with Israel and its lobby pushed to the side, the desert will bloom with flowers. A peace deal with Syria would surely follow, with a resultant end to hostile activity by Hezbollah and Hamas. Next would come a Palestinian state, depriving Al Qaeda of its principal recruiting tool. (The authors wave away the idea that Islamic terrorism thrives for other reasons.) Well, yes, Iran does seem to be a problem, but the authors argue that no one should be particularly bothered by an Iran with nuclear weapons. And on and on.

Tim Rutten, writing for the *Los Angeles Times*, also a paper not known for its positive predisposition to Israel in recent years, echoed Grimes's sentiments:

Anyone familiar with the tortured history of the Israeli-Palestinian conflict will have a hard time recognizing the history Mearsheimer and Walt rehearse. Every hoary old Israeli atrocity tale is trotted out, and the long story of Palestinian terrorism is rendered entirely as a reaction to Israeli oppression. The failure of every peace negotiation is attributed to Israeli deviousness under the shield of the American Israel lobby. There is nothing here of Palestinian corruption, division and duplicity or even of this unhappy people's inability to provide a reliable secular partner with whom peace can be negotiated.

And David Remnick, in the *New Yorker*, wrote that "[i]t's a narrative that recounts every lurid report of Israeli cruelty as indisputable fact but leaves out the rise of Fatah and Palestinian terrorism before 1967; the Munich Olympics; Black September; myriad cases of suicide bombings; and other spectaculars."

But if anything, the outrage surrounding Walt and Mearsheimer's thesis likely helped fuel their success. Neither their questionable motives nor the rebuffs from reviewers, from *Commentary* on the right and *The Nation* on the left, had any negative impact on the appeal of the thesis to an American public: it sold remarkably well and became a *New York Times* best-seller.

Behind all the rhetoric about the myriad ways in which Israel is the bully of the Middle East, the perpetrator of crimes against the Palestinians, and a country whose vulnerability is highly overstated, Walt and Mearsheimer had a more basic claim at stake: Israel, they implied, needed not more supporters, but fewer. If anything, they suggested, Israel deserved adversaries, not allies. In order to reach a reasonable settlement of the Israeli-Palestinian conflict, the world would have to stop coddling the Jewish state.

To many Israelis and other observers of the Middle East, what was most painful about this call for reduced international support for Israel was that it came at a time when such support was already at a low. The Jewish state was then already feeling as alone and abandoned as it ever had. Nonetheless, even serious academics such as Walt and Mearsheimer now felt that Israel ought to be even further isolated and pressured. As Israelis were already reeling from the realization that they were engaged in a war that would seemingly never end, these new calls for their isolation only contributed to their collective sense of desperation.

The euphoria that surrounded the famed United Nations vote on November 29, 1947, has long since subsided. The need for penance that the world apparently felt in the shadow of the Shoah has slowly evaporated, almost in parallel with the dwindling number of survivors. The very United Nations that voted to create the Jewish state has in subsequent years turned on Israel, becoming a relentless critic. Were the General Assembly to vote today on the creation of a Jewish state, it is highly unlikely that the resolution would pass. Indeed, in much of the international community, the image of Israel as the darling of the Western world, which Israel earned in its stunning June 1967 victory, has given way to that of a pariah. In ways that would have been unthinkable just three decades ago, Israelis now often feel that they have returned to the biblical image of Israel as "a people that dwells alone, not reckoned among the nations" (Numbers 23:9).

The Jews dancing in the streets of Jerusalem and Tel Aviv, whom Amos Oz describes so memorably, would not have believed on November 29, 1947, that matters could change so dramatically. It is true that the UN vote was not unanimous (it was thirty-three nations in favor, thirteen opposed, and ten abstaining), but it passed. And though the Arabs did respond by attacking, they lost the war they started. Israel's future looked bright, and after the worst period the Jews had ever known, it seemed they were finally getting a reprieve in the court of international opinion.

But by the early 1970s, the world had changed. The Palestinians had begun to express their own nationalist aspirations, often resorting to terror, as in the 1972 attack on Israeli athletes at the Munich Olympics. Not long after that attack, in November 1974, PLO Chairman Yassir Arafat was invited to address the General Assembly of the United Nations, the first very clear sign that the international tide was changing and that his terror was reaping its intended benefits.

Arafat's speech is remembered less than his dress; as he gesticulated at the podium, his pistol holster was visible for all to see (he'd been required to surrender the weapon itself when arriving at the UN). The point was clear, but he made it explicit nonetheless: "Today I have come bearing an olive branch and a freedom fighter's gun. Do not let the olive branch fall from my hand. I repeat: do not let the olive branch fall from my hand." But he was equally clear as to what it would take to get him to drop the gun: "Our resolve to build a new world is fortified—a world free of colonialism, imperialism, neo-colonialism and racism in each of its instances, including Zionism."

The Jewish state, Arafat was insisting, needed to disappear, and the UN willingly played host to this declaration of renewed war. (Dare we imagine what the world would have said had Ariel Sharon worn a pistol holster when *he* addressed the General Assembly in September 2005?)

But Arafat's speech, and the effective Palestinian declaration of war against the Jewish state, were but the beginning; the momentum only grew. The following year, 1975, the United Nations voted on

Resolution 3379, the now well-known "Zionism Is Racism" resolution. And this time, the vote was not at all close. Seventy-five nations voted in favor, and only thirty-five opposed. (For more than fifteen years, until Resolution 46/86 in December 1991, the United Nations refused to withdraw that accusation.) The tide had turned, and Israel had begun the journey to becoming the most endangered nation on the planet.

Though the U.S. representative to the United Nations, Patrick Moynihan, immediately responded that "[t]he United States will not abide by . . . this infamous act," Israel's sense of isolation grew even deeper. Israelis knew that Moynihan had it exactly right when he thundered to the UN that the resolution "is not an attack on Zionism, but on Israel." The noose was tightening. The United Nations, the ostensibly impartial mediator of international conflict, clearly had decided that Israel—not the Arabs or the Palestinians—was the sole offending party in the Israeli-Arab conflict. More than that, by equating Zionism with racism, it was raising serious questions about whether Israel should have a right to exist.

Like the UN, Arafat was also becoming more brazen in his delegitimization of the Jewish state. Even as he was awarded the Nobel Peace Prize in 1994 in the afterglow of the 1993 Oslo Accords and the resulting hope that the Middle East might finally know peace, he had no compunction about beginning his speech with a veiled call for Israel's destruction:

> Since my people entrusted me with the hard task of searching for our lost home, I have been filled with warm faith that those who carried their keys in the diaspora as they carry their own limbs, and that those who endured their wounds in the homeland and maintained their identity will be rewarded by return and freedom for their sacrifices. I have also been filled with faith that the arduous trek on the long path of pain will end in our home's yard.

"Our home's yard," of course, was now the heart of Israel. The image of "carrying keys" was an important one for Arafat and for all Palestinians, because the only reason to carry the keys to one's erstwhile home is that one intends to return to that home. The word "diaspora" was Arafat's way of saying that if the Jews had deserved a state, so, too, did the Palestinians. But he was not advocating equal treatment. The call for Palestinians to be able to return to their homes was a call for the end of a Jewish majority in Israel, for the erasing of the Jewish state, and for the re-creation of a Palestinian society in the cities that Israelis now called home.

Arafat understood all this, and so did his listeners. Nor was it lost on Israelis that Arafat had stood, first with a holster, and then advocating the destruction of Israel, not in Ramallah, not even in East Jerusalem, but first at the UN General Assembly, and then at the awards ceremony of the Nobel Prize in Stockholm. The world's most majestic and formal settings had turned into platforms not just for denigrating the State of Israel, but rather, for in effect calling for its annihilation.

Nonetheless, by the late 1990s, after the negotiations at Madrid, Oslo, the Wye Plantation, and others, it seemed that the Israeli-Palestinian conflict might be close to a settlement after all. But just months after the Camp David negotiations of July 2000 ended without closure, the Palestinian Terror War erupted.

As that war raged, the UN's World Conference Against Racism was held in Durban, South Africa, in 2001. Even as Israel was battling the Palestinian Terror War, as suicide bombers were wreaking havoc and sowing fear in Israeli society, what was supposed to have been a conference on the scourge of racism across the globe morphed into an Israel-bashing festival. Arab and Islamic states used their platforms as a means of raising once again the accusation that Zionism is racism.

In response to draft resolution language that read, "The World Conference recognizes with deep concern the increase of racist practices of Zionism and anti-Semitism in various parts of the world, as well as the emergence of racial and violent movements based on racism and discriminatory ideas, in particular the Zionist movement, which is based on racial superiority," the United States and Israel staged a walkout. Secretary of State Colin Powell said, "You do not combat racism by conferences that produce declarations containing hateful language, some of which is a throwback to the days of 'Zionism equals racism,' or supports the idea that we have made too much of the Holocaust, or suggests that apartheid exists in Israel, or that singles out only one country in the world, Israel, for censure and abuse." But the walkout proved symbolic at best; the conference continued with its anti-Israel undercurrents unaffected, much of the world essentially implicitly accepting the claim that what had once been the scourge of anti-Semitism was now the curse of Zionism. For those of us living in Israel at the time, the cognitive dissonance between what we knew to be happening in the battles raging just minutes from our homes and the absurdity and evil of the UN meeting was simply incomprehensible. At moments, it was so dizzying that it felt as if gravity had been suspended.

The following year, Israel experienced the unique treatment of the UN once again. It was April 2002, and Prime Minister Ariel Sharon ordered troops into the West Bank to destroy the terror infrastructure that was paralyzing Israeli society. A fierce battle erupted in the Casbah of the old city of Jenin. Israel suffered grievous losses (twelve reserve soldiers—some of them men with wives and children— were killed in one booby-trapped building alone), but the world's attention was quickly focused on a "massacre" of unarmed civilians that the Palestinians claimed had taken place. Israel denied those accusations immediately and vociferously, but to no avail. The world simply accepted the Palestinian claims.

Britain's *Guardian* reported that "Palestinians accuse Israel of a massacre, and there are convincing accounts from local people of the occasional summary execution." The London *Telegraph* headlined its article with "Blasted to Rubble by the Israelis," and followed with copy that read: "When we penetrated into the exclusion zone yesterday, by walking across a hilltop and finding an unguarded flank, it became clear why the Israelis had done their utmost to shield Jenin camp from prying eyes. . . . Hanging over everything was the sickly smell of rotting corpses, an unknown number of which lay under the rubble." France's *Le Monde* published a cartoon showing two identical scenes of rubble, entitling one "Warsaw 1943" and the other "Jenin 2002," again suggesting that whatever guilt the world bore for anti-Semitism had now more than been made up for by the evils of Zionism. But the ultimate outrage, as far as Israelis were concerned, was UN Secretary General Kofi Annan's response to Israeli protestations that no massacre had taken place. Annan said, "I don't think the whole world, including the friends of the Israeli Government, can be wrong."

The international community called for an investigation, and after some initial delays, a UN inquiry eventually did ensue. As Israel had predicted, it indicated that there had simply been no massacre. A few Palestinians had been killed, virtually all of them armed gunmen. The massacre had been fabricated, and yet, Israelis noted, neither the European press nor Kofi Annan ever apologized.

Yet Jenin was hardly the only example. If any one issue highlighted Israel's sense of isolation at the hands of international organizations that were purportedly unbiased and depoliticized, it was the international response to the security fence that Israel started to construct as a result of the wave of terror attacks. The world's litany of objections to the fence culminated in the International Court of Justice at The Hague ruling, in July 2004, that the fence had to come down. The court declared that it was "not convinced" that the fence helped address the problem of terror. Israelis knew that the Hague was wrong. Even Ramadan Salah, the Palestinian Islamic Jihad leader, had himself noted in an interview with Al-Manar TV that "the separation fence . . . is an obstacle to the resistance, and if it were not there the situation would be entirely different." But admissions by the terrorists themselves that the fence was working made no difference. The International Court of Justice declared, after years of terror unleashed against Israeli women and children in schools, restaurants, and buses, that the fence was the primary problem.

The proceedings at The Hague would have been humorous had they not been so offensive. Israelis noted that while The Hague saw fit to rule on Israel's fence, it has never investigated the 460-mile barrier built by India in the Kashmir region to prevent infiltrations from Pakistan (the construction of which began in the 1990s and continued through 2004), or the sixty-mile barrier built by Saudi Arabia along its border with Yemen to stop the smuggling of arms (which was begun in 2003). About those projects, the Hague had nothing to say. It was only the lives of *Israeli* citizens, it seemed to a society still reeling from the terror attacks, that did not justify the construction of a fence that could obviously be removed the minute that the threat disappeared.

Eventually the world changed its argument and moved from speaking about Israeli massacres, or of Zionism as racism, to open calls for Israel's destruction. Not surprisingly, this call emanated first from the Arab world, as it had when Egyptian president Gamal Abdul Nasser vowed in 1967 to drive Israel into the sea. This time, though, the source was Iran. In October 2005, at a conference entitled "The World without Zionism," Iranian president Mahmoud Ahmadinejad called for Israel to be "wiped off the map." Shortly thereafter, Ahmadinejad said that the Nazi Holocaust (which, in parts of the Western world, was an important element in the justification of the world's decision to create a Jewish state in the first place) was a "myth," a "fairy tale."

There were those who discounted Ahmadinejad's histrionics, suggesting that he was nothing but a loose cannon, a politician searching for rhetoric that would win him popular support. But these people missed the essential point. What is critical is not that Ahmadinejad called for Israel's destruction. What is of the utmost significance is that these calls for eliminating the Jewish state emanated from Iran just as Teheran was also apparently making significant progress toward the creation of a nuclear weapon. And though some pundits in the West continued to insist that Iran did not plan to develop nuclear weapons in order to destroy Israel, Iran itself had the clarity that the West did not. Former Iranian president Rafsanjani, speaking in a Friday sermon, for example, promised that "[i]f one day, a very important day of course, the Islamic world will also be equipped with the weapons available to Israel now, the imperialist strategy will reach an impasse, because the employment of even one atomic bomb inside Israel will wipe it off the face of the earth, but would only do damage to the Islamic world." Even the damage that such a bomb might do to Iran would apparently not be a deterrent.

Meanwhile the West, beyond some predictable hand-wringing, did little to stop Teheran. Bush made some veiled threats about bombing

Iran, but as of this writing, at least, beyond the talk of sanctions, nothing much has happened. Ahmadinejad's saber rattling also had another ominous dimension to it: Israelis did not fail to note once again that they were alone, and unique in that aloneness—one member of the UN had called for the destruction of another, and no serious repercussions followed.

As was to be expected, the virus soon spread beyond the UN and Iran. With time, the chorus of objections to Israel's very existence grew more explicit and began to extend to the world of academe and reputable publications, especially in Europe. The anti-Israel tenor of much of Britain's discourse was perhaps best epitomized by London Mayor Ken Livingstone's accusing Israel of ethnic cleansing.

Jacqueline Rose, a British academic (who happens to be Jewish), wrote that "we believe Zionism to be a form of collective insanity." In a book published by the august Princeton University Press, Rose raises the possibility that Hitler and Herzl both attended the same performance of Wagner in Paris, a performance that she suggests inspired both Hitler's *Mein Kampf* and Herzl's *Der Judenstaadt*. But her suggestion is patently absurd. It is virtually impossible that Hitler could have attended that performance, as he is not believed to have been to Paris before 1940. But even if he had attended the performance, he would have been a child at the time, and more likely than not, not yet preoccupied with the ideas that eventually framed *Mein Kampf.* Yet Rose can't seem to help herself; the desire to draw a connection between Nazism and the roots of Zionism is too tempting for her to withstand.

In 2005, Britain's Association of University Teachers (numbering 40,000 members) voted to adopt a boycott of Israeli academics, and in 2006, the even larger National Association of Teachers in Further and Higher Education decried Israel's "apartheid policies" and urged British academics to shun their Israeli colleagues.

No one can reasonably deny the suffering of many Palestinians, or claim that Israeli rule over the territories that it has tried to relinquish has always been benign. But Israelis could also not help but notice that while other conflicts across the globe took many more lives or were the focus of heinous violations of human rights, British academics said nothing about *those* regions of the world. Four hundred thousand people were murdered in Darfur, and British professors did and said nothing. Hundreds of people were detained and tortured in Zimbabwe, but no boycotts followed. Venezuela's most watched independent television station was shut down, but the British—for whom freedom of speech and expression should have been a major concern—did not respond. It was only with regard to Israel's policies that British academics became such activists.

Further compounding the illogic of the British academics' position was the fact that in boycotting Israeli university professors, the British were actually boycotting the one segment of Israeli society that leans most to the left, the very segment that had opposed Israel's policies in both Gaza and the West Bank long before the British academics decided to speak out on the issue.

Astute observers of Israel's condition understood that whether intentionally or not, the British boycott would eventually have another dangerous outcome. To the extent that this boycott and others like it could make Israeli academic life unbearably parochial (because those academics would not be invited to conferences in Europe, if the British got their way), ever greater numbers of Israelis committed to a flourishing academic career might have to choose to make their lives outside the Jewish state. These boycotts would result in much more than "mere" pressure on Israelis to change their positions. In time, they would demoralize and isolate Israel's top minds, thereby contributing to the academic brain drain that is already weakening the intellectual foundation of the state.

British academics were brazen when confronted with the unfairness of their position. When Dr. Jonathan Rynhold of Bar-Ilan University told British professor Tom Hickey, "You are imposing standards on Israel, and Israeli academe, that you do not demand of any other country, not even British academe, of which you are a part. And you treat the Israeli-Palestinian conflict as if it were completely one-sided," Hickey responded, "It *is* one-sided." Now, even reasonable people who disagree with Israel's policies, or who would prefer to see

Israel adopt a more conciliatory attitude to the Palestinians, never suggest that the conflict is one-sided. But the British academics had lost all sense of proportion. If the conflict was one-sided, then there was nothing short of ceasing to exist that Israel could ever do to make matters right. That, Israelis understood, was precisely the agenda; increasingly, Israelis sensed that they were utterly alone.

During a conversation with the owner of the *Daily Telegraph* newspaper, Conrad Black, about the Middle East crisis, the French ambassador to London, Daniel Bernard, referred to Israel as "that shitty little country." When his comment hit the press and Bernard was pressured to at least apologize, he refused to do so. Diplomats and politicians were now taking liberties with Israel that it would have been hard to imagine them taking with any other country.

To the mix of politicians and academics one could then add the world of public intellectuals. In the summer of 2006, Jostein Gaarder, a highly regarded Norwegian public intellectual (and the author of *Sophie's World*), vehemently objected to Israel's conduct of the Second Lebanon War. His response was simple: he wrote, "We no longer recognize the State of Israel. We need to get used to the idea: The State of Israel, in its current form, is history."

That Israel was at war or that the war had been precipitated by the kidnapping of Israeli soldiers from undisputed Israeli territory made no difference to Gaarder. That Hezbollah had taken over civilian neighborhoods of Beirut and had cynically used them as cover from which to shell Israeli civilians was of no concern to him, either. Nor was he bothered by the obvious fact that when people oppose the policies of the United States in Iraq, they do not suggest that the United States is, or ought to be, "history." But Israel was held to an entirely different standard. Just a few years after the heady, optimistic days of January 2000, Israel had become the only country whose right to exist was legitimate grist for the mill in respectable circles.

Nor was this opposition to Israel limited to politicians, opinionmakers, and intellectuals. Ordinary European citizens imbibed this attitude and soon made it their own. In 2003, as the Palestinian Terror War was still being viciously fought in the buses and restaurants of Israeli cities, a European Commission survey polled the attitudes of 7,500 European Union residents and asked them which country posed the most serious threat to world peace. Israel, amazingly enough, came in first. Fifty-nine percent of Europeans across the EU placed Israel ahead of North Korea and Iran, "with the figures rising to 60 per cent in Britain, 65 in Germany, 69 in Austria and 74 in Holland."

In the face of the UN's moral failure, the uncensored hatred and perverse historical revisionism being spewed forth from Teheran, and the damaged moral compass of much of Europe, Israelis and Zionists across the globe expected—or at least hoped—that the United States would remain a bulwark of sanity. Perhaps America would retain a more reasonable approach to the causes and potential solutions of the conflict in the Middle East. But even there, the picture grew darker than many had anticipated it would.

Those sympathetic to Israel, who hoped that the United States might remain the last bastion of sanity on this front, witnessed a magazine no less venerable than the *Atlantic Monthly* ask, "Will Israel Live to 100?" "Don't be seduced by the recent hopeful signs," the *Atlantic*'s Benjamin Schwarz insisted. "In the long run the Israeli-Palestinian conflict will remain a problem without a solution." The chances for Israel's survival, he intimated, were not good. Nor would the *Atlantic* let its attention to that question subside. Precisely three years later, the *Atlantic* published another cover story, this time by Jeffrey Goldberg. The cover had an Israeli flag composed not of blue and white, but of red, black, and green (the colors of the Palestinian flag), and asked, in bold lettering, "Is Israel Finished?"

Much more sobering was the fact that while the *Atlantic* was wondering whether Israel *could* survive, others were beginning to ask whether it *should*. The most distressing example was Professor Tony Judt's article, "Israel—The Alternative," in the *New York Review of Books*. Judt, himself Jewish and a former resident of Israel, argued in 2003 that Israel simply got on board the "nationalism train" too late.

The problem with Israel, in short, is not—as is sometimes suggested—that it is a European "enclave" in the Arab world; but rather that it arrived too late. It has imported a characteristically late-nineteenth-century separatist project into a world that has moved on, a world of individual rights, open frontiers, and international law. The very idea of a "Jewish state"—a state in which Jews and the Jewish religion have exclusive privileges from which non-Jewish citizens are forever excluded—is rooted in another time and place. Israel, in short, is an anachronism.

In light of those changes caused by the world "moving on," he wonders, "[W]hat if there were no place in the world today for a 'Jewish state'?" Instead of a Jewish state, Judt argues, there should be a binational state, of Jews and Arabs. The fact that Jews would immediately become a marginally tolerated minority in this state, or that once the state inevitably voted to allow millions of vengeful Palestinian refugees to return, that marginally tolerated status would almost certainly devolve rapidly into no tolerance whatsoever, was of no interest to Judt.

Moreover, as Judt certainly knows, the claim that Israel is a country in which "Jews . . . have exclusive privileges from which non-Jewish citizens are forever excluded" is a radical and conscious misrepresentation of Israeli democracy. Israeli democracy is surely not perfect, but Judt's description consciously casts Israel in a grossly unfair light. Furthermore, by Judt's criteria, Palestinian nationalism, which emerged almost a century after Jewish political nationalism, should have been even more of an anachronism than Zionism. If Zionism is illegitimate because it appeared on the international stage too late, is that not even more true of the Palestinians' quest for a state?

That a Jewish public intellectual, one who lived in Israel for a significant period of time, can make this argument, is the sort of blow that has Israelis reeling—at least those sufficiently worldly to know what people like Judt are saying. Israelis have begun to wonder, *Is there no safe harbor that can offer protection from the assault on Israel?*

If American, Jewish, Israel-experienced intellectuals will not provide that harbor, what or who will?

Nor, of course, is Judt the only American public intellectual to assail Israel's legitimacy. Adrienne Rich, the American poet, has written that Zionism is "so incendiary, so drenched in . . . ideas of blood and soil, in memories of victimization and pursuant claims of the right to victimize" that it "needs to dissolve before twenty-first century realities." And Joel Kovel, a member of the faculty at Bard College, who like Judt is a committed Jew, argued in his book entitled *Overcoming Zionism* and elsewhere that "to be a true Jew," Jews must "annihilate or transcend Zionism" and "annihilate the Jewish state."

Perhaps most notoriously, Jimmy Carter, long considered a friend of Israel and of the Jews, and a person whose seeming moral commitment prompted him to help found organizations such as Habitat for Humanity, seemed to have "flipped" in 2007 with the appearance of his book *Palestine: Peace, Not Apartheid*. The decision to use "Palestine," not "Israel," in the title speaks volumes about the Middle East that Carter envisions. Even more distressing, however, is the end of Carter's title. For merely by using the word "apartheid" with regard to Israel's policy, by effectively comparing Israel to South Africa, Carter delegitimized the very state he'd once brought to the negotiating table. Just as South Africa collapsed under international pressure and was re-created as a different country (albeit with the same name) with a different population in control, so too, Carter seems to suggest, should Israel collapse and a new country be born in its stead.

Someone as intelligent as Carter surely knows that the comparison between Israel and South Africa is absurd. Unlike blacks in apartheid South Africa, Israeli Arabs are full citizens. They earn degrees at Israel's universities, have established political parties, and are represented in the Knesset and in all walks of professional life. To be sure, there is much that Israel needs to do to improve the socio-economic lot of Israeli Arabs, as every modern country has to do with its minorities. But the word "apartheid" in Carter's title suggests that there is a legal, official policy of excluding Arabs from citizenship, and that is simply false. Nor is the implication that Israel is "racist" in any way fair. If it were, would Israel have whisked thousands of black

Ethiopian Jews out of Africa to the Jewish state? The very notion is offensive and baseless.

Through the years of this gradual but relentless reexamination of Israel's right to exist, it has never been lost on Israelis that the only country subjected to this question in respectable circles was Israel. North Korea, in violation of widespread international demands, attained and tested a nuclear weapon. There is strong evidence of widespread human rights violations in North Korea, and it is well known that it starves its own population, but no one has suggested for even a moment that North Korea ought to be dismembered. When Russia committed genocide against the Chechnyans, no one raised the issue of Russia's right to exist. When Turkey denies the genocide against the Armenians, no one asks whether Turkey should be dismantled. When China threatens to overrun Taiwan, or puts down the Tiananmen Square uprising, the only questions that are raised are about how to respond. Nor did the Chinese repression of Tibet, repeated again in 2008, arouse calls for China's dismantling. The question of whether China, or Argentina under Peron, or Cuba under Castro, or Iran under Ahmadinejad, has a right to exist is simply never raised.

One could ask, though, what difference it makes what an army of intellectuals and academics says, no matter how biased it may be? There are several reasons to care. Perhaps most importantly, it bears recalling, since these critics of Israel have raised the specter of Nazism, that the Nazis did not begin their mass murder of the Jews without groundwork having been carefully laid. Tours of virtually all serious Holocaust museums begin not with the death camps but with the massive cultural campaign of dehumanization and characterization of the Jews as evil incarnate that Nazi writers, artists, politicians, and many others worked on. By the time the actual genocide began, Europe had effectively been slowly and methodically prepared for the idea of a Europe without Jews. Ruth Wisse, in her provocative book *Jews and Power*, writes that Sebastian Haffner, a young German, noted that the Nazis had risen to power by engendering discussion "not about their own existence, but about the right of their victims to exist." That plan worked; by the time the Germans began the mass killing of Jews, the thought that Jews would be eradicated from Europe was no longer as shocking as it might have been had the Germans not prepared the world for that notion. And the lack of response, in Germany and beyond, was the tragic result.

Is it possible that what is happening in the world today, from the pens of people from Ahmadinejad to Carter, is the gradual and subtle preparation of the world for the idea of a world without Israel? Is this the delegitimization that is required so that the final step will seem less outrageous if and when it takes place?

Perhaps. But even if one were to argue that this is not the world's intention, the relentlessness of the attacks on Israel is clearly taking a significant toll. This barrage from international circles, coupled with the never-ending wars we have described, has created a sense of profound isolation for Israelis.

Many Israelis are not up for a persistent and long-term battle against international public opinion. They want to be *part* of that public opinion. And therefore, in ways that just a few years ago would have been unthinkable, they have actually begun to espouse some of the same positions that we've seen here. Unable to articulate thoughtful responses to these varied accusations and calls for Israel's end, some have joined forces with those calls, wondering aloud whether, in fact, the Jewish state still makes sense, whether it is still worth fighting for.

That closes the circle. Less than a century after the British declared in the Balfour Declaration that they were prepared to create a national home for the Jews in Palestine, the Arab world has unleashed ceaseless warfare, and the world has turned its back on Israel. And Israelis themselves are no longer certain whether the battle for their existence is worth its costs.

For the Jewish state to survive, Israelis need to recover a sense of purpose. They need to be able to articulate why the calls for their destruction are unfair, what Jewish statehood has done for the Jews, and why the Jews, like other national groups, have a right to the national self-expression that can come only with sovereignty. They need to steel themselves for the long fight that lies ahead, not only because international opinion has shifted, but because, as we will now see, a new combination of fanaticism and technology is going to make Israel's survival ever more difficult and tenuous, requiring its population and its supporters to be ever more committed and ever more tenacious.

Chapter Five

THE NEXT SIX MILLION

The second holocaust will be quite different. One bright morning, in five or ten years, perhaps during a regional crisis, perhaps out of the blue, a day or a year or five years after Iran's acquisition of the Bomb, the mullahs in Qom will convene in secret session, under a portrait of the steely-eyed Ayatollah Khomeini, and give President Mahmoud Ahmadinejad, by then in his second or third term, the go-ahead.
                                    —Israeli historian Professor Benny Morris

There were days, particularly in the euphoric years between 1967 and 1973, when Israelis had begun to believe that Israel had grown invincible. Those were the days of conventional wars, of standing armies employing nonchemical and nonnuclear weapons. Israel— or so Israelis once allowed themselves to believe—would no longer be subject to the threat of annihilation at the hands of the Arabs. Those were also the days when Israeli society pulsed with a sense of purpose, a deep pride in the Jewish recovery that statehood made possible. Today both of those sentiments have changed. As we have seen, the sense of purpose that once lay at the core of Israeli society has begun to fade. And on the military front, Israelis are now beginning to come to terms with the realization that even the most powerful military in the Middle East cannot necessarily keep them safe.

Until recent times, confidence in Israel's military defense capability had rarely been rattled, much less seriously shaken. Even the bloody and costly Yom Kippur War, in which Israel was caught off guard and suffered thousands of casualties, did not fundamentally change that view. Yes, Israelis understood, from then on Syria would have to be watched much more carefully. And yes, Israel's intelligence services would need to be better heeded by the civilian government. But if Syria's surprise attack—which at one point had threatened to slice the country into two indefensible halves—could be repelled, Israel was fundamentally safe. There might be high costs, but Israel would not be destroyed. Indeed, it is now clear that following the Yom Kippur War in 1973, the major Arab powers of Egypt, Jordan, and Syria made a conscious decision not to engage Israel in full-scale military confrontations, a policy from which they have not strayed in thirty-five years, even, for example, when Israel bombed what appeared to be a Syrian nuclear facility in September 2007.

Nonetheless, Israelis are no longer nearly as certain as they once were that they do not face the threat of complete destruction. A lethal combination of the advance of technology and the explosion of fundamentalist Arab effectiveness has done much to change the balance of power—some would say the "balance of terror"—throughout the world.

When U.S. president Bill Clinton ordered the firing of cruise missiles at Afghanistan and the Sudan in August 1998 in retaliation for attacks on the U.S. embassies in Kenya and Tanzania, he had no reason to fear retaliation from those countries or the terrorists they were harboring. Americans could, and did, debate the wisdom of Clinton's action—some felt it was too little, too late, while others felt that he was unnecessarily leading the United States into armed conflicts that it did not need—but there seemed little danger that Afghanistan or the Sudan could strike back. Against countries like those, and even against the terrorists who emanated from there, the United States seemed invincible. The Americans had cruise missiles employing GPS technology capable of striking anywhere with astonishing accuracy.

What could the Muslim fanatics against whom Clinton was striking possibly do in return?

Americans found out on September 11, 2001. True, the 9/11 attackers used human pilots rather than GPS cruise missile technology, and much more preparation was required in order pull off that attack. But the result was devastating, and not only in terms of those killed and wounded. What bin Laden showed the world on 9/11 was that, despite the seeming imbalance of power in the world, technology now afforded options to the weak no less than it did to the powerful.

In the aftermath of the attack, Americans came to understand that the greatest threat to the United States was not the former Soviet Union, or China, or even North Korea. In the wake of the assault on the Twin Towers and the Pentagon, the single greatest threat to the United States was not a nation-state at all. It was terrorists who, using technology that was ever more rapidly available, could wreak unprecedented havoc on American cities. And there was little that the U.S. military could do to stop it.

In the years following 9/11, Israel began to draw similar conclusions about its own safety. As horrific as the Palestinian Terror War was, those four long, blood-soaked years had no chance of destroying the state. In its War of Independence, Israel lost a full one percent of its civilian population. And Israel survived. In 2000, for Israel to have lost another one percent of its population, 50,000 people would have had to be killed. But the horrors of the Terror War notwithstanding, the numbers of Israelis lost—civilian and military—didn't come close to that figure. The fear was palpable, the grief often unbearable. But no one thought, not even for a moment, that the country would collapse because of that sort of low-tech terror.

Nonetheless, Israelis were having to confront the fact that the spread of technology could, in fact, make them vulnerable in ways they had not anticipated. Just as Americans have come to recognize that the most powerful army in the world cannot necessarily keep them safe, even in New York or Los Angeles, so, too, have Israelis come to understand that the Israel Defense Forces cannot necessarily keep them safe in Israel.

This new Israeli sense of vulnerability is heightened most dramatically by Iran. Unless antimissile technology were to advance far beyond where it stands today, a nuclear Iran will render Israel pathetically vulnerable to the scenario that Benny Morris has described, quoted at the outset of this chapter. It is ironic, but painful nonetheless: the number of Israelis now exposed to a potential nuclear attack from Iran approximates the number of Jews killed during the Shoah.

And here, the delegitimization of Israel that we discussed in the previous chapter and the gradual preparation of the world for a new reality of a world without Israel, become important once again. Even those with a relatively rudimentary knowledge of the history of the Shoah understand that the Nazis' "Final Solution" did not emerge out of thin air. Hitler and the Nazi propaganda machine had been preparing Europe, and the world beyond, for the idea of a world without Jews for quite some time. Already in 1919, Hitler declared that his goal was the "removal of the Jews altogether." Six years later, in *Mein Kampf*, he wrote that had "some twelve or fifteen thousand of the Hebrew corruptors of the people been poisoned by gas before or during [the First World] War," Germany might not have lost. In 1938, he said at a meeting chaired by Hermann Goering, "Should the Reich become involved in an international conflict in the foreseeable future, we in Germany will obviously have to think about settling our accounts with the Jews." The quotations go on and on.

A great deal of cultural groundwork was laid to prepare the populations of Europe for the eradication of the Jews. The now infamous cartoons that emerged from Germany for years and years before the war, depicting the Jew as vermin-infested, as the hooked-nosed villain at whose feet the blame for Germany's ills could be laid, were more than mere drawings. The demonizing of the Jew in art, literature, and law communicated consistently and not terribly subtly that in order to recover its former grandeur, Germany—and Europe—would have to dispense with the Jews. Nonetheless, despite all of Hitler's many warnings for all those years prior to the unfolding of the "Final Solution," the world reacted as if it were surprised when it eventually did happen.

Today, once again, the combination of technology and fanaticism makes possible the obliteration of a substantial portion of the world's Jews. Once again, certain elements in Europe and the United States (to say nothing of the Muslim world) seem to be preparing themselves for that eventuality. And once again, the world is basically silent.

Very few public figures have had the clarity of vision that Irwin Cotler exhibited when he suggested that Mahmoud Ahmadinejad be tried for inciting genocide. Cotler, the former Canadian justice minister, was one of the few to make explicit the analogy to Nazi Germany: "What you have today is the toxic convergence of the advocacy of the most horrific of crimes, namely genocide, embedded in the most virulent of ideologies, namely anti-Semitism, dramatized by the parading in the streets of Teheran of a Shihab-3 missile draped in the emblem with the words, 'Wipe Israel off the map.'"

For some reason, the international community has chosen not to take Ahmadinejad's threats seriously. Yes, there have been sanctions against Iran, but Ahmadinejad was allowed into the United States and given a platform at Columbia University. Even thoughtful people dismiss Iran's leader with the most unconvincing of proofs. Juan Cole of the University of Michigan has claimed that "Ahmadinejad did not say he was going to wipe Israel off the map because no such idiom exists in Persian." And Stephen Walt, whom we discussed in the preceding chapter, said in Jerusalem in June 2008, quite simply, "I don't think he is inciting to genocide."

But as scholars such as Joshua Teitelbaum of Stanford University have pointed out, these are thoroughly implausible readings of Iran's president's utterances. Teitelbaum notes that it's a common theme of incitement to genocide that the intended victim is described not simply negatively, but in specifically nonhuman, or dehumanized, terminology. This, too, Nazi Germany and Ahmadinejad's Iran have in common. The Nazi weekly *Der Stürmer* "portrayed Jews as parasites and locusts," while Ahmadinejad, in a speech on October 26, 2005, claimed that "[i]n the Middle East, [the global powers] have created a *black and filthy microbe* [italics in the original] called the Zionist regime." Or consider Ali Khamenei, Khomeini's successor, who opined that "Iran's position, which was first expressed by the Imam [Khomeini] and stated several times by those responsible, is that the cancerous tumor called Israel must be uprooted from the region."

Why are Walt so many others certain that Ahmadinejad isn't serious? And what if they are wrong? Is it possible that they know that they are wrong but want to convince the world otherwise?

But what if Iran were neutralized? What if the United States succeeded in fomenting some form of regime change? What if military action (by the United States, Israel, or some other actor) destroyed or delayed Iran's nuclear capabilities, once or several times? Would that really make Israel safer?

It would buy time, no question. But Israel must face the devastating truth that even without Iran, the technology genie is out of the bottle. Egypt has already announced its intention to develop nuclear capacity for peaceful purposes. So has Jordan.

To be sure, Israel has treaties with Egypt and Jordan. But what if the regimes in those countries were to change *after* they have become nuclear powers? Egypt regularly crushes its radical Muslim opposition. That might seem to be a positive fact for Israel in the short run; but this iron-fisted policy further foments hatred of Egypt's regime and of the West in general. What would happen if Egypt did develop nuclear power, or nuclear weapons, with absolutely no intention of using them against Israel, and that technology eventually fell into the hands of Muslim radicals after they took control of Egypt's state apparatus?

Similar concerns exist with Jordan. To be sure, Jordan has a reasonably palatable monarch, but like Egypt, it is not a democracy. And Jordan has an enormous Palestinian population, which it rules, and represses, also with little mercy. (The instability of Jordan's populace has increased dramatically with the flood of hundreds of thousands of angry and now often impoverished Iraqi refugees across the border into Jordan.) What if the balance of power in Jordan were to shift after Jordan, too, had achieved peaceful nuclear capacity?

Treaties, sadly, will not protect Israel. Proximity may offer some protection (as a direct nuclear strike by Jordan, for example, could endanger Jordan, too). But in the hands of fundamentalists who do not care about their own survival, these weapons could be used,

proximity notwithstanding. Nuclear technology is going to spread in
the Middle East. It is going to be virtually impossible to control, and
with Muslim fundamentalism spreading even more quickly than the
nuclear technology, the confidence that Israelis once had that their
armed forces could protect them now seems sadly naive.

It is worth noting, incidentally, that some have argued that Iran
does not actually have to "push the button" to have its nuclear capacity begin to undermine the stability of the State of Israel. Ephraim
Sneh, a longtime Israeli government official, has said—and many
agree—that merely living in the crosshairs of an Iran with a nuclear
capacity would render Israeli life too tenuous for those with any degree
of mobility. The mere notion that the entire population of the country
could be wiped out at any moment, even if years of inaction go by,
Sneh and others insist, would lead any Israelis who *could* leave to do
exactly that. That would, of course, rob Israel of its elites—economic,
academic, industrial, scientific. It would rob Israel of the very people
on whom Israeli flourishing depends. Thus, more slowly but perhaps
not any less effectively, it would bring about the end of the Jewish
state—precisely what Ahmadinejad has said must be done.

Yet technologically enabled fanaticism is a problem not only in relation to Iran and nuclear weapons, but also in relation to enemies
much closer to home. That was perhaps the most painful lesson of
the Second Lebanon War. In the summer of 2006, the spread of technology and its use by radical Muslims did not have to be nuclear for
Israeli security to be profoundly affected. The great irony of that war
was that despite the tremendous mismatch in technological sophistication between the two sides, Israel could not keep its citizens safe.

Israel employed massive air power, naval power, and land incur-
sions to battle Hezbollah that summer. Some of Hezbollah's weapons
were more sophisticated than others, but relative to Israel's equipment, they were rudimentary. Indeed, one of the starkest images of
the war was the evening news broadcast of Israel Air Force videos
showing pickup-truck-based launchers firing their missiles, but
then quickly darting down the street and disappearing into a garage.

The videos made clear the huge technological differential between Israel's F-15's and these pickup trucks. But the technology gap didn't matter as much as Israelis expected it would. Even with what they had, Hezbollah kept the northern third of Israel wracked with fear.

The question of how much damage Hezbollah's missiles could do relative to the destructive capacity of Israel's arms misses the point entirely. What matters is the undeniable fact that Israel's massive fire-power was unable to keep its citizens out of bomb shelters for the thirty-four long days of the war in 2006. The economy of the north ground to a halt, and families and businesses lost their entire savings just trying to stay alive. Buildings were destroyed. Towns were rendered empty. Children were terrorized. And some people were killed. Hezbollah's missiles were as powerful and accurate as they needed to be.

This, then, is the key change in Israeli life: even without Iran and without nuclear weapons, the Arab threat can actually make the Jewish state unlivable, and therefore untenable. No longer do Syrian tanks have to come rolling down the slopes of the Golan Heights; no longer do the Syrians or the Egyptians have to hope that their air forces can penetrate Israel's well-protected defenses. Significant penetrations of that sort are still unlikely, but as the summer of 2006 demonstrated, such penetrations are not necessary to render life in Israel all but impossible and thoroughly unbearable.

The threat to Israel's very existence has returned.

Finally, the changing nature of technology is such that nothing need unfold in the Middle East for Israel to be dramatically affected. Technology and fanaticism could meet far away from Israel's borders but still have powerful reverberations for the Jewish state.

New York City has already been the target of Muslim terrorism. What if Palestinian militants were to manage to smuggle a dirty nuclear bomb into New York City, perhaps in one of the thousands of still uninspected shipping containers that cross the Atlantic Ocean every day? Imagine that Hezbollah were to inform the United States that unless Israel allowed Lebanese refugees to start flowing across the border by the hundreds of thousands, the bombs would be detonated within forty-eight hours. Or imagine if they demanded that every Israeli soldier in the West Bank be removed within that same time period. What would the United States do? It could never evacuate Manhattan in that amount of time. The United States might have no alternative but to force Israel to do what Hezbollah demanded.

The point here is not to play out all the possibilities—they are virtually limitless. The point is that a bomb thousands of miles away from Israel, even if it were never detonated, could radically change the course of Israeli history.

The problem, then, isn't only Iran. Nor is it simply nuclear weapons, or Israel's shrinking size. It is, at the end of the day, the intersection of fanaticism and technology, which has completely altered the ways in which Israelis must think about their safety and their future.

Because the inexorable progress of technology cannot be reversed, and because that technology is likely to become available to ever-increasing numbers of fundamentalist enemies of the Jewish state, Israel and its citizens are likely to live with uncertainty forever. Living with uncertainty is possible, though, provided one has a profound sense of purpose. Absent security *and* absent purpose, Israeli life will become untenable. Since Israel cannot reverse the spread of technology, it is going to have to make the recovery of purpose a primary national goal. We will address that recovery of purpose in the last chapters of this book. First, however, we turn to some additional challenges that Israel faces, and that it must begin to both admit and address.

Chapter Six

ISRAELI ARABS IN
A JEWISH STATE

Israel cannot be defined as a democratic state. The only way to make Israel a democratic state is to eliminate its Jewish character.

—*The Future Vision of Palestinian Arabs in Israel,*
published by the National Committee for the
Heads of Arab Local Authorities in Israel

Gentlemen, bow your heads." Thirty-five years after I used to hear that phrase in assembly each eighth-grade morning, I still remember the scene clearly: several hundred of us middle school and high school students, boys more than gentlemen, in our coats and ties, beginning our day at the private school I attended for a couple of years in Baltimore. The school day started with assembly, which in turn always ended with the Lord's Prayer. And just before the prayer, the headmaster would say, sternly but not unkindly, "Gentlemen, bow your heads."

I didn't bow my head. In the two years that I spent at that (quite excellent) school, I experimented with a few alternatives. At first I tried the "slump," which allowed me to keep my head up, but to have it no higher than anyone else's bowed head, so I wouldn't be terribly conspicuous. But the simplest mode, I eventually discovered, was simply to sit in my chair and not bow my head. That, after all, my parents had told me, was the deal they'd cut on my behalf with the school when I'd been admitted.

That latter pose, which worked well in some ways, did succeed in getting me summoned to a conversation with the chaplain. He was a nice fellow, collar and all, and he took me aside one day to explain that there was really nothing Christian about the Lord's Prayer. "Thy Kingdom come," he assured me, was nothing that Jews didn't also pray for. It might not be a bad idea, he came close to suggesting, just to say the prayer.

I was a pretty timid eighth grader, just back from two years of living in Israel. Now enrolled in this Episcopalian school, I was quite conscious of the fact that I was not the typical student there. Still, somehow, timidity notwithstanding, I made it clear that the Lord's Prayer was not for me. I seem to recall mentioning, in what was undoubtedly a quivering stammer, that given that it came from Matthew and Luke, it wasn't *really* all that ecumenical. The chaplain was kind, and let the matter drop.

Though many years have passed without my recalling those assemblies, the last few years in Israel have brought them back to mind, and I've come to admire even more what that school did. They never forced me to say the prayer. Nor did they really pressure me. They had admitted me (and a number of other Jews) to the school, and we were treated with extraordinary respect. But at the same time, they never felt they had to hide what was then the pervasive Christian character of the school just because we Jews were enrolled there. They were who they were; we were welcome to study there, but what the school stood for wasn't up for grabs.

It was, I thought, eminently fair.

So why, in the years following the Second Lebanon War, did I find myself thinking once again about those assemblies and the Lord's Prayer? It was not because of Baltimore or my school, but rather because of Israel's Arabs. What was troubling me was their comportment during the war, and then a series of documents that they began to publish in the months following the war about the kind of state they wanted Israel to become.

I had begun to have these concerns even during the 2006 war, which was not going well. Prime Minister Ehud Olmert had promised a nation holding its breath that Hezbollah would soon be routed, that peace would return to the north, and that the kidnapped soldiers would be returned to their families. But things were not working out that way. Night after night, the evening news on Israeli television subjected us to ever more video of destroyed buildings across Israel's northern third, to the panic and frustration of thousands of people considering fleeing the north for the center of the country, and to reports of deaths among both civilians and the army.

One of the stories broadcast covered an Israeli Arab family from a village in the north who, earlier that day, had lost two children to a missile that Hezbollah had fired from Lebanon. Understandably, both the parents and the wider family were grief-stricken. The camera showed the damaged building outside of which their children had died, and the puddle of dried blood on the street. It was infuriating. The randomness of the attacks on Israel, I thought, so blatantly disregarded innocent life that Hezbollah was even willing to endanger the Arab villages in Israel. It didn't matter who they killed, as long as they terrorized Israel. We were at war, it felt, with pure and unadulterated evil.

But then, as the interview with the grieving family continued, they began to vent their fury. The guilty party, they insisted as they shouted into the camera, was Israel. Israel, not Hezbollah, had killed their children. It made no difference that Hezbollah had fired the missile that killed their children; Hezbollah's men, they insisted, were freedom fighters, waging battle in a just cause against the country of which they simply happened to be citizens.

I think that was the moment at which something clicked for me. It wasn't as if I learned anything from that interview that I hadn't known before. Israeli Arabs live lives of tremendous dissonance. In Israeli society, they are in many respects second-class citizens. They do not feel part of the Jewish rebirth that Israel has made possible, and they face discrimination in a variety of areas. But even as second-class citizens, they are infinitely better off than even wealthy Arabs in Palestinian-controlled areas. Their access to education, health care, and the most basic services of a developed society far exceeds what the Palestinian Authority could offer them. As a result, despite their second-class status, polls continually show that virtually none would consider leaving Israel and moving to Palestine, even were a Palestinian state eventually to emerge.

At the same time, the differences between the plights of Israeli Arabs and Palestinian refugees are more an accident of history in 1948 than anything else. Some fled, some stayed—but those who stayed obviously did not do so out of Zionist convictions. They either hoped that Arab forces would derail the newly formed Zionist state, or thought they could better protect their property by staying. Many were poor; and even as they watched the leadership of the Arab communities fleeing to Lebanon, Syria, and Jordan, they themselves had far fewer options. In some cases, families split, a portion remaining in what became Israel, with others now languishing as refugees in neighboring Arab countries.

For years many Israelis, myself included, believed that improving the lot of Israeli Arabs by raising their standards of living and education could get them to gradually become more loyal to the State of Israel. Yet one of the enduring results of the Second Lebanon War has been that many Israelis, like me, have begun to wonder whether the "problem" of Israeli Arabs is not more intractable than we'd previously allowed ourselves to believe. Could it be, we wondered, that it was not only Hezbollah that was still fighting the first war? Might it also be Israeli Arabs, sixty years after the creation of Israel, who were still hoping that the state could be derailed? Was it possible that even improved socio-economic standing would do little to help the Jewish state win the loyalty of Israel's Arabs?

During the war, a number of Israeli Arab leaders began to express positions that intimated precisely that. Azmi Bishara, a member of the Knesset and the chairman of the Israeli Arab Balad party, said, speaking of Hezbollah, "Solidarity with these heroes is the least [we can do]." Wasil Taha, another Arab member of the Knesset, said that "resistance is not terror, but it is a moral value. As for terror, [Israel is the party that] carries it out." And Nimer Nimer, an Israeli Arab author, claimed as the war was being fought, "What happened in Nazi Germany 60 years ago occurs today in . . . Gaza and Beirut."

To them, Hezbollah's militias were not terrorists, but heroes; not only did decency require of Israeli Arabs that they show solidarity with Hezbollah, but Israel now was equated with Nazi Germany. While no one can deny the poverty and suffering of Gaza's and Beirut's populations (though Israel's role as the creator of that suffering is highly contestable), any comparison of those situations with the wholesale murder and enslavement of millions of people, Jews and non-Jews alike, is morally debased. But Israel's Arabs as a group did not dispute the vulgar analogy; they either agreed, or were silent.

Arabs in Israel, Israelis began to sense, are not like African Americans or Jews in the United States a century ago, seeking an improved position within their current society. Israeli Arabs want much more than a protected and honored place in a Jewish Israel. Many of them clearly want the Jewish character of the state eliminated.

To be sure, there is much more that Israel can—and should—do to improve the conditions of Israel's Arabs. Increased spending on infrastructures in Arab villages is long overdue. Arab schools deserve larger allocations, and Israel ought to close the income gap between Jews and Arabs. Israel might even benefit from teaching its Jewish students more about the history of Israel's Arabs and what happened to them in the War of Independence. But Israel should take these steps because it is the right thing to do, not because any such actions are likely to make Israeli Arabs fully loyal to the state.

It is time to be honest; given their history, and their families on the other side of the line, Israel's Arabs are unlikely to become passionate patriots. It is sad but true, and frankly understandable. Israel can either pretend otherwise, or address the issue head-on. If anything, the Second Lebanon War provided part of the wake-up call.

Not surprisingly, the divide between Jewish and Arab Israelis became the subject of some intense media coverage when the war finally ended. Shortly after the cessation of hostilities, *Haaretz* reported that 18% of Israeli Arabs said that they had supported Hezbollah during the war. Another 36% said that they had supported neither side. Some Jewish Israelis were relieved that "only" 18% said that they'd backed Hezbollah. Others, however, were concerned that a total of 53% were unable to say that they had supported Israel, the very country of which they were citizens. Was a dormant volcano about to erupt?

For a short while after the war, discussion of the issue died down; but the lull did not endure for long. Between December 2006 and May 2007, Israeli Arab organizations published four manifestos in which they articulated their demands for the kind of state they wanted Israel to be.

In December 2006, the National Committee for the Heads of the Arab Local Authorities in Israel published a document (which was subsequently endorsed by a much wider swath of Israeli Arab leadership) entitled "The Future Vision of the Palestinian Arabs in Israel," which insisted that Israel's 1.4 million Arabs are "*the* indigenous people of the homeland" (emphasis added) and said that they wanted to share power in a binational state and work to block social policies that discriminated against them.

What was significant about this demand, and the others that followed, was not its insistence on equality. Who could be surprised by that, and who would object? Nor was it necessarily the notion that Israeli Arabs were now demanding recognition not as individuals but as a group. Israel, after all, had been founded precisely because the Jews, too, had sought rights as a collective, not as individuals dispersed in the lands of others.

Rather, what raised eyebrows was the language with which the document describes the origins of the State of Israel:

> Israel is the outcome of a settlement process initiated by the Zionist-Jewish elite in Europe and the west and realized by Colonial countries contributing to it and by promoting Jewish immigration to Palestine, in light of the results of the Second World War and the Holocaust. After the creation of the State in 1948, Israel . . . continued conflicting with its neighbors.

The claim is subtle but clear. What raised the concern of many formerly sympathetic Israelis was not the word "colonial" per se. After all, even early Zionist leaders such as Ze'ev Jabotinsky had explicitly acknowledged that his brand of Zionism contained distinct elements of "Colonisation" [sic]. But absent from this new document is any sense that there was a *reason* that the Jews immigrated to Palestine. What is nowhere acknowledged is that two peoples had long aspired to make Palestine their home. This the authors do not acknowledge, choosing instead to portray the Jews as mere interlopers who had no explicable business building a life in the homeland of the Palestinians.

Once again Israel was being portrayed as a country with no justification, no genuine raison d'être. And this time, the accusation came not from Europe or from the halls of American academe; now the charge was being leveled by a significant swath of Israeli society.

A few months later, in March 2007, not long after the appearance of this manifesto, another Israeli-Arab organization, Adalah, proposed a constitution for Israel. Though many Jewish groups had long been working on a variety of draft constitutions, this was the first instance in which an Arab group had joined the fray.

As with the first document, the hostility to the very enterprise of the State of Israel is palpable throughout: "The State of Israel must recognize its responsibility for past injustices suffered by the Palestinian people [and] recognize the right of return of the Palestinian refugees based on UN Resolution 194." That the return of the refugees would immediately make Jews a demographic minority in Israel goes unstated, but the intent and purpose are clear. The state that this constitution would create would not be a Jewish state. "The State of Israel is a democratic state, based on the values of human dignity, liberty and equality," it says, nowhere mentioning Judaism. The demand is that the symbols of the state be determined by a group whose members "will be members of parliament from parties that by definition and character are Arab parties or Arab-Jewish parties." One needs to know how to read this. To suggest that an Arab-Jewish party will determine the symbols of the state is a subtle means of advocating changes to the national anthem, the flag, and the centrality of Jewish holidays in Israel's national culture. Thus, this document, too, is a mildly disguised attempt to end the existence of Israel as a Jewish state.

A third document, which appeared in May 2007, was entitled "An Equal Constitution for All?" It was published by the Mossawa Center, an advocacy center for Arab citizens in Israel, and its tone is much more genial and less adversarial than the others just mentioned. On the surface, it seemingly accepts the Jewish nature of the state: "The Jewish majority must remember that the State is not only Jewish but also democratic." But matters are not that simple. The document says that declaring that Israel is the state "of the Jewish people" is tantamount to telling "16% of the general citizens of the State of Israel that they have no country at all." This document, too, calls for far-reaching changes to symbols such as "*Hatikvah*": "This is an exclusive Jewish-Zionist anthem, and it is clear to all that it cannot serve as the anthem for Arab citizens."

Some of the implications of the almost deferential language are not clear. For example, when the authors write that "allocating immigration and citizenship quotas expresses the State's strength, and it must exercise this strength fairly, justly and equally," what do they mean? Are they advocating an end to the Law of Return? (The Law of Return, of course, is a symbolic statement that Jews must never again find themselves without a place to go.) Perhaps this is meant to be a subtle demand for the return of Palestinian refugees. But even politically left-leaning Israeli author-activists who have long advocated far-reaching Israeli steps to reach accommodation with the Arabs, such as David Grossman and Amos Oz, have formally expressed their opposition to a Palestinian right of return, recognizing that its implementation would be the end of the State of Israel.

Finally, a fourth document, known as the Haifa Declaration of May 2007, proved no more conciliatory. Here, too, the "history of Israel" that the authors provided led many Jewish Israelis to wonder whether rapprochement was even a possibility. The document states:

> Towards the end of the 19th century, the Zionist movement initiated its colonial-settler project in Palestine . . . which

aimed at occupying our homeland and transforming it into a state for the Jews. . . . The Zionist movement committed massacres against our people, turned most of us into refugees, totally erased hundreds of our villages, and drove out most of our inhabitants out of our cities [sic].

As in some of the other documents, the authors go to great lengths to make clear that "Israeli Arabs," as such, are simply a figment of Israel's imagination:

[R]econciliation requires the State of Israel to recognize the historical injustice that it committed against the Palestinian people through its establishment, to accept responsibility for the *Nakba*. . . . Reconciliation also requires recognizing the Right of Return and acting to implement it in accordance with United Nations Resolution 194, ending the Occupation and removing the settlements from all Arab territory occupied since 1967, recognizing the rights of the Palestinian people to self-determination and to an independent and sovereign State.

Not surprisingly, the document also calls for a "change in the constitutional structure and a change in the definition of the State of Israel from a Jewish state to a democratic state established on national and civil equality between the two national groups."

By asking Israel to abandon its Jewish character, these Israeli Arabs are asking Israel to do something that would eliminate its very reason for being. All four of these documents essentially asked the Jewish state to self-destruct.

The question, of course, was (and is) whether Israelis would understand what was at stake. Some on the right were bound to resent any Arab demand for equality, no matter how legitimate those demands might be. And on the left, Israel is not short of Jews who see no value in a Jewish state, and who have long been advocating a binational system, or a "country of all its citizens." The question, however, was what those in the center—people committed to social equality but also to the Jewishness of the Jewish state—might say.

As one would expect in a country like Israel, where the politics are divisive and the population is often split between left and right with more rancor than one might think necessary, even many centrist Israelis disagreed. Some assumed that the views expressed in these four documents were those of a small group of leaders and did not necessarily represent the opinions of rank-and-file Israeli Arabs. Others chose to downplay the radicalism of the documents, arguing that Israel Arab leadership was simply asking to "be heard" so that a dialogue might ensue. Thus, Hagai Meirom, treasurer of the Jewish Agency for Israel, insisted that the threat to Israel "is not the Arab minority itself but rather the fragile relationship between Arabs and Jews in this land. The solution to this threat lies in dialogue. It is my belief that we do not need to forgo the essence of the state of Israel. There is still a possibility to create co-existence."

But many others were much less sanguine. Dan Schueftan, deputy director of the National Security Studies Center at Haifa University, argued that "equality is not the issue. As far as the Arabs are concerned, nothing short of the destruction of the Jewish enterprise will be enough, even if Israel closes the gap."

The Israeli thoughtful and middle-of-the-road position was perhaps best reflected by Avi Sagi and Yedidiah Stern, in a much-quoted op-ed article in *Haaretz* entitled "We Are Not Strangers in Our Homeland." Sagi and Stern began their piece by acknowledging the legitimacy of many of the contentions of Israel's Arabs, claiming:

> We pushed the Arab citizens into an alley with no exit: they are experiencing prolonged discrimination that cannot be justified. Their right to full civil equality is not being realized. Decent Israelis cannot remain silent in the light of the state's ongoing failure in its treatment of minority groups. Moreover, decent Jews cannot ignore their responsibility to protect the national minority from manifestations of racism. We did not make an effort to consolidate civil partnership; we did not create inviting conditions for honorable coexistence. The outcry of the poor Arab, who is discriminated against as a person and

who feels excluded and alienated as the member of a minority group, is resonating across the country. It raises doubts about the depth of our true commitment to the values of a "Jewish state" and a "democratic state."

But this admission did not lead them to accept the demands expressed in the Arab documents that had recently appeared. Instead, they argued that if the previous Arab generation had been overly passive, the new leadership was being aggressive in a way that Israeli Jews could not countenance:

> Accordingly, they launch a frontal assault against the state's Jewish character. If the previous generation of Arabs, the "stooped generation," was content to aspire to civil equality, the present "erect generation" is challenging the right of the majority to maintain a Jewish nation-state.

And then, in a stinging rebuke of the Arab's denial of Jews' legitimate right to settle the land, the authors asked if anyone could really believe that Jews, too, had not longed for Palestine for thousands of years. Did "Next Year in Jerusalem," perhaps the zenith of the Passover seder, not mean anything? Were the Zionists simply fabricating when they wrote at the start of the Declaration of Independence, "The Land of Israel was the birthplace of the Jewish people"? No, they responded, "We are not strangers in our homeland." And finally, the authors concluded with a warning:

> The Arab elite is leading its followers into dangerous realms. They must understand that the members of the Jewish people, including the salient supporters of civil equality for all, will not forgo the realization of their right to self-determination in this space, the cradle of the Jewish nation. The Jewish people has an inalienable right to the existence of the State of Israel as a Jewish state. . . . The Jewish people does not intend to divest itself of its aspiration to realize its nationhood in the political space of the State of Israel.

To a degree that would have been difficult to predict, the four documents and the subsequent discussion of them in Israeli circles alienated even many on the Israeli left who had long been activists on behalf of Israeli Arabs. "You lost me," more than one claimed, insisting that when the battle for equal rights for Arab Israelis morphed into a plan to rid Israel of its Jewish character, these former allies had to turn and walk away.

Some Israeli Arab leaders were not willing to let well enough alone, however, and the campaign of explicit hostility toward Israel grew ever more intense. Shortly after the appearance of these documents and the return of the Israeli-Arab predicament to Israeli headlines, Azmi Bishara, mentioned above, suddenly announced—from abroad—that he planned to resign from the Knesset. At first the reasons for Bishara's announced resignation were not entirely clear.* Never one to miss an opportunity to lambaste Israel or to heighten tensions between himself and the establishment, Bishara insisted that he was simply too democratic for Israel. Furthermore, he claimed in a radio interview, "We [Arabs] are the original owners of this land. They want us to act like guests in our own country and to prove all the time that all is well. All is not well. We are Palestinian Arabs, the children of this land, and we will act in a manner fitting for a people who oppose occupation and aggression." Again, as they had been during the Hezbollah war, Jewish Israelis were witness to a claim that their mere existence violated the moral order.

Nor was Bishara the sole example. In March of that same year, YNet, one of Israel's main news Web sites, ran a headline reading, "If we organize effectively, we can liberate Jerusalem."

---

*It was subsequently revealed that Israel's security services suspected Bishara of having given information to the enemy during the Second Lebanon War, helping Hezbollah improve the aim of its rockets by giving them more precise information about where previous rockets had fallen. Bishara thus had fled Israel to avoid arrest. Israel, it should be noted, has the death penalty only for Nazi criminals and those who commit treason. At this writing, Bishara has not yet been arrested.

Previously, when Israelis read language like that, it came from such people as PLO Chairman Yassir Arafat, who even after the signing of the Oslo peace accords and even after he'd ostensibly recognized Israel's right to exist, used the phrase "liberation of Jerusalem" as a veritable refrain. But this article wasn't about Arafat urging the liberation of Jerusalem (Arafat was dead by then), or Ahmadinejad, or any of the likely cast of characters. This time, the encouragement to liberate Jerusalem came from Ibrahim Tsartsur, an Arab member of the Knesset. This was a democratically elected member of Israel's Parliament, meeting in Ramallah with leaders of the Arab world, urging a multitude of international Arab communities to focus on the liberation of Jerusalem. "Just as the Moslems liberated Jerusalem from the Crusaders, so too, we must believe today that the liberation of Jerusalem is not an impossible mission." Nor was Tsartsur the only MK (member of the Knesset) present. Muhamad Barakesh, the chairman of the Hadash party, expressed views no less vitriolic.

Again, the envelope had been pushed. The analogy was not with Nazi Germany, or with South Africa (another favorite of Palestinians, just as it is of Jimmy Carter), but with Israeli Jews as Crusaders. These were elected members of the Israeli Parliament making an analogy between Israel and the Crusader invasion of the Middle East. The Crusader image is a powerful idiom in the Arab world; it communicates the hope that just as the Crusaders were a fleeting phenomenon in the Middle East and eventually were forced to leave, so, too, will the Jews of Israel eventually have to flee.

But while the Crusader analogy has long been in use, something about members of Israel's Parliament using it struck a distressing chord among Israelis. MK Otniel Schenler (of Ariel Sharon's centrist Kadima party) expressed what many were feeling when he said that Tsartsur's remarks were a clear indication of the hypocrisy and two-faced nature of the Arab MK, and that it was now undeniable that Israeli Arabs were becoming a fifth column in the Jewish state.

He was not alone in his worry. Later that month, *Haaretz* reported that a recent survey had shown that 68.4% of Israeli Jews feared an Israeli-Arab civil uprising, and 63.3% said that they were so frightened of Israeli Arabs that they would not enter an Israeli-Arab town *inside*

Israel's pre-1967 borders. The sentiments were reciprocated, incidentally. The very same poll showed that 73.8% of Israeli Arabs said that they feared suffering violence at the hands of Israeli authorities, while 71.5% feared being attacked by Israeli citizens.

In another incident that led Israelis to worry, Israeli Arabs actually chose to appeal to international bodies, including the UN, over a dispute with the government. Ali Haider, an Israeli Arab attorney at the helm of this appeal, explained that during the riots of 2000 (in which twelve Israeli Arabs were killed by Israeli police, but for which no police were indicted, due to lack of evidence of malfeasance), "the Arabs demonstrated because they identified with their brothers and sisters in the territories—and the situation in the territories has worsened. . . . If the government doesn't act soon, the events of October 2000 will seem like little more than a promo for the events of 2008."

Their "brothers and sisters" were not Jewish Israelis, Haider made clear. And his threat regarding the future was not even slightly veiled.

With time, even American Jews on the political left began to worry. At the New Israel Fund, a fund that had traditionally supported endeavors designed to improve the lot of Israeli Arabs, major donors began to have their doubts. "There is a big question here," one donor told *Haaretz*. "We support a democratic and Jewish Israel. . . . [But] the [manifesto] suddenly created a conflict. If the assistance to Arab organizations that promote democracy means the erosion of the Jewish interest, perhaps other ways should be explored." Awareness that Israel faced a potentially serious demographic time bomb had now spread across the political spectrum.

What makes matters even more complex and dangerous is the fact that Israel's current demographic balance may be shifting. Indeed, it is clear that Israel's Jews may not remain a clear majority for the indefinite future. Should that change, the Jewish character of Israel will be even more threatened.

In today's Middle East, demography is no less contentious a topic than borders or history. Both Israelis and Palestinians have invoked demographics to make the case for specific policies or strategies.

Yassir Arafat, for example, unwilling to make peace with Israel, repeatedly assured Palestinians that the "womb of the Palestinian woman will defeat the Zionists." At the very same time, then Deputy Prime Minister Ehud Olmert, exhorting Israelis to endorse Ariel Sharon's slowly emerging plan to "disengage" from Gaza, was warning that "Above all hovers the cloud of demographics. It will come down on us not in the end of days, but in just another few years."

It is therefore not surprising that even Israeli estimates and predictions of Jewish and Arab populations, both inside pre-1967 Israel and in the territories captured by Israel in the Six Day War, vary, often dramatically, from one study to another. The most widely cited Israeli authority on the subject of Israeli demography, however, is Professor Sergio DellaPergola of the Hebrew University. In a much-discussed article that appeared in 2003, DellaPergola offered a variety of projections as to what the percentage of Jews in pre-1967 Israel would be in several decades. In 2000, he asserted, Jews constituted 81% of "Israel without [the] territories." By 2020, he predicted, that number would decrease to 77%, and by 2050, according to his "medium projection" (there were more ominous possibilities, he admitted), the percentage of Jews would stand at 74%. Were Israel to hold on to the territories and make those Palestinians under its control Israeli citizens (a scenario that no one in Israel who wishes to maintain a Jewish state advocates), Jews would constitute 37% of the total population.

As DellaPergola notes, even the drop to 74% of Jews inside pre-1967 Israel (or 65.8%, according to an alternate scenario he presents) would have potentially devastating effects on Israel's long-term stability:

> [A]n emerging Israeli Arab minority in the range of 30 percent calls to mind international comparisons with other ethnically split societies. In the case of Cyprus, which went through bitter conflict and eventually a territorial and political split, the minority group was far smaller—the ethnic balance during the 1960's was 82 percent Greek vs. 18 percent Turkish. Other recent examples of ethnically split societies can be found in most of the republics that constituted the former Yugoslavia.

In these cases, too, ethnic cleavages have triggered harsh struggles.

Today, more than sixty years after the creation of Israel, the balance between Jews and Arabs remains approximately what it was in 1949. The number of Jews in Israel has grown more than tenfold, due in no small measure to massive waves of immigration. But Israeli Arabs have managed to keep pace almost exclusively through natural reproduction. With the major waves of Jewish immigration almost certainly largely over, it seems inevitable that the gap is going to close.

How can Israelis maintain the Jewish nature of their state in the face of these shifting demographic sands? There is no easy answer. But the combination of demography and the growing sense that Israeli Arabs will not forever accept Israel's Jewish nature has many Israeli Jews wondering when the gingerly erected house of cards they call home could begin to collapse.

No one can reasonably deny that Israeli Arabs are in a difficult situation. A century ago, their ancestors had every reason to expect that they would long remain the majority culture in what was then Palestine. When Jewish immigration began, however, they made many strategic mistakes. They rejected the UN's vote of November 29, 1947, and chose to begin hostilities against the emerging state. The Israel that emerged was larger and more defensible than the one that the UN had voted to create. As the Arab leadership fled, the rank-and-file local Arabs were neglected by their own and shunned by a fledgling state that saw them (perhaps rightly) as a persistent danger.

Even those on the Israeli left often acknowledge that Israel's Arab community is a serious challenge to a state that wishes to be both Jewish and democratic. The complexity is perhaps best reflected by a much-discussed interview with Professor Benny Morris, a member of the "new historians" school of Israeli historians. It was Morris who, in his *The Birth of the Palestinian Refugee Problem, 1947–1949*, debunked the Israeli myth that all the Arabs who'd fled had done so of their own accord. He showed that some of those who'd fled had been forced out and that others had left when a climate of fear was intentionally created. Morris quickly became the object of tremendous hostility from Israel's right, and even from some of the centrist Zionist camp.

Yet, in an interview with *Haaretz* in January 2004, Morris stated rather matter-of-factly, "Ben-Gurion was a transferist. He understood that there could be no Jewish state with a large and hostile Arab minority in its midst." Morris then continued, "Without the uprooting of the Palestinians, a Jewish state would not have arisen here."

In the pièce-de-résistance of this interview, Morris concluded about Ben-Gurion:

> I think he made a serious historical mistake in 1948. Even though he understood the demographic issue and the need to establish a Jewish state without a large Arab minority, he got cold feet during the war. In the end, he faltered. . . . If the end of the story turns out to be a gloomy one for the Jews, it will be because Ben-Gurion did not complete the transfer in 1948. . . . The non-completion of the transfer was a mistake.

What could be more illustrative of the complexity of the problem of Israel's Arabs than the statement by a man long associated with the left that Ben-Gurion should have transferred even more of them out of Israel during the War of Independence? Without arguing the merits or weaknesses of Morris's claim, he has pointed to exactly the sense of dispossession that Israeli Arabs understandably feel, and to which they have responded by calling for the end of Israel as a distinctly Jewish state. Yet he has at the same time highlighted the strategic thinking Israel must undertake if it wishes to remain both Jewish and democratic.

By publishing the four documents mentioned in this chapter, Israeli Arabs have now joined the battle over Israel's legitimacy. And now that the newest arguments about Israel's "right to exist" stem from a segment of the Israeli population that will only grow with time, that battle is infinitely more threatening than most Israelis have previously allowed themselves to imagine.

In time, it is likely that Israeli Arabs will find this adversarial position a mistake. First, many individual Israeli Arabs may not feel well
represented by the overt hostility of these manifestos; their status in
Israeli society may be endangered by a position that they do not personally endorse. Second, if Israel were ever to become a non-Jewish
state, it would have trouble surviving. Without the support of international Jewry, it would quickly sink into the economic mire that has
swallowed the rest of the non-oil-exporting Middle East. If Israel's
Arabs do not wish to move to an eventual Palestinian state, they need
a strong and vital Israel. Their position thus undermines even their
own self-interest. And third, Israeli Arabs may find that they have
pushed a once sympathetic Jewish public to utter nonsympathy.

But how likely is it that Israel's Arabs will recognize the dangers
with which they are flirting? Like Palestinian leadership under Arafat,
Mahmoud Abbas, or Hamas, the leadership of Israel's Arabs has
rarely demonstrated strategic brilliance. Israeli Arabs do not want to
leave Israel and move to the West Bank. Nor do they genuinely believe
that Israel plans to give up its Jewish nature. Of what use, therefore, is
the creation of this hostile engagement with Israel's Jewish majority?

At the same time, however, it is not only Israel's Arabs who have to
rethink their position. There was an era, decades ago, when someone
like Golda Meir could write unabashedly in the *New York Times,* "We
dispossessed no Arabs. Our toil in the deserts and marshes of Palestine created more habitable living space for both Arab and Jew. . . .
Whatever subsequent ills befell the Arabs were the inevitable result of
the Arab design to drive us into the sea."

The reality, of course, was much more complicated. A much more
nuanced view is expressed by Professor Ruth Gavison, who accords
legitimacy to the narratives of both sides:

> We hear the constant repetition of the claim that Zionism is,
> by its very nature, a form of both colonialism and racism. On
> the other hand, many Jews refuse to accept that Arab objec-
> tions to Zionist settlement are not only legitimate, but also
> inevitable. . . . [F]ew are willing to admit that the original
> Zionist settlers did not come to an uninhabited land, or that

they posed a real threat to local Arab interests. As long as each side continues to deny the other's narratives, hopes and needs, reconciliation and compromise over the long term are unlikely.

Gavison, one of Israel's leading jurists and legal philosophers (and at one point, the leader of the Association for Civil Rights in Israel, a leading left-of-center human rights advocacy organization), proposes a world in which both sides acknowledge the deep suffering of the other. And she implies that were that to happen, reconciliation between the two sides might become a real possibility.

The critical question, though, is whether her optimism is well founded. How long can Israel permit itself a Gavison-like wager before it takes concrete steps to save the Jewishness of the Jewish state? For it is not impossible that Professor Gavison is overly optimistic, and that in the long run, despite the best efforts of Israel's Jews, the Arab citizens of the Jewish state will remain unalterably hostile to the very idea of a Jewish Israel. At some point, it could be too late for Israel to begin to respond.

What, then, are the options that Israel might have at its disposal? Now, more than ever before, these are questions that Israelis cannot allow themselves to ignore.

Chapter Seven

THE WITHERING OF ZIONIST PASSION

Wenn ihr wollt, ist es kein Märchen.
If you will it, it is no dream.
—Theodor Herzl, *Altneuland*, 1902

[T]he greatest [threat] of all . . . does not come from Iran,
nor from terrorist groups, nor from any external source. It
comes from within us. . . . Without motivation, we will not
endure. . . . What are we aspiring to here? Without [answers],
we will not endure. . . . We are like a mountain-climber that
gets caught in a snowstorm; the night falls, he is cold and tired,
and he wants to sleep. [But] if he falls asleep, he will freeze to
death.
—Professor Israel Aumann, Israeli Nobel Laureate, 2007

It was the summer of 2007, and with my eighteen-year-old son,
Avi, and a friend visiting from Los Angeles, I'd driven north from
Jerusalem, past Tel Aviv, a bit beyond Caesarea and then inland, to a
small agricultural village way off the beaten track. As instructed, we
pulled off the road onto an unmarked dirt driveway, and then, just a

few meters beyond, we found a tractor in the field, and among the trees, a huge corrugated metal shipping container. It was the sort of container that gets stacked high on cargo ships, but this one was different. Now it had a satellite dish on top and a door in front. Inside, I saw a bed and some clothing hanging neatly on the back of a chair. Outside the container were a plastic table and some chairs, and standing by them were the two men we'd come to see.

Their names were Mahmoud and Kareem, they told us.* They were refugees from the Sudan, recently released from Israeli prison after having been caught crossing the border from Egypt. The summer of 2007 was when the Sudanese refugee problem "broke" in Israel and became a major news item. What should Israel do with all these people? On the one hand, thousands of refugees were making their way from the Sudan, and if word got out that they were being given free passage across the border, Israel could easily be overrun. That would create a humanitarian crisis in a small country that could not afford to support thousands of African refugees; in due course, these additional refugees, even without any such intention, would also further diminish the Jewish demographic majority that we discussed earlier.

But on the other hand, many Israelis were also asking, how could a nation built on the stories and memories of Jewish refugees—a nation that each Passover recounts the Israelite escape from Egyptian slavery and the journey to the Promised Land—ignore these people, or worse, send them back to Egypt? Could a state that had been fashioned to a great degree in the shadow of the Shoah now ignore human beings fleeing another genocidal catastrophe?

We sat around the plastic table as the two men, thin as rails, their deep black skin hugging their bones, began to tell us their story. They started not with the horrors of the genocide in the Sudan but with their decision to come to Israel. "I'd read the Bible," Mahmoud said in his broken English, "and I knew that the Jews are good to strangers. I must go to Israel."

---

*These are not their real names. To avoid any possible repercussions to them, I've altered their names here.

I felt myself stiffen. For a moment I was sorry that I'd brought my son with me; for I was certain that I knew what we were going to hear next. This was going to be one of those "Your Bible says you're kind to strangers, but when I got to Israel, you threw me into jail" moments. I was going to feel ashamed, I was certain, and embarrassed in front of my son. As, on the verge of turning eighteen, he wasn't far from getting drafted, I worried that we'd hear more stories about abuse by Israeli soldiers, and that in addition to being ashamed of his country, he'd have even more complicated feelings about the army he was about to join.

But the die had been cast; we'd driven hours north to go hear them, hoping that by learning their story firsthand, we might be able to tell it more widely and thus encourage more Israelis to help. So now, so as not to be horribly rude, there was nothing to do but listen to their story.

They actually didn't say much about their lives in Darfur. We did eventually learn that Mahmoud had been rather wealthy there; his family had owned more than four hundred head of cattle (a herd of that size, I imagined, makes one reasonably wealthy almost anywhere). We heard that in one attack, his ten brothers and sisters were killed along with his mother, leaving only him to care for his father. He told of the long trek through the desert from the Sudan to Egypt, of his father's death along the way. We heard about his life in Egypt, how his wife (whom he met there) became pregnant several months later, how they were separated at a demonstration in front of the UN office in Cairo, and how she was killed by Egyptian police as the demonstration was dispersed.

And then, he said, having lost everything in Darfur, he decided he would flee to Israel. He and Kareem told us of their treacherous crossing of the Sinai Desert, walking only at night to avoid being robbed or killed by the Bedouin there, of slowly making their way north, without maps, not entirely certain where they were heading. Their knowledge of geography and of Middle Eastern politics wasn't terribly sophisticated, but they knew that if they went too far west, they'd end up in the Gaza Strip, which they didn't want. And they thought (incorrectly) that if they went east, they'd be in Jordan, which they were also anxious to avoid. So without maps or flashlights, without a guide or any means of navigation, they tried to aim for the "middle," and hoped for the best.

Eventually, after weeks of walking through the desert, they came to some barbed wire, which they correctly assumed was the border. They delicately worked their way through the barbed wire and stood quietly on the other side, hoping that they were in Israel. Within a minute, they said, the quiet was shattered by the roar of jeeps, and through the blinding glare of searchlights mounted on the military vehicles, they saw that they were surrounded by soldiers, guns at the ready.

We already knew the end of the story—that they'd been thrown into Israeli jail—so again, I braced myself. Mahmoud continued. "I looked at the soldiers, and on their shirts (and he pointed to where a breast pocket would be), I saw lettering that I did not recognize. I knew we were in Israel. And I knew we would be okay."

I held my breath. So far we'd avoided the horror story I still feared was coming.

Because Mahmoud and Kareem were among some of the earlier Sudanese refugees to make their way to Israel (they'd been in Israel quite some time by the time I met them), the soldiers didn't know who these people were, or what to do with them. So they ordered them into the jeeps, and with no standing orders on which to draw (their commanding officers were asleep at that time of the night), they took them back to base. They gave them soup, made some beds for them, and put them to bed. "We'll figure this out in the morning," the soldiers, in their broken English, explained to the worn refugees.

Eventually Mahmoud and Kareem were jailed, along with the other refugees making their way across the border. As Sudanese refugees, they were, after all, citizens of a country technically at war with Israel, and they'd entered Israel illegally. But they were freed after some months, and by the time we met them, they were living on an agricultural collective in the Galilee, trading labor for food and lodging, preparing to move to Tel Aviv as soon as the judge permitted them to move about the country.

"How was it in jail?" my friend from Los Angeles asked them. Again, I felt my hands gripping the arms of my chair. "Very good,"

Mahmoud said. "No," my friend insisted, certain that Mahmoud had not understood. "In *jail*, how was it for you in *jail*?"

"Yes," Mahmoud persisted, "very good." Israeli jail, he said, wasn't like Egyptian jail. In the Egyptian jail where he'd been held after being arrested for demonstrating outside the UN office, sixty people were crowded into a cell that couldn't hold them all. Therefore, in order to get some sleep, thirty would sleep on the floor while thirty stood at the edges of the cell until, a few hours later, they changed places. In Israeli jail, he said, each got his own bed. And they were fed three hot meals a day.

A few hours later, as we were preparing to depart, we exchanged cell phone numbers. As Mahmoud was typing our numbers into his cell, he asked my son to remind him what his name was. "Avi," my son said. Mahmoud looked at Kareem and smiled, and then said to us, "Avi. That was name of one of very nice guard in prison. He was very kind man." We told Mahmoud that we would see him again. Did he think that he would try to stay in Israel? "Yes," he said, "this very good country. The Jews very good people."

Avi looked at me with a combination of surprise, bewilderment, and the hint of a smile. It wasn't the story we'd expected. It wasn't the horror story about Israeli soldiers we'd grown used to hearing. It wasn't a tale of occupation, or of abuse, or of incompetence. It was a story of reasonable goodness, of decency, of something to be proud of.

What struck me more than anything else, as we started the car and began the long drive back to Jerusalem, was how surprised I was at not having been castigated, at not having heard how cruel Israelis had become, at not having been accused of unjustifiably throwing someone in jail, or worse. I had just known it was coming—and I'd been wrong.

It was quiet in the car on the way back. Their stories had been horrifying, and there was a lot to absorb. And we were tired. But the quiet, it seemed to me, was about more than that. I, at least, was asking myself, "How did we get here?" What has happened to us that we Israelis just "know" that we're no good, that we're a failing country, and that the moral fiber of our society has long since eroded? Why have we forgotten then Prime Minister Menachem Begin's decision to admit dozens of Vietnamese "boat people" to Israel, insisting that their plight, so similar to that of Jews fleeing Europe, simply had to touch Jewish hearts? Why do we assume every story about Israel is going to be a critique? Why had it not even occurred to me that we might hear a story that could make us proud?

Some of the self-loathing that now characterizes Israeli life, and that is steadily eroding Israelis' sense of purpose and their stamina for the long haul that still lies ahead, can be traced back to the 1967 war. Inside Israel, what once had been seen as the victory that might actually bring an end to the Israeli-Arab conflict now is seen by many as a turning point in Israel's self-perception and in the international community's portrayal of Israel's legitimacy (or its lack thereof).

At the end of June 1967, Israelis were relieved that they'd managed not to be driven into the ocean as Nasser had threatened, but they were also confident and proud. True, there had been losses during the war, and people throughout the country were mourning. And yes, Israel was now in control of large numbers of Palestinian civilians, but that, too, seemed a small problem relative to the magnitude of Israel's victory.

Some Israeli public intellectuals claimed immediately that while the victory had been extraordinary, it would be foolhardy to hold on to the newly occupied territories. Perhaps most vocal was Professor Yeshayahu Leibowitz, who claimed that Israel's moral fiber would be irrevocably weakened by controlling another people. David Ben-Gurion, Israel's first prime minister, was already retired by then, but he was equally vocal. Israel should retain Jerusalem, he said, but should immediately seek to trade the other territories for peace.

For complicated reasons, this did not happen. Israelis believed that they were now invincible. The Arabs still refused to talk to Israel. In some Jewish religious circles, a nascent messianic triumphalism (which would soon morph into the settler movement) was taking hold. Over the course of time, to a certain extent as a result of the Israeli occupation of the West Bank and the Gaza Strip, Palestinian nationalism was either created or awakened, depending on whom one asks, and its spokespeople learned to cultivate the affections of the international community through a combination of terror and public relations. As the years passed, the world tired of what it called Israel's "occupation," ignoring the facts that Israel had captured those territories in a war that it did not seek, and that successive attempts to return significant portions of those lands to Arab partners willing to negotiate a peace settlement had all been stymied. The international community seems to have forgotten that despite the devastating defeat he had suffered at the hands of the Israelis, Egyptian president Nasser pressured the Khartoum conference three months after the war ended to insist that there would be "no recognition of Israel, no peace and no negotiations with her."

Yet it was not only the international community that lost patience with what one observer has called Israel's "accidental empire." Some Israelis also tired of being occupiers, or of serving their military time in the territories. Even Professor Benny Morris, whom we cited in a previous chapter as chastising Ben-Gurion for not evicting *all* of the Arabs from Israel during the 1948 war, spent time in military prison for refusing to serve in the territories.

Occupation, regardless of its origins, exacts terrible tolls on both sides. It demeans the occupied. It can make the occupier callous, insensitive to the impact of occupation on those to whom he is just a soldier, not a human being. Eventually, cognizant of the toll it was taking on their society, and also because of international pressure, Israel decided to end the occupation. Yitzhak Rabin pledged himself to that goal, but was assassinated by a right-wing fanatic who was opposed to returning any land to the Palestinians.

The peace process continued, but Palestinian leadership snatched defeat from the jaws of victory. When Israeli Prime Minister Ehud Barak made it clear that he, too, wanted to cut a deal with the Palestinians, Arafat and his associates unleashed the Palestinian Terror War. Ironically, it was now dawning on Israelis, *they* were the ones trying to push Palestinian statehood forward, while the Palestinians showed no interest in making progress. *Israelis* were the ones who wanted out of the territories (though many Israelis were vociferously opposed, of course), but there was no Palestinian leader willing to make the basic concessions that would have assured Israel a modicum of security. To leave the territories without a responsible, peace-committed party on the other side would have been suicidal. Sadly, Israelis found themselves simply unable to get out of the territories many of them had never sought in the first place.

Ariel Sharon picked up where Rabin had left off, and got Israel out of Gaza. But the Disengagement from Gaza also backfired. The Palestinians elected Hamas, the shower of *kassam* missiles began, and with Sharon comatose, no one in Israel seemed to know how to put a stop to it. Then Ehud Olmert was elected, this time on a platform of getting out of the West Bank. But just as he was getting started on that process, Gilad Shalit was kidnapped on the Gaza border. Two more soldiers, Eldad Regev and Ehud Goldwasser, were kidnapped in the north. The Second Lebanon War immediately ensued. By the time it was over, the potential for a deal with the Palestinians seemed farther away than ever, and Israelis who had wanted to return the territories found themselves burdened with both land and people they could not keep but could not give up.

Though they understood that they were stuck, Israelis were still sensitive to their declining cachet in international circles. Gone were the days when Israel was thought of in the romantic terms of the kibbutz or of "making the desert bloom." Instead, Israel was now more often compared to South Africa. And, as Professor Tony Judt of NYU, who had written in the *New York Review of Books* that Israel was an "anachronism," remarked, "such comparisons are lethal to Israel's moral credibility. They strike at what was once its strongest suit: the claim of being a vulnerable island of democracy and decency in a sea of authoritarianism and cruelty."

But Israelis saw few alternatives. Organizations such as Peace Now or Gush Shalom (the Peace Bloc), which once might have seemed noble even to those who disagreed with their policies, now seemed almost pathetically Pollyanna-ish. *To whom, exactly, would you like to return the territories?* became the question, spoken and not. And no reasonable answer was forthcoming. Who would not want "peace now"? But, many wondered, who could possibly be so naive as to imagine that that peace was achievable?

Suddenly the war in 1967 now seemed to many not a great victory, but a profound and unfortunate turning point in Israel's history; even justified victories, it seemed, could contribute to Israel's impending doom. A deep sense of gloom began to pervade Israeli life.

That malaise, coupled with the virtual collapse of Israel's international standing, troubled most Israelis. But the deadlock had an even more pernicious effect on some. It began to elicit in some Israelis a sense that there *must* be a reason that the peace process was not moving forward. Blaming the enemy is easy, they argued, but not helpful. Many Israelis essentially argued that if the Palestinians would not change, then Israelis must. They turned the frustration engendered by a conflict that would not end into self-blame, suggesting that they themselves must be the real reason for the impasse. With time, that post-Zionist or even anti-Zionist ethos permeated much of Israeli academe, and from there went on to color many dimensions of Israeli discourse.

To be sure, not all of this malaise and self-loathing was a result of the Six Day War and the "occupation" that followed. Compelling claims have also been made that the post-Zionist ethos of Israeli universities can be traced to their very creation, and to the binationalists who were central in their founding. But whatever the source, the drumbeats could hardly be escaped or ignored.

And the effects were undeniable. Just months after the Second Lebanon War ended, two eminent Israeli scientists and Nobel prize winners, Professor Yisrael Aumann and Professor Aaron Ciechanover, gave an interview to *Yediot Ahronot*, Israel's best-selling daily newspaper, in which they asserted that they were worried about Israel's future. Ciechanover said, "What we see [is an] all-encompassing disease, I would even call it a fatal disease: The depletion of spirit. This is a cancer that has spread through Israeli society, through all its body parts." Aumann, a national hero due to his recent Nobel Prize award and colorful personality (and who is quoted in the epigraph at the beginning of this chapter), opined, "I . . . am very pessimistic and despaired. We lack now the desire to exist, we lack the patience to exist."

When Iranian President Mahmoud Ahmadinejad was invited to speak at Columbia University in 2008, Professor Amnon Rubinstein, a prominent Israeli intellectual and former minister of education, attended the lecture. What most astonished him was not Columbia's invitation or Ahmadinejad's comments, but an Israeli student in the audience. In an op-ed article in the *Jerusalem Post*, Rubinstein lamented the fact that he saw this *Israeli* student applauding Ahmadinejad, despite the latter's advocating the destruction of Israel. This student, Rubinstein insisted, was not a lone lost soul. Rather, he felt, she was the product of a worldview promulgated by the wider world of Israeli academics, who are "seized by a frenzy of hatred toward the state that provides their livelihood."

Nor is the phenomenon limited to faculty at academic institutions. It includes a former speaker of the Knesset and a number of popular writers. It includes some of Israel's most-read journalists whose weekly columns regularly vilify the Jewish state (Amira Haas and Gideon Levy are the two most prominent examples). It includes David Landau, then the editor of Israel's most prestigious daily newspaper, *Haaretz*, who told U.S. Secretary of State Condoleeza Rice that Israel was a "failed state," that the Israeli government wanted "to be raped," and that it would be like a "wet dream" for him to see this take place. It includes a professor who wrote a book arguing that Zionists invented the notion of a Jewish people, and some of Israel's most promising university students (who will constitute much of the next generation of Israel's leadership), who can no longer speak engagingly about Israel without questioning its very legitimacy.

All of this brings us back to Theodor Herzl's famed aphorism, quoted at the outset of this chapter: "If you will it, it is no dream." Herzl's point, of course, was about the *possibility* of making the dream come to be. The creation of a Jewish state, he insisted, was not beyond the realm of the possible.

Today, however, one reads Herzl's famed line and tends to focus not only on the notion of *possibility* but on the requirement of *will* if the dream is to succeed. Today Herzl can be read not as encouragement, but as warning: *If you do not have the* will *to make this dream happen, or to perpetuate what has already been built, it will be lost. It all depends on your will.* Perhaps nothing is more illustrative of the loss of that will in Israeli society than the fact that 50% of Israeli schoolchildren do not even know who Herzl was. Could there be any more apt a metaphor for the loss of purpose that now has Israel in its grip?

The will that Herzl urged upon Jews is withering. After the collapse of Oslo, the loss in the Second Lebanon War, and the evaporation of any significant hope for a settlement of the Israeli-Palestinian conflict anytime soon, it is virtually undeniable that one of Israel's greatest challenges comes not from across its borders but from within them. The real threat to Israel now comes from Israelis themselves. What remains to be seen is whether Israel's elites will so undermine their society's sense of justice and purpose—and the narrative that has sustained them—that rank-and-file Israeli citizens soon will see no reason to defend what previous generations built.

The Jewish state is at stake, then, because the *idea* of the Jewish state is under attack. And it is under attack not only from Tony Judt, or Jimmy Carter, or Jostein Gaarder, but from Israelis themselves, often from among the ranks of Israeli leadership. And that challenge, Israel cannot afford to ignore.

The Jewish state was only an idea when Herzl convened the First Zionist Congress in 1897. Within fifty years, that idea had become reality; sixty years after Israeli independence, Israel had built a thriving economy, world-class universities, and cutting-edge health care systems. It has absorbed millions of immigrants and withstood decades of Arab aggression, and it continues to seek solutions to the conflicts on its borders.

One of the fundamental lessons of the history of Zionism is that of the power of ideas. What was once but an idea is now, despite all its travails, a thriving country. The story of Zionism, the story of the power of an idea to move a people, is one of the most dramatic narratives in the history of humanity. As the historian Barbara Tuchman has noted, of all the peoples of the Western world from three thousand years ago, it is only the Jews who live in the same place, speak the same language, and practice the same religion. One hundred years ago that claim would not have been true. It is true today because of the revolution called Zionism, a revolution whose most important fuel was the power of an idea.

Israel's future depends on the perpetuation of the Jews' belief in that idea. The critical question for the future of Israel is whether Israel and Zionism can wean themselves from their addiction to self-loathing without losing the ability for self-criticism that is key to any moral and constantly improving society. Can Israelis learn to be appropriately self-critical without undermining the entire edifice on which their nation is built?

What Israelis need to do, now more than ever before, is to learn to live with the frustration of the stalemate that grips their region, to continue to hold out hopes for peace even if that peace seems farther away than ever, and to remind themselves—even while acknowledging their failures, mistakes, and inadequacies—of the justice of the cause that has always been at the core of the rebirth of the Jewish people in their "national home." Yes, for some, it might be easier to assume that if peace is not growing closer, it *must* be someone's fault; and since the world sees the Palestinians as the victims, the fault *must* lie with the Jews. But truth and simplicity do not always overlap; Israelis will need intellectual fortitude in the coming years no less than they've needed courage on the battlefield for the past decades. They will need to learn that simply because the Israeli-Palestinian conflict cannot now be settled does not mean that Zionism is the cause of the conflict.

Israel's academics and its other harsh critics from within are completely correct, of course, that were Israel to declare defeat, the conflict would end. If Israel would accept a one-state solution, a single democratic entity between the Jordan River and the Mediterranean Sea, for Jews and Arabs alike, hostilities might end (though the safety of the Jews in that new country would likely be tenuous). But just because Israel *could* end the conflict at such a horrific cost does not mean that it *should*.

It bears remembering that there is a purpose to Zionism, a revitalization of Jewish peoplehood at the core of Israel that cannot unfold anywhere else. Israelis dare not evaluate their own successes by comparing themselves to other countries. A return to a sense of purpose, and even uniqueness, is thus the key to Israel's working its way out of the present conundrum. Israelis can triumph over their tendency to self-loathing by remembering that Israel was never meant to be a state like all other states. Israel was created for a distinct Jewish purpose, and thus will always be different.

Perhaps what is needed now is a decision *not* to be like all other states. Perhaps it is time to recognize, accept, and acknowledge (or even celebrate?) the fact that in order to survive with purpose, Israel needs to be different. Perhaps, by deciding to be different, Israelis could overcome the malaise that threatens to consume them.

Pointing to some of the ways in which Israelis will need to think differently about themselves and their society is the task to which we now turn.

Chapter Eight

MORE THAN JUST A
HEBREW-SPEAKING AMERICA

The Jewish spirit . . . is essentially modern and essentially American. . . .

Indeed, loyalty to America demands rather that each American Jew become a Zionist. For only through the ennobling effect of [Zionism's] strivings can we develop the best that is in us and give to this country the full benefit of our great inheritance.

—Louis D. Brandeis, June 1915

Just eleven minutes after David Ben-Gurion declared Israel's independence on a Friday afternoon in Tel Aviv on May 14, 1948, the United States became the first country to recognize the new Jewish state. President Harry Truman's relationship with both Jews and Zionism had long been a complicated one. He was powerfully affected by the horror of what had happened to European Jewry during the Shoah, but he remained resistant to plans for a Jewish state. His wife, Bess, had had many misgivings about Jews even crossing the threshold of their personal home (though obviously, once they arrived at the White House, she lost control over such matters). Why, then, had Truman rushed to recognize Israel, even over the objections of many in the State Department?

Some of his motivation may have had to do with his Jewish long-time friend and business partner Eddie Jacobson. But more than that, something about the fledgling state apparently reminded him of the United States in its earliest years. When the United Nations Special Committee on Palestine (UNSCOP) was debating whether or not the Negev should become part of the still-to-be-created Jewish state, Truman was in favor. He felt that "the Negev represented for the Jews what 'the Frontier' had represented for the Americans a century before." Most influential, perhaps, was Chaim Weizmann's plea to Truman that "the greatest living democracy [should be] the first to welcome the newest into the family of nations."

Indeed, Israel's role as the only genuine democracy in the Middle East is now the most often cited justification for U.S. support for Israel. John F. Kennedy, like many others, made that claim explicitly. Commenting on Israel's unique qualities, he opined that it "can neither be broken by adversity nor demoralized by success. It carries the shield of democracy and it honors the sword of freedom."

U.S. presidents from Truman on have focused on the values that Israel and the United States share. Interestingly, even when in 2002 George W. Bush pressed Israel to make accommodations that might move the stalled peace process forward, he suggested that Israel needed peace in order to preserve the values that made it similar to America: "Israel also has a large stake in the success of a democratic Palestine. Permanent occupation threatens Israel's identity and democracy. A stable, peaceful Palestinian state is necessary to achieve the security that Israel longs for. So I challenge Israel to take concrete steps to support the emergence of a viable, credible Palestinian state."

AIPAC (the American Israel Public Affairs Committee), by far the most effective organization devoted to strengthening the United States's ongoing commitment to Israel, sees much more than democracy in the values that the two nations share. As one AIPAC document declares:

Both nations were founded by refugees seeking political and religious freedom. Both were forced to fight for independence against foreign powers. Both have absorbed waves of immigrants seeking political freedom and economic well being. And both have evolved into democracies that respect the rule of law, the will of voters and the rights of minorities.

Attempts to show the similarities between the values held and represented by both Israel and the United States often implicitly suggest, however, that Israel is essentially a Hebrew-speaking, miniature version of America. This image of Israel has long been particularly attractive to American Jews, for whom, perhaps, the sense that Israel and the United States are "birds of a feather" might lessen the potential accusation of dual loyalties. If defending Israel is tantamount to defending American values, what tension could there possibly be between the loyalties?

Thus, American Jewish leaders point to Israel not only as a bastion of democracy in a despotic Middle East, but as a country with a vital free press, consistently free elections even in periods of turmoil, a history of absorbing immigrants, and the like. Israel's leadership in technology, medical advances, world-class universities, weaponry, and military prowess are often cited, as well.

Israelis, too, relish the similarities. On Israeli radio stations, American music is heard more often than Israeli music. Israelis want to wear what Americans are wearing, watch the TV shows that come from Hollywood, and read—usually in translation—what Americans are reading. Part of this, of course, is simply the impact that American culture has across the globe, from Europe to the Far East. To a certain extent, Israel is no different than England or the Czech Republic when it comes to the influence of American culture. But in ways that are difficult to quantify or adequately characterize, Israelis seem to want to transform their country into America—and thus a "real" country—with a lust that is different from how other countries consume American products and culture.

All of this seems humorous at times, innocuous at others, and occasionally worrisome, mostly because of the conspicuous consumption that such values bring in their wake. But behind all this lurks a much more significant question, a deeper dimension of self-perception with which Israelis are going to have to wrestle: can Israel survive if its sense of self is that of a Hebrew-speaking miniature America still in formation? I believe not.

The most perplexing, and frankly, the most disturbing conversations that I have had in Israel have been those with Israeli friends and colleagues who finally admitted that they couldn't understand why anyone would actually *choose* to leave the life that America makes possible and to come to Israel, where everything is smaller, more expensive, more dangerous, and more tenuous. "Isn't the standard of living much higher there?" the less worldly ones ask, not only as if there were any question about that, but also as if that was what mattered most.

When responding to those questions, I've always tried to distinguish between "standard of living" and "quality of life." I've tried to explain what it means to be home, to be part of the rebirth of the Jewish people after two thousand years of exile; what it means to be not on the edges of Jewish history but on center stage. I'm not sure how effective I have been in those discussions, but I usually leave them with the sense that the prevalence of the question points to a fundamental failure of Israeli education. So long as America remains the model of how Israelis measure success, Israel will struggle to make the decisions that it needs in order to secure its own future as a Jewish and democratic state.

The comparison to the United States is problematic for a variety of reasons. First of all, it places the Jewish state in an implicit contest in which it cannot really compete. Israel will never have the security, the wealth, the quiet borders, the vast expanses of open space, and the governmental institutions of pure liberal democracy that the United States has. Even more important, however, another issue looms: if Israel actually were to become the mini-America that many Israelis would like it to be, it would lose its uniqueness and, along with it, its very reason for being.

For the vast majority of immigrants who have come to Israel over the years, the plan hasn't been to create another America but rather to help build a *Jewish* state. That it would share many important values with the United States has been obvious to some of them. But it has been no less clear that Israel's greatest contributions—to both the Jews and the world—would stem precisely from where it elected to differ. Yet that willingness to differ has begun to fade, in part because technology makes American advancements and values so ubiquitous, but also because the core values upon which Israel was founded have begun to fade. What is at stake, therefore, is more than Israel's foundational values; what is at stake in perceiving Israel as a miniature America is the danger of losing the very sense of purpose that once lay at the core of the Zionist enterprise. For Israel to survive, that core has to be recovered. And for that to happen, Israel is going to have to shed its self-image as an America-wannabe.

Given the centrality of democracy to Americans' sense of self, and the fact that none of the Arab states surrounding Israel (with many of which Israel has been at war for all of its history) is a genuine democracy, it is only natural that supporters of Israel point with tremendous pride to Israel's democratic character.

Reasons for this abound. Israel's commitment to democracy implies a set of shared values with America. Its status as the sole democracy in the Middle East suggests, to some, that Israel has a unique relationship with the United States and, as a result, has unique strategic value for the United States. And in the face of Israel's many shortcomings, its unyielding democratic commitments enable its supporters to insist that despite everything, the Jewish state is a rousing success story, democracy being, as Churchill so aptly put it, the "worst form of government except for all the others." (It is therefore not surprising that critics of Israel—Stephen Walt and John Mearsheimer (discussed in chapter four), for example, in their critique of the "Jewish lobby" and its alleged power in Washington—have sought, however ineffectively, to debunk the claim that Israel is a genuine democracy.)

Yet there is a lurking danger in this tendency to justify Israel's existence, strategic value, or policies by referring to the similarities between the U.S. and the Israeli democracies. The danger is that the parallels that are so often drawn lead many people to believe that because the purposes, goals, and natures of the two countries are similar, their democracies, too, either are, or should be, very much alike.

But why should that be the case? While democracy may well be part of the *purpose* of American national life, the Jewish state was not created *in order* to be a democracy. It was founded in order to change the condition of the Jews. While the United States may have been founded by white Protestants, and while those founders may well have expected that people like them would remain the backbone of America far into the future, there is nothing about the *purpose* of America that requires that. Were the United States to become largely Asian, or Hispanic, or Arab in a century or two, there is no need to assume that America's core values would necessarily have to change. America is not *about* the thriving of a particular ethnicity or religion (despite what Pat Robertson may believe).

Thomas Jefferson's letter to Roger Weightman, written on June 24, 1826, put it better than almost any other document. Expressing his regrets that, due to ill health, he would be unable to attend the celebration of the fiftieth anniversary of American independence, Jefferson penned what might be characterized as a deathbed blessing for the United States. "May it be to the world," he wrote, "what I believe it will be, (to some parts sooner, to others later, but finally to all,) the signal of arousing men to burst the chains, under which monkish ignorance and superstition had persuaded them to bind themselves, and to assume the blessings [and] security of self-government."

It is a noble idea. It has had profound influence around the world, including in Israel. It is a vision of American life in which no ethnicity need take precedence over another, which therefore permits the United States to adopt a far-reaching liberal democracy.

But while Jefferson's is a noble vision, it cannot be Israel's. Israel simply is not and cannot be about "arousing men to burst the chains . . . and to assume the blessings and security of self-government." While few American Jews or left-leaning Israelis wish to acknowledge this fact, Israel cannot allow itself the same liberty. Were it to do so, how could it possibly fulfill its *purpose*? Can Israel retain a raison d'être without the notion that the thriving of the Jewish people is core to its mission? But how can it do that and remain democratic? Are there alternatives? Should Israel become nondemocratic? Less democratic?

Professor Ruth Gavison has pointed out that "the real tension is not between Israel's 'Jewish' and 'democratic' aspects, but between competing ideas within democracy, which are forced to find a balance between complete civic equality and freedom for the majority to chart the country's course." Making her claim even more explicit, she asserts that "the Jewish character of the State of Israel does not, in and of itself, mean violating basic human rights of non-Jews or the democratic character of the country." She is, of course, fully aware that the distinct Jewishness of the state makes many Arabs feel like second-class citizens, but she denies that this means that Israel is somehow not democratic. She writes: "Non-Jews may not enjoy a feeling of full membership in the majority culture; this, however, is not a right but an interest—again, it is something which national or ethnic minorities almost by definition do not enjoy—and its absence does not undermine the legitimacy of Israeli democracy."

Many observers, inside Israel and out, are deeply troubled by the notion that in a democracy, "non-Jews may not enjoy a feeling of full membership." But it boils down to the state's reason for being. Gavison, again, reflects on Israel's purpose:

> The idea of national self-determination doesn't mean that all the population of a country belongs to one ethnic or national group. It means . . . this country does have a specificity and that specificity is the materialization of the right of a specific people with a specific culture, with a specific history, to self-determination, to enlisting the power of the state to protect themselves physically, culturally, and, in terms of identity, against the forces of assimilation or liquidation or attack by other groups around them.

What Gavison has in mind for Israel, therefore, is not a pure liberal democracy; instead, her vision approximates "ethnic democracy," a democratic system described by Professor Sammy Smooha that "combines the extension of civil and political rights to permanent residents who wish to be citizens with the bestowal of a favored status on the majority group." Because ethnic democracy is a system in which "the state belongs to the majority and serves it more than the minority," some legal philosophers consider it a "diminished" form of democracy, and for that reason, many Israelis and supporters of Israel are distinctly uncomfortable endorsing it. Yet even Smooha, a critic of ethnic democracy and a (Jewish) passionate defender of the rights of Israel's Arabs, admits that "the democratic framework is real, not a facade."

The democratic framework may be real, but there is no question that for those not part of the majority ethnicity, it is diminished. The feeling that Israeli Arabs have that they are not fully "mainstreamed" in Israeli society is real and undeniable. The pain that this causes them is also real. Even Jews who may insist that there is no alternative if the Jewish state is to remain Jewish must admit the sense of relative deprivation that Israeli Arabs feel. The fact that Israeli Arabs may have significantly more civil rights than they would have in Palestine is only partially relevant; relative to their Jewish fellow citizens, they *are* deprived. And no serious discussion of this issue can proceed without acknowledging that.

The problem for Israel's Jews, however, is that the Arab citizens of the Jewish state insist that, as a consequence of that relative deprivation, the Jewish state must abandon its primary commitment to Jews and the Jewish people. One Israeli Arab spokesman, for example, has insisted that when Israelis discuss the creation of a constitution, Israeli Arabs "increasingly find themselves being used as fig leaves to provide cover for the effort to consolidate a Jewish consensus around the project of constituting Israel as 'Jewish and democratic.'" The objection here is not simply to a diminished place for Israeli Arabs; we can understand why any Israeli Arab would find that troubling. The problem, for Israeli Jews and for those who care about the Jewish state, is that the fundamental objection is to the notion that Israel can be, or should be, a *Jewish* and democratic state.

But current trends in Israel notwithstanding, understanding and even sympathizing with Israeli Arabs and their frustrations about Israel's being a Jewish state does not require Israeli Jews to capitulate to it. The critical question for Israel's future is not what form of democracy in Israel might arouse the least objection. Instead, the question that matters most is what form of governmental system could both guarantee civil liberties to all of Israel's citizens and at the same time preserve Israel as the sort of state that can contribute to the survival, and the flourishing, of the Jewish people. That, after all, is precisely what a homeland is for. That is the purpose of the Jewish state.

A homeland, perhaps in a way that will always differ from liberal democracies at their core, does not view citizenship simply as a "bundle of rights," with people bonded together solely or primarily for the protection of those rights. Implicit in a national homeland is more a "moral" community, a "strong" community, as the political philosopher Michael Sandel notes. To such a community, Sandel claims, we "owe more than Justice requires or even permits, not by reason of agreements I have made but instead in virtue of those more or less enduring attachments and commitments which taken together partly define the person I am." These are the bonds of one history, of shared memory and aspirations. They transcend the kind of community that can be created by oaths of allegiance, or devotion to the same flag.

The State of Israel has long been devoted to this notion of "thick" community, as Sandel calls it, in which one nation is central, one set of memories is sacred, one set of national aspirations and dreams is the very purpose of being. The persistent presence in Israel of music and museums, and of military and literature, that we have mentioned throughout, is part and parcel of this project. Such a project can never be ethnically value-free. It is a project about the Jews—it is, to paraphrase Lincoln, "of the Jews, by the Jews, for the Jews."

To be sure, Israel was created as a democracy. That cannot be meaningfully disputed. The Israeli Declaration of Independence speaks of commitment to the notions of "liberty, justice and peace," to "the full social and political equality of all its citizens, without distinction of race, creed or sex," and to the "full freedom of conscience, worship, education and culture." One of Israel's Basic Laws, laws which have been adopted over the past decades and are essentially an informal constitution, explicitly defines Israel as a "Jewish and Democratic State."

It is that coupling of "Jewish" with "democratic" that understandably troubles Israel's Arabs. We can easily understand why many Israeli Arabs resent and oppose Israel's "Law of Return," which guarantees automatic citizenship to all Jews, should they wish to come to Israel. The issue isn't the alleged inequity of the law, but what the law symbolizes. The Law of Return makes clear that Israel has a unique relationship with the Jewish people; Israel's relationships extend even to those Jews who do not live in Israel and who are not citizens. Might Israel have even more of a commitment to British or Australian Jews (who are not citizens of Israel) than it does to Israeli Arabs? The mere suggestion understandably has infuriated the Arab citizens of Israel.

But that may, in fact, be implicit in the Law of Return. Those Jews of other lands may not be citizens now, the law suggests, but they are potential citizens; they are part of the "thick" community of which Sandel speaks and to which Israel is committed. And as a result, they may not necessarily make policy and they do not vote, but they are "on the radar screen" of the Jewish state in a way that no other people ever could be. Strange though it may sound to the ears of those who have been raised in more classic liberal democracies, that is the very point of the State of Israel.

This delicate balance between civic rights for all and one ethnicity at the center of Israel's agendas occasionally makes for cases of national policy when it is very difficult to know what the right thing to do might be. In 2007, for example, Israelis and Israel-supporters abroad wrestled with the question of whether to force the Jewish National Fund (JNF) to sell lands in its possession to Israeli Arabs. Israeli Arabs understandably claim that it is outright discrimination for portions of the country's land not to be available to them. But proponents of a bill that was introduced to the Knesset in July 2007, a bill that would allow the JNF to continue its policy of selling land only to Jews, argued that those lands had been bought by Jews across the globe who had collected pennies, nickels, dimes, and larger sums in order to make a *Jewish* homeland possible. To use those lands for purposes other than that which the donors had in mind, the argument went, was a violation of the will of those people who had acquired the lands for the Jewish state in the first place.

Obviously, at issue was much more than what the original donors, many of them already dead, would have wanted. The real issue was the future of the JNF now that the state had been created, and even more important, defining the limits of the Jewishness of the Jewish state. As the war of words on the subject reached Israeli op-ed pages, the sides were clearly aligned. There were those who wished to see Israel become as close to a liberal, democratic state as possible, and others who insisted that certain steps had to be taken to ensure that Israel communicate, both internally and externally, that it was created by the Jewish people and for the Jewish people.

Another, even more interesting, test of the delicate balance of Israel as a Jewish and democratic state had arisen years earlier in Israel's 1984 national elections. Two political parties—one an Arab party that many people accused of denying that Israel should be a Jewish state (the Progressive List for Peace, PLP) and one a right-wing Jewish party that insisted that Arabs should be transferred out of Israel (Kach, led by Rabbi Meir Kahane)—ironically had one thing in common. They both argued that since Israel had a sizable Arab minority, there was no way that it could continue to be Jewish and democratic. Where they disagreed, of course, was on what had to give.

Both parties succeeded in electing a small number of representatives to the Knesset. But the overt racism of Kach proved so unpalatable to many Israelis that in 1985, the Knesset approved a law that barred parties from running for the Knesset if they (a) negated the existence of Israel as a Jewish state, (b) negated the democratic nature of the state, or (c) incited to racism.

On the basis of that law, Kach, the right-wing Jewish party, ultimately was disqualified from the electoral process in the 1988 elections; the court decided that it was a racist party. The PLP, however, was *not* disqualified. Had the PLP been denying the legitimacy of Israel as a Jewish state, the court said, it would have been disqualified.

But the court insisted that the evidence presented had not proven that claim satisfactorily.

Those who argue that an ethnic democracy cannot sustain the rights of minorities should note that even as the courts considered the implications of a law that insisted that Israel was a *Jewish* state, it was the Jewish party that was disqualified, while the court permitted the Arab party to run. Ironically, in this particular instance, the law defining Israel as a Jewish state actually asserted the civil and democratic rights of the Arab population even as it limited those of a Jewish political party.

At the same time, though, no one should delude himself; the secondary status that Israeli Arabs feel is real and their frustration often justified. It would be unfair to point to this case and say, "See! The Jewish state defends the rights of Arabs, even over and above those of Jews." Israeli society will never be that simple. For if Israel has a purpose, that purpose must have something to do with Jewishness. If the Jewish character of the country is to be safeguarded, Israel's supporters will have to accept that Israel's democracy can never be the model of pure liberal democracy that political life in the United States approximates. That is difficult for many American Jews, and for Israelis, all of whom have been taught to think differently about Israel and who have been raised on references to the similarities between the United States and Israel. But there is no alternative.

Because the idea that Israel can never be an American-style liberal democracy is so difficult for so many people, and because it cuts against the grain of how many American Jews (and Israelis, among others) have been taught to think about Israel, it is worth pressing the point. Consider, therefore, the profound differences between the core values of those two countries as reflected in their respective declarations of independence. Whereas Jefferson's text begins with "When in the course of human events," Ben-Gurion's opens with the claim "The land of Israel was the birthplace of the Jewish people."

Even those opening phrases speak volumes about the need to distinguish between the purposes of the two nations that so often are compared to each other. The United States was designed to end "the long train of abuses and usurpations" by the "present King of Great Britain." Israel's declaration makes no mention of any accounts to settle with any king or any other ruler. In some sense, then, America would be a success if British tyranny could be brought to an end (recall Thomas Jefferson's letter to Roger Weightman). But Israel is different, its Declaration of Independence suggests, for Israel is about the "Land of Israel" and its role as the "birthplace of the Jewish people." The U.S. Declaration of Independence, in contrast, makes no mention of a specific people or a particular religion.

"We hold these truths to be self-evident," the American declaration insists, "that all men are created equal, that they are endowed by their Creator with certain unalienable Rights, that among these are Life, Liberty and the pursuit of Happiness." There is no gainsaying the universalism of the American vision.

In contrast, however, the Israeli Declaration of Independence, written under Ben-Gurion's controlling watch, makes clear that Israel was necessary because the Jews had been "exiled from Palestine," and "strove through the centuries to get back to the land of their fathers and regain their statehood." If the American vision is universal (although its rights and liberties took a long time in coming to women and African Americans, of course), that is not the case with Israel. Israel was designed to be a "Jewish state," an "independent Jewish nation," dedicated to "the great struggle for the fulfillment of the dream of generations—the redemption of Israel."

Other Americans have sketched the fundamental qualities of "The American Idea" differently. In its 150th anniversary issue, the *Atlantic Monthly* asked a group of leading Americans to reflect on the core of the American idea, and to ruminate on whether it could survive. And what *was* this core American idea? Not everyone agreed. For John Updike, the great novelist and literary critic, the American idea is about the individual, "to trust people to know their own minds and to act in their own enlightened self-interest, with a necessary respect for others." For Cornel West, the African American intellectual and activist, what is great about America is democratization, "the sublime notion that each and every ordinary person has a dignity that warrants his or her voice being heard in shaping the destiny of society." Eric Schmidt, the CEO of Google, not surprisingly, argues that "the American idea has always involved innovation." Steven Weinberg, a Nobel Prize–winning physicist, argues, "If any one idea can justly be called the American idea, it is that a child's circumstances at birth should not determine the station in life that that child will occupy as an adult."

Noble ideas all, these are further examples of profound qualities of certain dimensions of America that are quite laudable. But they probably cannot serve as the foundation for what Israel should become. It's not that one wouldn't want Israel to incorporate these values, or any of the others suggested, into the fiber of Israeli society. Indeed, one could argue that all of these, and more, are already part of the core of Israel's value-set. Cornel West's notion, to cite only one example, that in a democracy "every ordinary person has a dignity that warrants his or her voice being heard in shaping the destiny of a society" is surely part of Israel's discourse. Has Israel brought this goal to bear on every corner of society? Of course not; no democracy has. Still, there are probably few Israelis who would dispute that Israel is or ought to be committed to West's ideal.

The question, though, is not whether any of these qualities should be or could be *part* of Israeli society, but whether they can be the *foundation* of what makes Israel unique. The critical point is that all the respect for individual rights, democratization, or innovation in the world will not lead Israeli citizens to commit to their state. Those Israelis who seek a society predicated fundamentally on those values can find them in abundance elsewhere. Staying in Israel, and committing to the ongoing struggle that Israeli survival will entail, requires a very different set of axioms at Israel's core.

The long-term challenges to Israel's survival are not Iran's looming nuclear capabilities, relentless terror, a war that will not end, or Europe's abandonment of the Jews. These can all be dealt with by a population that knows why it exists and that is committed to its own survival. The core challenge is to produce the sort of citizenry who can articulate why their country exists in the first place and who can then fashion a political framework that matches the purpose of the country.

Were Israel to take the values of American democracy to their full and logical conclusion, it is quite likely that it would simply cease to be a Jewish state. That is precisely why Arabs continue to demand the right of return for the 1948 refugees and all their descendants. That is also the motivation for the explicit demands in the four documents produced by Israel's Arabs that we saw in chapter six. That is what animates Tony Judt's argument that the nation-state is a thing of the past. And that is what lies behind the calls of left-leaning Jewish Israelis to transform Israel into a "country of all its citizens," or in other words, to end the project called the Jewish state.

The United States and Israel differ dramatically not only in the foundational ideals of their formative documents or the views of their current citizens as to what the purposes of the respective countries are. The two nations have also lived very different histories, particularly when it comes to what has been required of them in the defense of their populations.

Israel has not been at peace for a single day since its creation. Not so, of course, the United States. True, both the United States and Israel seemed to know that their declarations of independence would lead to war. Indeed, Thomas Paine's *Common Sense* had based part of its argument for independence on the assertion that the colonies would be able to defeat the British navy. And war in Israel had essentially broken out long before it declared independence on May 14, 1948, as Arab armies had begun to attack soon after the UN vote of November 29, 1947.

Yet, though the United States has fought its share of wars, most were fought abroad, and the almost two hundred and fifty years of American independence have been characterized largely by peace, particularly on U.S. shores. Not so with Israel. War began even before the country was created, and it has never ceased. Nor, tragically, is the conflict likely to be resolved at any point in the near future.

Thus, in America, a conception of the well-lived life, what some call an image of human flourishing, has emerged in which war is perceived as an anomaly. In this view of how human life ought to be lived, war is something to be avoided at all costs; it is somehow a violation of humanity's natural state. Therefore (although this may be changing in the face of the onslaught of Jihad-inspired terror), Americans have by and large not had to fashion a younger generation committed to (or even comfortable with) the notion of the American as warrior. Americans have built their armed forces of late largely on the backs of the less advantaged, who saw the military as a means of climbing up social and economic ladders. (According to one study, rural areas have suffered 27 percent of American casualties in Iraq, but account for only 19 percent of the population.)

Mainstream Americans do not participate in America's wars to the same extent that mainstream Israelis participate in Israel's wars. Most college students at America's elite universities do not give serious consideration to serving in the military. Even civilian service to their country is far from the minds of most. True, some do develop an interest in Teach for America or other programs modeled on the Peace Corps. But the percentages are minuscule, and even those who volunteer for Teach for America do so precisely because it is essentially volunteering. It never even occurs to most of them that their country might consider obligating them, and all their peers, to do something of that sort. And they certainly don't see themselves likely to volunteer to serve in Iraq or Afghanistan.

But Israel has always faced threats to its very existence that the United States has not faced in centuries. As a result, Israeli youth have been taught to view service very differently from their American counterparts. This ethic developed even before the state was created, and it continued as war engulfed the newly born Israel. Even today, despite increasing numbers of draft dodgers in some sectors of society, the vast majority of Israeli young people accept the obligation to serve as natural, and indeed many of the most outstanding high school students compete vigorously to be accepted into the most elite combat units, which often happen to be the most dangerous. They do this because their culture, their teachers, and their parents imbue them, from a very early age, with a belief that citizenship requires of them not only service, but even profound risk. Were Israel's youth to adopt the attitude of America's most talented youth, were they to cease to willingly risk their lives for their country, the Jewish state would quickly be unable to defend itself. Very soon thereafter, it would probably cease to exist.

Indeed, the conception of the ideal human life that emerges from America's most hallowed institutions might be one of the most dangerous aspirations Israelis could adopt. For in the world that they inhabit, Israelis sadly need to see themselves as engaged in a long-term conflict. Does emulating America and the American way of life prepare Israelis for that long-term engagement?

The image of Israel as a miniature America ignores what is unique about Israel, and thus could prove very dangerous for Israel in the not too distant future. Ultimately, younger generations of Israelis will devote themselves to sustaining, protecting, and enhancing Israeli life only if they can say something intelligent about what it means to be a Jew and how being a Jew can be a wholly different experience in a Jewish state from what it could be anyplace else. As long as Israelis see themselves as being in relentless pursuit of a Hebrew-speaking American or Western European sort of life, they will discuss these issues less and less. Israel's younger generations will have no way to explain why they should risk everything, again and again, to ensure the survival of the Jewish state.

Indeed, such results are already becoming apparent. A 2008 report issued by the Israel Defense Forces suggested that only 52% of able-bodied men that year had been drafted. Though the statistics included Israeli Arabs, who are not drafted, and ultra-Orthodox Jews, who usually do not serve, they pointed to no less than seven thousand men who should have been drafted and who instead avoided joining the army, through false claims that they were religious, conscientious objection, feigned medical conditions, simply leaving the country, and a variety of other means. The report also noted that the rate of those not serving was continuing to climb.

Israelis need to be able to say why serving matters. They need to be able to speak thoughtfully about why what they are defending is worth the price it inevitably exacts. Otherwise, the State of Israel will soon find that it cannot sustain or defend itself.

Difficult though it is clearly going to be, shedding the notion of American democracy and values as "default," and anything else as an aberration, is going to be critical if young Israelis are to sustain the sense of purpose that their circumstances will require.

There is yet another difference between U.S. and Israeli systems. This, too, is a difference that Israel will have to maintain if it is to be true to its very purpose. This difference is the separation of church and state (or a "wall of separation," to quote Jefferson's famous 1802 letter to the Danbury Baptists) in America, and the absence of this separation in Israel. Importing the assumptions behind the First Amendment's "Establishment Clause," which asserts that "Congress shall make no law respecting an establishment of religion," would be foolish in Israel. Even those who argue (correctly) that Israel's rabbinate has too much power, and who assert (also correctly) that non-Orthodox forms of Jewish expression are regularly treated unfairly, usually acknowledge that Israel does have and should continue to have some significant Jewish quality if it is to fulfill its function. But on this issue, as with many others, Israelis have yet to devote the necessary time and attention to asking what, exactly, they are trying to build, or how they might seek to be different from other countries.

Interestingly, as is commonly known, the word "God" is absent from Israel's Declaration of Independence. As Yoram Shachar's research illustrates, this omission has a poignant history. One of the earliest drafters of the Declaration was a man named Shalom Zvi Davidowicz, a European yeshiva student who had gone to America, become a Conservative rabbi, and then immigrated to Palestine. In Davidowicz's draft, the Declaration had a distinctly religious overtone, including in the first section a reference to a Divine Promise of the Land of Israel to the fathers of the nation.

Subsequent drafts omitted this section, rendering the Declaration a much more secular document. For the hardened secularists who had abandoned the religious Jewish communities of Europe in favor of lives of physical labor, social commitment, and secular beliefs, the mention of God would contravene everything they hoped the country would become. But the secularization of the Declaration did not sit well with everyone expected to sign it. The religious signatories, as one would expect, very much wanted God mentioned in the document. For them, after all, the creation of the state was in many ways the fulfillment of a long-standing religious aspiration.

Ultimately the crisis over whether to include God in the Declaration was resolved by the use of the phrase "Rock of Israel," a Biblical metaphor for God that is also found throughout the traditional prayer book. The ambiguity of the term allowed everyone a moment of satisfaction. For the secularists, "Rock of Israel" could mean Jewish power, a Jewish return to the land, or a host of other nonreligious associations. For traditionalists, "Rock of Israel" was a phrase for God that every religious Jew instinctively understood as such.

Thus, the compromise allowed all the various groups to sign the document. But here, too, it simply delayed the critical conversation about the kind of society that Israel would become, about what form of democracy would take root. Should the Orthodox rabbinate have exclusive control over marriages, divorces, and conversion? On the one hand, if there is not a uniform code for who is Jewish, or who is genuinely divorced, how can Israeli society function? But on the other hand, what about those Jews who want something other than what the Orthodox rabbinate offers? Reform or Conservative Jews, for example? Or atheists, who might wish to be married without the participation of a rabbi? At present, some of those people leave Israel and go to Cyprus to get married, since Israel recognizes marriages performed abroad for legal (nonreligious) purposes. Others choose simply not to be registered by the rabbinate, but to be recognized by the Ministry of the Interior as married, with no formal religious validation of the marriage. Is that a solution? Does the Jewish state want Jews to have to leave its borders to have the kind of Jewish weddings, or conversions, that they seek? Does it want Jews who seek a different form of religious ceremony to have no choice but to eliminate any religious dimension from their marriage rites? If not, how could Israeli society function with a completely free-market approach to religious matters?

Other questions abound in the struggle to create a society that is both Jewish and democratic. Should buses in Israeli cities run on the Sabbath? Who has more rights, those who wish to have the Sabbath feel like a dramatically different day, with quiet on the streets and stores closed, or those who argue that it's their right to have access to travel, a right that should not be hindered because of the religious preferences of others? How should Israel balance its democratic principles with the sense that *something* should be Jewish about the country? But who should decide what that *something* is? And what are the rights of those who disagree?

Should the very religious, ultra-Orthodox Jews have to go into the army? What if the army's environment would force them into contact with lifestyles that are not in keeping with their religious commitments? But why should any large subsection of Israeli society not do its share to defend the state? Should all Israeli schoolchildren study the Bible and some Jewish religious content? How can that be forced on parents who are avowedly secular—not only uninterested in religion but fundamentally opposed to it? To what extent should Israel's Arabs be required to study the Hebrew Bible, or classic works of Zionist literature? If they are exempted, they become even less pre- pared to engage in the public discourse that is—and ought to be—at the heart of Israeli life. But these texts are not "theirs" in any mean- ingful way. Is it appropriate for Israel to oblige Arab students to study them? Should Jewish Israelis also study the Koran?

And most vitally, can a state whose children are Jewishly illiterate engender a conversation with those children when they become adults about why Jewish statehood is critical, and why the Jewish state is worth defending?

These are the sorts of questions that Israelis know they must address. That conversation is slowly beginning. Professor Ruth Gavison (mentioned above) joined with Rabbi Yaakov Medan (the often right- wing head of the Har Etzion Yeshiva in Alon Shevut, about ten miles south of Jerusalem) to write a "social contract" between religious and "freethinking" Jews, defining what each would give up to make living in a shared society possible. Just a few years ago, such a joint project would have been unthinkable.

Other signs of progress are also evident. Jewish studies programs are attracting more and more "secular" Jews eager for some Jewish con- tent in their lives, as long as they can get it outside the confines of what they consider the religiously oppressive and coercive regime of the Orthodox rabbinate. Israel's popular news Web sites, which just years ago had no Jewish content on their home pages, now have a great deal.

These Web sites are purely market-driven; if the content is there, it is because the purveyors of the material believe that there are readers who wish to read it and that advertising revenue will go up if it is offered. Israel's bookstores are filled with increasing numbers of volumes about Judaica that are designed for the people whose parents wanted to flee Jewish life with all their might, but who themselves are seeking roots once again (a subject to which we'll return in a later chapter).

Occasionally issues of Israel's Jewishness and the balance between a Jewish quality to the state and freedom of expression reach the courts. When that happens, observers gain a valuable window into the ongoing struggles involved in what Israel is still trying to create.

One poignant example occurred in April 2008, when a municipal judge overruled the conviction of four merchants who had sold *hametz* (unleavened bread) on Passover. The judge argued that the law prohibited only the display of such food, not its sale. Her ruling, as might have been expected, unleashed a firestorm of arguments, and even threats from one political party to abandon the coalition and to force new elections. But more significant for the long term were the ruminations of more thoughtful Israelis, even secular ones, who recognized that there was a tension between "freedom of religious expression" (or freedom *not* to observe the religious dictum) and the formation of a national identity with Judaism at its core.

Foreign Minister Tzipi Livni, herself a secular Jew, did not minimize what was at stake. "Ostensibly, the ban on the public display or sale of bread on Passover is a minor and marginal issue, but I believe that this is not the case," she said. "In my view, this prohibition is part of the substantive question of how we wish to characterize our identity in the national home for the Jewish people." What Livni was essentially saying was that the ban on *hametz* on Passover ought to be seen as part of Israel's civil religion. Commenting on the simmering tensions, Nahum Barnea, one of Israel's most thoughtful and widely read columnists, mused on precisely what differentiates Israel from other countries. Even sixty years into its existence, he said, Israel "is still trying to define itself, something most states don't have to do."

That is precisely the point. "We are still debating our existence," Barnea continued, "not only in terms of policy but in terms of ideology. What is Israel? What is a Jewish state? And how can *hametz* help us find the answer?"

How, or whether, *hametz* can help Israelis find the answer is not at all clear. But what many Israelis sensed was that, strange though it might sound to American ears, what kinds of food Israeli stores were permitted to sell on Passover could not be exclusively a free-market decision. The radical (though not perfect) divide between state and religion that characterizes American life ought not be imported to Israel. Israel will require a very different system, and a much closer intersection of the two. That, too, will be one of the ways in which the American and the Israeli models will have to differ if Israel is to persevere.

Many of the most compelling questions around Israel's fundamental nature remain unanswered. At the heart of Israel's discontent—even beyond its enemies and the world's harsh judgment—is the lack of consensus, or even clarity, about the questions as to what kind of country Israelis are building. How democratic should it be, and should it be democratic at all? How Jewish should it be, and how should it be Jewish? Is it "of the Jews, by the Jews, and for the Jews," or does it have a more universal purpose?

None of this had yet been resolved when the state was declared. The lack of consensus is most obviously reflected in the fact that even though the Declaration of Independence asserted that "a Constitution [was] to be drawn up by a Constituent Assembly not later than the first day of October, 1948," almost sixty years have passed, and no constitution has been written.

For Israel, though, the real problem is not that there is no constitution. The country functions reasonably well with its system of Basic Laws. The issue is not the text but the shared sense of purpose that creating the text would require. Israel has no constitution not because its greatest legal minds have not thought about how to write one; it has no constitution because there is no consensus about the fundamental values that ought to inhere in the Jewish state. The conversation to clarify those values could well become explosive, but it can no longer be dodged; indeed, it must become one of the most pressing matters on Israel's agenda.

Life in Israel is going to continue to exact a high price from Israelis, in no small measure because the conflicts with Israel's enemies appear to be unsolvable for the present. For a long time, Israelis understood that they had no choice but to pay that price. But that is true no longer. Increasingly Israelis are asking, both for themselves and for the sons and daughters whom they will one day drive to the induction base to be drafted by the army, "Why pay this price if I can't say what it is that I'm being asked to defend?" Learning to articulate what they are being asked to defend depends, in no small measure, on Israelis' ceasing their quest to become a Hebrew-speaking, miniature America.

Even at the start of the process, though, one conclusion seems relatively clear: the unadulterated American model simply cannot work if the goal is the sustenance of Israel as a Jewish state of any sort. Now, perhaps more than ever before, articulating how Israel might be unique, and not an inadequate version of another country, is a requirement of the utmost urgency.

Chapter Nine

ISRAEL'S ARABS, ISRAEL'S CONUNDRUM

> Each state has a purpose that is particular to it: Expansion
> was the purpose of Rome, war that of Lacedaemonia; religion
> that of the Jewish laws; commerce that of Marseilles, public
> tranquility that of the laws of China . . . [and] political liberty
> [was the purpose of England].
>
> —Montesquieu, *The Spirit of the Laws*

A great deal has changed since Montesquieu penned the words above, and today few readers would agree with his assessment of the purpose of *any* of the countries he lists. Even so, he makes a claim that remains worth considering: namely, that states can have a purpose.

Is there a *purpose* to the Jewish state? Is Israel simply the nation-state of the Jews by virtue of the fact that a large number of Jews live there, or that Hebrew is an official language of the state? Or does Israel have some greater and more profound purpose, and if so, what might that purpose be?

Throughout these pages, we have argued that restoring the notion of purpose to discourse about Israel is critical to saving the Jewish state.

But the purpose of Israel is not *religion*, we've argued, as least not as Montesquieu meant that. Rather, it is the healing of the Jewish people, the creation of a space in which Jews can thrive as they could nowhere else.

The fact that few Israelis or supporters of Israel outside the country speak about the *purpose* of Jewish statehood has weakened Israel immeasurably. For in the face of relentless international attacks on Israel's legitimacy, an inability to articulate why the Jews need a state leaves Israel's supporters speechless at precisely the moment when they cannot afford this. When such prominent intellectuals as Tony Judt argue that it's time for Israel to come to an end, it is not enough merely to disagree viscerally. Something articulate and profound needs to be said, and to too great an extent, Israel's supporters have been rendered mute by the criticism leveled against them.

One of the many reasons that Israel's supporters have been rendered mute is the unspoken but important awareness that a sense of purpose for Israel, if it is about the thriving of the Jewish people, cannot— by definition—include Israel's Arabs to the same extent that it includes Israel's Jews. That is not to say that Israel's Arabs cannot be citizens, or that they do not deserve better treatment and equal protection under the law. But there *is* an inherent tension between the inclusive and universal values of many Israelis and many of Israel's supporters on the one hand, and the demographic reality that Israel's Arabs create on the other. For sixty years, Israelis have dodged any serious conversation about that tension. But if Israelis are to save their state by renewing a conversation about its purpose, that long-overdue conversation can be delayed no longer.

The tension between universal values and a specific commitment to Jewish thriving has always been a factor in Israeli life. Israel's Declaration of Independence says that the Jewish state "will uphold the full social and political equality of all its citizens, without distinction of race, creed or sex." But it also says, in the previous sentence, that it "will be open to the immigration of Jews from all countries of their dispersion," a commitment that later was codified in 1950 as Israel's

Law of Return. The Law of Return guarantees citizenship and the right to immigrate to all Jews, but only to Jews. Others can apply for citizenship, but Jews do not have to. They are guaranteed automatic citizenship simply by virtue of their Jewishness.

To the founders of a country created in the shadow of the Shoah, this made perfect sense. If the country was about saving the Jews, then Jews had to know that they could come to their newly created homeland and refuge, no matter what. And they had to know that this commitment was part of the very essence of the country's purpose.

But Israel was then, and remains, approximately 20% Arab. Can the Law of Return mesh with the desire to create a society based on equality without regard to race, religion, or gender? Not at all easily. It is thus not surprising that, as we saw in a previous chapter, virtually every Israeli Arab organization, in arguing for improved rights for Israeli Arabs, demands the nullification of the Law of Return. From their point of view, the Law of Return clearly makes them second-class citizens. The law suggests that Israel is "of the Jews, by the Jews, and for the Jews." Therefore, the Arabs insist, no matter how much Israel's courts might enforce Israeli Arabs' civil rights, the mere existence of the Law of Return relegates them to a diminished status.

What, we might ask, did the Knesset intend when it passed the Law of Return? It had in mind a sense of *Jewish* purpose. Israel was not meant to be just another democracy, or simply one more member of the UN General Assembly. It was a country with a mission: the saving and ingathering of the Jews. And given that, nothing could make more sense than admitting Jews just because they were Jews.

What did Ben-Gurion think these Arab inhabitants, who are invited to "play their part in the development of the State," would feel about a state that is "of the Jews, by the Jews, and for the Jews"? What about "*Hatikvah*," the national anthem, which opens by proclaiming, "Still, deep in our heart, a Jewish spirit still sings"? Or the state's flag, designed to look like a *tallit*, a Jewish prayer shawl, with a Star of David in the middle? Or Jewish religious holidays, which are effectively national holidays? Or even the state's language, which is a modernized version of the language of the Hebrew Bible? (Arabic is technically also an official language of the state, but that is observed more in the breach than in practice.)

Israel's early leaders were aware, from the very outset, that those Arabs remaining in a sovereign Jewish state would be problematic. Ben-Gurion himself realized that Arabs who remained inside Israel's borders would constitute an internal threat. And Eliezer Kaplan, who in 1948 was serving as the treasurer of the Jewish Agency, said, "Our young state will not be able to stand such a large number of strangers in its midst." Indeed, on the famed night of November 29, 1947, one longtime resident of the Yishuv (the pre-state Jewish community) noted in his diary, "In my heart there was joy mixed with sadness: joy . . . that we were a nation with a state, and sadness that we lost half the country [to the partition] and, in addition, that we [would] have [in our state] 400,000 Arabs."

Given the widespread recognition that it would be difficult for an emerging Jewish state to assimilate a significant number of Arabs, it is not surprising that even then, the option of transfer was given serious consideration, by Jews as well as non-Jews. As early as 1937, the British Peel Commission "recommended that the bulk of the three hundred thousand Arabs who lived in the territory earmarked for Jewish sovereignty should be transferred, voluntarily or under compulsion, to the Arab part of Palestine or out of the country altogether," and suggested that 1,250 Jews living in those areas slated for Arab sovereignty be moved as well, in "an exchange of population." Even some Arabs seemed to understand the need for transfer. Ibrahim Pasha Hashim, Jordanian King Abdullah's prime minister, apparently representing the views of Abdullah himself, said in 1939 that "[t]he only just and permanent solution lay in absolute partition with an exchange of populations; to leave Jews in an Arab state or Arabs in a Jewish state would lead inevitably to further trouble between the two peoples." And years later, when the 1948 war erupted, Ben-Gurion hinted that the war offered the opportunity for a massive transfer of populations:

> From your entry to Jerusalem through Lifta-Romema . . . there are no [Arabs]. One hundred per cent Jewish . . . I do

not assume that this will change. . . . What has happened in Jerusalem . . . could well happen in great parts of the country. . . . [It] is possible that . . . there will take place great changes . . . and not all of them to our detriment. Certainly there will be great changes in the composition of the population of the country.

And as mentioned in an earlier chapter, even Benny Morris, one of Israel's "new historians" and thus often associated with the left, has suggested that Ben-Gurion made a serious historical mistake in 1948. "Even though he understood the demographic issue and the need to establish a Jewish state without a large Arab minority, he got cold feet during the war. In the end, he faltered. . . . If the end of the story turns out to be a gloomy one for the Jews, it will be because Ben-Gurion did not complete the transfer in 1948. . . . The non-completion of the transfer was a mistake."

The transfer never did take place, and the concerns of those observers in November 1947 were never addressed. Now, more than sixty years later, Israel's Arab population is showing signs of becoming increasingly radicalized. Its numbers are growing, and fewer and fewer Israeli Jews are sanguine that their Arab fellow citizens are instinctively loyal to the state. What, then, is to be done? Left unaddressed, the situation will only grow more severe as the percentage of Arabs in the country's population continues to climb. But what is the alternative? Is there anything that Israeli Jews can legitimately and fairly do to safeguard the Jewish majority of their country, and with it, its very reason for being?

There are essentially two ways of addressing Israel's future demographic balance. One, of course, is to limit, or even decrease, the number of Israeli Arabs, a subject to which we will return. But another, taken seriously by few but still strongly advocated by some (former Prime Minister Ariel Sharon being a prime example), is that of massive immigration of Jews to Israel.

What would happen if Jews from across the world decided, en masse, to make *aliyah* and to live in Israel? The United States alone has somewhere between 5 million and 6.5 million Jews (the numbers are highly contested, but this range appears to be reasonably safe). If even a third of those Jews moved to Israel, the proportion of Jews to Arabs in Israel would shift significantly. But it is clear that no massive immigrations of this sort are going to transpire, from the United States or from anywhere else.

France, too, has a sizable Jewish population, approximately 600,000. But while French Jews are beginning to make their way to Israel in significant numbers (there are neighborhoods in Ashkelon, Eilat, and other Israeli cities where all the roadside billboards and advertisements are in French, with no English and very little Hebrew to be seen), they won't make a substantial difference. In fact, after the election of French president Nicolas Sarkozy in 2007, some French Jews who had already moved to Israel decided to move back to France. The well-known pattern was reconfirmed: Jews immigrate to Israel almost exclusively from countries in which they do not feel secure. They are not coming from France, and barring some wholly unforeseen change, they are certainly not going to come from the United States.

When more than a million Russians came to Israel during the 1990s (we'll avoid the question of how many were "technically Jewish" according to Jewish law, which is a problem in and of itself), they came because Jewish life in the Soviet Union and in post–Soviet Russia was oppressive. It is precisely the *lack* of adverse conditions that explains why the few hundred thousand Jews in Britain produce only a trickle of immigrants (and the United States produces barely more).

One of the great disappointments for Zionist ideologues of the early part of the previous century was that those Jews who came to Israel were *fleeing* to Israel. Those who did not have to flee, by and large, simply did not come. One can certainly understand why. The standard of living in Israel is lower, life is more dangerous, and many do not know the language and are not sure how they would make a living. Leaving family and aging parents can be difficult. A move to Israel is no simple matter.

Yet, had the early Zionist thinkers been told that the only Jews who would come to Israel would be those who needed to leave their host countries, and that on the whole, "free" Jews would not choose to be part of the new Jewish state, they would have been shocked—and unconvinced. As Ben-Gurion said, "For hundreds of years, a question-prayer hovered in the mouths of the Jewish people: would a country be found for this people? No one imagined the frightening question: would a people be found for the country when it would be created?"

The writer Yossi Klein Halevi captures the kind of faith that moving to Israel has often required. He tells of an Ethiopian immigrant to Israel, Asher, who reflected on why he was not fleeing the barrage of Katyusha missiles during the Second Lebanon War. "When we left our village to walk to the Sudan," Asher said, "my father brought a shovel. I asked him why, and he says, 'so that we'll be able to bury those who will die on the road and carry on to the land of Israel.'"

That's a kind of real faith in why life in Israel matters, Klein Halevi correctly notes. But thus far, it's the kind of faith that has been in evidence with "fleeing Jews" who have left places where they were not welcome, not with Jews who have real choices. Given that the major Jewish populations outside Israel now reside in counties in which Jews are welcome, *aliyah* is not likely to solve Israel's demographic problem.

If the demographic balance cannot be solved by bringing sufficient numbers of Jews to Israel, many therefore argue, the solution will have to be found in controlling the number of Arabs. One way of doing this, it has been suggested, is to move not the people themselves, but the borders within which they live.

Many of Israel's Arabs live in villages that are spread across the Galilee (where Arabs constitute 50% of the population) and the Negev. Therefore, there is no way to adjust Israel's borders so as to make those villages part of the Palestinian Authority, or part of a Palestinian state, should one emerge.

However, there *is* one place in Israel where an adjustment of the border might place a significant group of Israeli Arabs on the other side of the border. This is Wadi Ara, also known as the "Triangle." Wadi Ara is contiguous with the West Bank, which, in turn, in all likelihood will become Palestine in some future political settlement.

Approximately 15% of Israel's Arabs live in this area. Thus, either ceding this territory to Palestine or "trading" it for those swaths of land in the West Bank where there are Jewish settlements (a trade that has been advocated by some right-wing Israeli political parties) would alleviate some of the demographic pressure.

Those in favor of the move argue that diminishing Israel's Arab population by even 15% would make a difference. But the issue is much more than one of numbers; what may matter is the *kind* of people who live in Wadi Ara and who would therefore be removed from Israeli society. The largest town in the Wadi Ara area is Um el-Fahm, which is not only a significant population concentration, but is Israel's first and foremost Islamic fundamentalist city. Its leadership is thoroughly uninterested in any cooperation with Jewish Israel. The movement there is headed by Sheikh Ra'id Salah, who has served as the mayor of Um el-Fahm, and by Kamal Hatib, who lives in Kafr Kana and co-leads this faction in the Galilee. What these two share is their commitment to complete separatism—cultural, religious, and social—for Israel's Arabs. While they cannot permit themselves to become involved in national politics and to run for places in the Knesset (that would require taking an oath of allegiance to the State of Israel, which they refuse to do), they do participate in local politics, where, they argue, they can slowly shift the culture to one founded more explicitly on Muslim values and Islamic law.

It is critical to understand what this conflict is about. This population is not simply hostile to Israel's policies or resentful of its treatment of Israeli Arabs; rather, it is unalterably opposed to the existence of a Jewish state in Palestine. That this population is a potentially significant danger to Israeli society is beyond dispute. Therefore, some argue, the value of moving the border westward, so that Wadi Ara finds itself in Palestine rather than in Israel, is not only numeric. It would take this highly antagonistic population and attach it to the emerging state that represents its values, and it would remove this dangerous population from inside Israel's borders (by moving the border, not the people). Some Israelis argue that such a move would also make it clear to Israel's other Arabs that they have a choice to make: they can come to terms with the existence of a Jewish State of Israel and see themselves as committed partners in building it (however understandably difficult that may be), or they can begin to prepare for the eventuality that Israel will not be able to long abide increasingly subversive minorities.

The Arab residents of Wadi Ara oppose such a move by overwhelming margins, for understandable reasons. The standard of living in Israel is significantly higher than it is in the Palestinian Authority, even for Arabs who have yet to receive their fair share of Israel's bounty, and it is likely to stay higher. Israeli Arabs (or Palestinian Israelis, as they prefer to be called) benefit from Israel's advanced medical system, a modern technological infrastructure, a robust freedom of the press, freedom of expression, and protection for women (from honor killings, for example), among many other advantages. Hundreds of Palestinian homosexual men have made their homes in Tel Aviv, knowing full well that if they were exposed in the Palestinian Authority they would be summarily murdered. The sorts of "disappearances" of Hamas's opponents that became common in the Gaza Strip once Hamas took over (many of these "opponents" were Christians uninvolved in the fighting, while others were leaders of the opposition Fatah faction) simply do not happen in Israel. Even living under the watchful eye of Israel's security forces is a price most are more than willing to pay for the freedoms that life in Israel brings.

Still, the question remains. Is moving the border this way a wise move for Israel? There is no simple answer. According to most readings of international law, Israel would still have obligations to this population even if the border were moved; the villages could be transferred out of Israel, but their inhabitants would retain their rights to Israeli citizenship (and their right to leave their village and to move back into Israel if they wished). Legally, Israel could do nothing to prevent that. As one study notes, "[I]t is quite doubtful that such a step, which was originally meant to maintain a Jewish majority in the respective areas . . . can achieve its objective—given the possibility that the Palestinian residents of these areas may choose to relocate to within the new borders of Israel." That study concludes, "It would be inappropriate to promote such a solution as far as its sole intent remains continuation of Jewish majority in the State of Israel."

Nonetheless, even though moving the border poses legal difficulties, we ought to recall that this happened across Europe throughout the twentieth century, without profound harm to the populations involved. Consider Vilna, a prime example. Now called Vilnius, Vilna was once a primary seat of Jewish learning and culture in Europe. Today Vilnius is the capital of Lithuania, but it has a long history of being annexed and ceded by a variety of countries. In 1795 it was annexed by Russia, but it was later captured by Napoleon, and during World War I, it was occupied by the Germans. It then changed hands repeatedly, among the Poles, the Russians, the Lithuanians, and the Germans.

By and large, Jewish life survived and even flourished in Vilna throughout most of these shifts (until the Nazis annihilated the population). And relative to the warring conditions in which the Jewish community of Vilna often found itself, what is proposed for Wadi Ara would be mild, indeed.

There are countless other examples. The city that the Jews know as Lovov, also long a seat of Jewish cultural and religious thriving, is now part of the Ukraine and is called Leviv. The Russians, when they possessed it, called it Lewow. The Austrians controlled the area until World War I, and called it Lemberg. And so on.

One would have to be foolish to suggest that these transitions did not impose hardship on the native populations. But they happened, and they happened often. And by and large, they transpired without widespread bloodshed among the civilian population. Nor are these events considered moments of supreme human suffering or horrific violations of human rights. They are seen, instead, as almost expected examples of border-shifting as part of wider conflicts.

Israel's Arabs are also part of a wider conflict, and in many cases, they have taken the side of Israel's enemies. There are increasing incidents of terror being carried out by this population. In the space of a few months in 2008, for example, an Israeli Arab murdered eight students at Jerusalem's Merkaz Ha-Rav Yeshiva, another used a bulldozer to commit an attack in which three Jewish Israelis were killed, and four more were arrested on suspicion of having provided or having planned to provide information on Israeli civilian targets to al-Qaida in two separate plots. In addition, Israeli Arab leaders use ever more venomous language in their dismissal of Israel's legitimacy. The bottom line is clear: if Israelis want to survive as a Jewish state, they will have to ask themselves the painful question of how far they will go to address the growing threat posed by Israeli Arabs, and what they are willing to do to preserve the state they have built at such a high cost.

To be sure, there are many reasons not to move the border in this way. There is the matter of those Arabs (the majority) who would remain in Israel. A decision to "offload" 200,000 full Israeli citizens would undoubtedly be highly demoralizing for those Israeli Arabs (about 1 million more) who would not be removed. It might communicate to them the sense that Israel doesn't really want them, setting back any attempt to build better relations with them. The other possibility, of course, is that they already believe that Israel does not want them, and nothing Israel does will convince them otherwise. After all, some Israelis point out, these Arabs (who are Israeli citizens) commemorate the *Nakba*, the Arabic term for the "Catastrophe" of May 14, 1948. How likely is it that they will embrace the Jewish state?

Some Israelis raise strategic reasons not to move the border. They point out, for example, that the distance from Tel Aviv to the Jordan River, running straight through the West Bank, is already treacherously short (less than fifty miles), and suggest that making the country even narrower would be foolhardy.

While other objections are also raised, the point is clear. Shifting Israel's borders is an option, but it is replete with legal, moral, and strategic complexities. None of these complexities rules out the step completely, but they do suggest that it is not a foolproof solution. Given the fact that the solution would address only a small percentage of Israel's Arabs, moving the borders for this reason might not be worth the price it would exact.

What, then, is the alternative? If massive *aliyah* from the United States and France (the world's two largest Jewish communities outside

Israel) is not likely, and moving the border appears overly complicated and insufficiently effective, what then? Some people have suggested that instead, Israel will have to consider moving massive numbers of Arabs out of Israel into neighboring Arab countries.

In Israeli discourse, the mere suggestion of "transfer" immediately evokes the memory of Meir Kahane, who as we saw above, was excluded from the political process for advocating precisely that, and more recently, of Avigdor Lieberman, a right-wing Israeli politician also accused by many of being a racist for advocating the transfer of populations.

On the surface, there are almost innumerable reasons to denounce transfer as immoral or unfeasible. Forced population transfers are now considered an international crime against humanity by many authorities. Israel would likely encounter strong international resistance, if not actual troop deployment, if it tried to carry out such a move against the wishes of the population being transferred. Does anyone really imagine that the international community would simply sit by and watch the forced expulsion of hundreds of thousands of Israel's Arabs, who would claim, often legitimately, that their families had been living on their lands for centuries?

Beyond the objections to Israel's moving these people, there is the fact that no other country in the world wants them. The Hashemite rulers of Jordan have long been worried about the size and hostility of the Palestinian population of Jordan. In September 1970, we should recall, a month that the Palestinians refer to as "Black September," Jordanian forces attacked Palestinians who had entered Jordan, killing thousands of them. Many more were exiled; Jordan clearly has no interest in admitting large number of Palestinians (which is what Israeli Arabs are) today. Egypt has long expressed absolutely no desire to assist the residents of Gaza, an area it controlled before Israel captured it. Syria, formally at war with Israel and also not positively predisposed toward the Palestinians, has no reason to accept a flood of newly displaced, marginally impoverished refugees from Israel. After all, like Jordan, it's done virtually nothing to settle the 1948 refugees who have already made their way to Syria. Nor do the Lebanese, who have yet to address the 1948 refugee problem, want more. There is, therefore, with the possible exception of a Palestinian entity that might one day be created on the West Bank, no place to which these populations could even be transferred.

Furthermore, it should be noted, despite the undeniable second-class status that Israeli Arabs endure, they do not want to leave. A recent Harvard University study found that 76.9% said that they would rather live in Israel than in any other country. Thus, they are not likely to leave Israel willingly, especially to a fledgling Palestinian state with a history of significant human rights abuses. For this reason, most Israelis not on the far right consider the mere idea a nonstarter, both morally and pragmatically.

However, we should note that the picture is not nearly as one-sided as it is often portrayed. First, Israelis are keenly aware that population transfers do not need to be catastrophic for those moved, if there is a willing host country (which there isn't right now, but which international pressure might succeed in creating). From 1947 on, as it became clear that the State of Israel would be founded, approximately 750,000 Jews were forcibly evicted from Arab lands to a country that barely had the resources to absorb them. None of these people ever received compensation from their former "host" countries, and the nascent State of Israel had little to offer them. But Israel took them nonetheless, for while it lacked resources, it had, in abundance, a desire to help them. All those refugees were made citizens, and in the years that have passed, their descendants have steadily (if sometimes too slowly) climbed Israel's social and economic ladders.

Being evicted from your country need not condemn you to poverty, as long as someone is willing to take you in. Jews from Arab lands found that "someone" in Israel; Palestinians, despite the bluster of Israel's Arab neighbors, have not. And that makes all the difference. An international community interested in a long-term settlement in the Middle East might have to focus not only on how Israel must compromise, but on what other Arab nations will need to do to accommodate populations that might have to be shifted.

Indeed, there have been cases of population transfer that have been conducted bloodlessly, and that have contributed to the creation of peace between formerly warring neighbors. There was a transfer of populations between the Greek and Turkish sides of

Cyprus, for example, after Turkey occupied 38% of the island in 1974. Though various UN organs determine the numbers of those who were transferred in slightly different ways, estimates of the number of Greek Cypriots who were moved range from 165,000 to 200,000, while the estimates of Turkish Cypriots moved range from about 45,000 to 65,000. Yet, despite all this movement and undeniable dislocation, people were not killed. The Republic of Cyprus not only faced invasion and the loss of significant territory; it also had to deal with massive numbers of Greek Cypriots returning and some Turkish citizens leaving. And all this happened with no loss of life. If that was the case in Cyprus, some ask, why could it not happen in Israel?

To all of the above we should note yet an additional factor: many Israelis believe that transfer has already taken place as part of the ongoing attempt to settle the conflict. Here they refer not to the Arabs who were displaced in 1948 and 1949, but to the Jews who were forced out of Gaza in the summer of 2005. Interestingly, the several thousand Israeli Jews who were removed from Gaza at that time when Israel left that territory made a point of referring to themselves not as *mefunei azah* (evacuated from Gaza), but as *megorashei azah* (*transferred from Gaza*). Furthermore, these people point out, all discussions of giving the West Bank to the Palestinians invariably assume that the Jews in the West Bank will be forced to leave. There are approximately a quarter of a million Jews there, not counting those in greater Jerusalem. Is that not also transfer, they ask?

Their point is clear. If the Peel Commission felt that transfer was the only workable solution, if Jews have already been transferred out of Gaza and even Israeli governments have put the transfer of hundreds of thousands of Jews out of the West Bank on the bargaining table, why is discussing the transfer of Israeli Arabs inherently illegitimate? If Jewish governments could require Jews to leave their homes, their communities, their livelihoods, and more, all in an effort to move one step closer to a final resolution of the regional conflict, then why cannot the same government countenance moving other populations for the same goal?

To be sure, it feels different on the international stage when the (predominantly Jewish) Israeli government moves Jews into Israel

than it would if that same government were to move Arabs out of
Israel. But still, Israeli proponents of transfer do at least have a point.
If population movement is a potentially legitimate tool in reaching a
final settlement, then it is conceivably a legitimate tool with regard to
populations other than Jews.

Finally, we should note, not all the scholarly literature is absolutely
opposed to population transfer. Chaim Kaufmann, for example, writing in the MIT-sponsored journal *International Security*, while not
explicitly supporting transfer, suggests that at times, it can be the only
way to settle a conflict, or that it may be inevitable, given the directions
that that conflict is heading. In those cases, he argues, the question
isn't simply *whether* to separate the populations, but rather, *how* to
do so. It is possible, he notes, to move populations "with protection,
transport, subsistence and resettlement organized by outside powers"; ultimately, failure to prepare for the resettlement of populations
that may be inevitable given the ethnic strife in which the region is
embroiled "does not protect people against becoming refugees, but
inflicts disaster on them when they do."

What should Israel do in this instance? Is transfer, despite its lep-
rous character in most discussions thus far, so obviously unthinkable?
Perhaps some accommodation could be made with the countries bor-
dering Israel (Egypt, Jordan, Syria, and eventually Palestine) to take
in Israel's Arabs, so that the populations could be separated peacefully,
as was done in Cyprus. Alternatively, perhaps the international community could raise sufficient funds and offer massive cash settlements
to those Israeli Arabs willing to relocate so as to move the conflict
closer to settlement. Is there any way that the international community can see its way to separating two populations that have been at
war for more than a century, in the hope that the region might finally
know some peace?

I cannot recall writing anything that has filled me with more pain
than some of the suggestions contemplated in this chapter. When
I have had wonderful Israeli Arab students with whom I've developed long-term friendships, or when simple social interactions with
Palestinian Israelis—at the doctor's office, in the university library, or
on the street—are pleasant and respectful, I feel tremendous hope that

the lurking danger facing Israel can somehow be addressed. I still find myself hoping that the optimists in Israeli society are right, and that my worries are misplaced.

Nonetheless, I fear that those moments of coexistence, in which I still take pride and pleasure, simply camouflage an issue that Israel's Jewish majority can no longer afford to avoid. Therefore, despite the great pain, these potentially agonizing solutions to an undeniable problem have to be raised, if for no other reason than to bring into sharp focus the challenges that Israel faces, so that Israelis might finally confront head-on the *kinds* of choices that they will soon have to make.

Those who seek to restore purpose to Israeli life will have to decide how to preserve Israel's Jewish majority. For it is that majority that enables Israel to serve as such a beacon of hope for Jews. That, in turn, invariably will entail more than rhetoric. It will require abandoning the pretense that Israel is just like other countries, the charade that claims that Israel can deal with its minorities precisely as other democracies do. Perhaps there are possible solutions that no one has yet considered. I hope that there are. More immediately, however, significant gains will have been made if Israelis, and Israel's supporters abroad, ask themselves honestly and directly what the purpose of Israel's existence is. If Israelis genuinely believe in that purpose, they will then have to be willing to discuss what they are actually willing to do to protect the existence of the state that has saved the Jewish people.

Chapter Ten

CREATING THE NEW JEW

The anti-Jewish riots in Kishinev, Bessarabia, are worse than the censor will permit to publish. There was a well laid-out plan for the general massacre of Jews on the day following the Russian Easter. The mob was led by priests, and the general cry, "Kill the Jews," was taken up all over the city. The Jews were taken wholly unaware and were slaughtered like sheep. The dead number 120 and the injured about 500. The scenes of horror attending this massacre are beyond description. Babes were literally torn to pieces by the frenzied and bloodthirsty mob. The local police made no attempt to check the reign of terror. At sunset the streets were piled with corpses and wounded. Those who could make their escape fled in terror, and the city is now practically deserted of Jews.

—*New York Times* account of the 1903 Kishinev pogrom

On February 6, 1903, Michael Ribalenko, a young Christian Russian boy, was murdered in the town of Dubossary, approximately twenty-five miles north of the city of Kishinev. It was clear that Ribalenko had been murdered by a relative, but that did not stop several Russian newspapers from insinuating that he'd been murdered by a Jew.

The rumors about Jewish involvement in the crime eventually took on a life of their own, and in short order, they led to three days of rioting and attacks on Jews. The *New York Times* offered the account of what transpired that appears at the beginning of this chapter.

The actual number of dead was lower than the *Times* reported, approximately forty-seven, but news of the devastation quickly made its way around the Jewish world. Hayim Nahman Bialik, already widely acknowledged as the Jewish people's poet laureate, went to Kishinev, seeking to learn more about what had happened. The poem that he wrote based on his experience, "In the City of Slaughter," quickly became a classic.

It is a lengthy, complex, and painful epic poem. In the middle of the poem, Bialik describes the basement of a house, where the marauding Cossacks mercilessly rape the Jewish women, time and again. While the savage assault is unfolding, according to Bialik's rendition, the Jewish men hide behind casks, unable to stop the attackers, too afraid even to try. These "sons of the Maccabees," Bialik calls them with his bitter irony, are symbols of what Bialik believes has gone wrong with European Jewry. The Maccabees, he expects us to recall, were a band of Jewish warriors who, though vastly outnumbered, were able to recapture the Temple Mount from the Greeks in 167 B.C.E.

But the Jews are Maccabees no longer, Bialik suggests. In fact, for Bialik, the villains of the scene are not the Cossacks; rape and murder are simply what Cossacks do. The problem with what happens in Kishinev, Bialik intimates with his biting pen, rests with the Jewish men. It's bad enough that they are too weak to defend their wives, their sisters, their mothers, and their daughters, though that is clearly lamentable. But worse than that, they are too frightened to even try.

After the attack is over, some of the men in Bialik's poem step over the bodies of their wives and daughters and run to the rabbi's house to ask a question. "Is my wife," the *kohanim* ("priests" in the Jewish tradition) in Bialik's poem want to know, "still permitted to me?"

"*That* is what worries you?" Bialik virtually screams. The people you love are broken, wounded, raped, and lying on the ground, and all that concerns you is a question of Jewish law, the matter of whether your wives are still sexually permitted to you? Why didn't you kneel by her side? Hold her. Tell her that you'll take care of her. Tend to her wounds. Tell her that you still love her, and always will.

The exile of the Jew from his own land, Bialik claims, has not only robbed the Jew of his strength and his courage. It has eaten away at his very humanity. Exile has destroyed him. And Jewish ritual, which might once have created purity and holiness in a spoiled world, now rots his soul by turning his attention away from what really matters. The European Jew cannot fight. He cannot feel. He is not human.

For Bialik therefore, and for many of his contemporaries, the point of Zionism, of the return to the Jewish homeland, was not simply to offer hope, refuge. The reason that Jews needed to return to their land was that Jews needed to create the Jew anew.

Bialik was hardly the only Zionist artist or ideologue who believed this. If Bialik made his case for a "new Jew" metaphorically, then Max Nordau (1849–1923), one of Theodor Herzl's earliest supporters, called explicitly for the creation of *Muskeljuden*, muscle-Jews, who would transcend what the ravages of exile had done to the Jew.

> For too long, all too long have we been engaged in the mor-
> tification of our own flesh. . . . Or rather, to put it more
> precisely—others did the killing of our flesh for us. Their
> extraordinary success is measured by hundreds of thousands
> of Jewish corpses in the ghettos, in the churchyards, along the
> highways of medieval Europe. . . . In the narrow Jewish street
> our poor limbs soon forgot their gay movements; in the dim-
> ness of sunless houses our eyes began to blink shyly; the fear
> of constant persecution turned our powerful voices into fright-
> ened whispers, which rose in a crescendo only when our mar-
> tyrs on the stakes cried out in their dying prayers in the face of
> their executioners. . . . Let us take up our oldest traditions; let
> us once more become deep-chested, sturdy, sharp-eyed men.

Whereas Bialik recalls the Maccabees and their revolt against the Greeks, Nordau cites Bar Kokhba, the zealot who led a (failed) rebellion against the Romans. But what they share is the image of a long-since-extinct Jew that had to be revived, a belief that when situated on their homeland, even if under the Greeks or the Romans, the Jews had been full human beings.

The problem with Europe was not its Christian anti-Semites, or even its Cossacks. The problem with Europe was the sort of Jew that it had rendered. Europe's Jews needed to be healed, to be transformed. Exile and powerlessness were killing the Jew; but Zion would allow the Jew to be recrafted and reimagined in the image of what once had been.

That is why Israel's Declaration of Independence begins by evoking the Bible. "The Bible," claims Moshe Halbertal, one of Israel's most prominent intellectuals, "tells a heroic story of the national drama whose focus is the land of Israel. . . . Unlike the Talmud, [the early Zionists] held, the Bible had the potential to become a national epic. Its drama unfolded in the hills of Judea, and it connected the national claim to the land with a historical past."

And that is why one of the earliest Zionist projects after the creation of the state was the renaming of rivers, streams, towns, hills, and valleys with biblical names, replacing the Arabic names they'd acquired, even when it was impossible to determine with certainty what a specific place had actually been called in the Bible. Even the land would be renamed to evoke an era in which Jews knew how to defend themselves, an era long before the celebration of passivity had "corrupted" Jewish sensibilities.

There is perhaps no better way to illustrate what the Zionists wanted to do to the image of the Jew than to recall two well-known photographs that have come to represent two radically different eras: Jewish powerlessness under the Nazis, and Jews at the height of their power, when they captured the Old City of Jerusalem from the Jordanians. The former period is represented in the minds of many Jews by a black-and-white photograph of a Jewish boy, probably no older than eight or nine, dressed in his finest coat and hat, his dress black socks pulled up almost to his knees. He is the model of innocence, of European-Jewish financial and social success, and yet, he is pitiful. His family's apparent wealth did nothing to save him, and we see him in this famous photograph, a small child, his hands raised in the air, with the Nazi's gun pointed directly at him. There is no one around him. His parents are not at his side, and no onlookers have come to comfort him. He is alone, unprotected, utterly unable to do anything on his own behalf. He is technically alive, but he might as well already be dead.

In contrast to the helplessness of this boy, a very different image captivated Jews after 1967. This photograph was taken by David Rubinger, perhaps Israel's greatest documentary photographer, at the Western Wall in the aftermath of the paratroopers' conquering of the Old City during the June 1967 Six Day War.

This photograph, too, is of soldiers and Jews. But in this image, three Israeli paratroopers stand in front of the Western Wall, shortly after capturing it. Side by side, shoulder to shoulder, they are young but not weak. This time, the Jew is a soldier, a symbol of power; he is not a frightened boy with his hands held high in surrender. He is home, in Jerusalem, at the Western Wall, not in a Nazi-dominated Europe. The European dress cap has been replaced by a helmet, the dressy overcoat by an army uniform and soldier's equipment. Yet the soldier has his helmet off, and there is no glee, no gloating. Situated where the ancient Temple had once stood, he is powerful but approachable, in control but not cruel, newly arrived at the ancient city of his forefathers, home once again.

The soldier in the middle of the picture, interestingly, is bareheaded. He is a model of Israel, of the new Jew, but he is not a religious model. If there is religious resonance in the photograph, it is because the background is the Western Wall. But these soldiers are looking *away* from the wall, not toward it. Rubinger's image captivated the heart of the Jewish world because it suggested that the state had succeeded—the new Jew had been created.

The project of creating the Jew anew permeated prestate and early post-Independence life in more ways than one could count. During the British Mandate, youth movements training soldiers-to-be violated a law prohibiting hiking to the desert near the Dead Sea where Masada stood. Masada, the ancient Judean fortress where 960 defenders ultimately committed suicide rather than fall into Roman hands, was a virtual magnet for these young men and women. And after they had reached the mountaintop, they would declare, "Masada will never fall again."

After the state was created, Israeli paratroopers completed their training by uttering the same words in the same spot. If the defenders of Masada had no choice but to take their own lives, the ceremony on that mountain two millennia later clearly meant to suggest that the State of Israel was designed to change that. Masada would not fall again; the emaciated Jew of Europe had been left behind, once and for all.

Even Jews who came to reject the militarism of much of Israel's public culture, and even those who came to be associated with the political left and advocated accommodation with Israel's enemies, understood that statehood would put an end to the merciless persecution of the Jew, and they, too, took pride in that. Amos Oz, the great Israeli novelist mentioned earlier, is a well-known political liberal, and thus is a case in point. Oz has some profound pacifist tendencies. He broke with his kibbutz's tradition, for example, when he refused to allow his *chuppah* (wedding canopy) to be held aloft on four rifles. But still, he took pains to recount in his autobiography the story of his father on the night of November 29, 1947—his father's whispered wish that what would emerge from the creation of Israel was not only a state but a new kind of Jew, no longer fearful of the world. That alone, his father seemed to believe, would make the state worthwhile.

But the creation of a new Jew has been a complex and multifaceted process. Had the early Zionists' only demand of the "new Jews" been that they learn to defend themselves, they could probably declare victory. But Bialik, for example, had more in mind than mere self-defense. In his poem "In the City of Slaughter," he wanted the re-created Jew to be able to defend himself, but he did not think that new Jews would be created simply by their living in a new place. They also needed to live in a new way, without the outmoded and backward practices of Jewish ritual life. Thus he urged the new Jew to shed the ballast of unthinking Jewish religious practice, a point he made through ridicule when he suggested that the men went to ask their rabbi if their wives were still permitted to them.

This rejection of the religious dimension of Jewish tradition permeates much of the greatest literature that appeared just as the state was created. Indeed, if the Bible saw the great, defining moment of Jewish history as the revelation of the Torah on Mount Sinai, Zionist ideologues denied that claim, insisting that the defining moment of Jewish history was the creation of the state.

Nowhere is that claim more explicitly and harrowingly expressed than in Nathan Alterman's famous poem "The Silver Platter." Alterman, one of the great poets of the period of Independence, wrote the poem in response to the pithy remark by Chaim Weizmann (who would become Israel's first president) that "a state is not handed to a people on a silver platter." Alterman's poem was published for the first time on December 26, 1947, a month after the UN vote and just months before Ben-Gurion declared Israel's independence.

In "The Silver Platter," Alterman describes the entire nation gathered together to receive the revelation of "the one miracle and only." As the nation is assembled, a boy and a girl, the only characters in the poem, walk slowly toward the assembled throngs. The two are almost immobile, and say nothing. Awe-struck, the nation watches the young man and woman caked in dirt or blood, and then asks them who they are. "We," the boy and the girl reply, "are the silver platter on which the Jewish state has been given to you," whereupon they collapse. With that, the poem ends.

As with "*Hatikvah*," with Bialik's poem, and with much of early Zionist literature, it is impossible to understand Alterman without knowing the biblical text to which he was alluding. The poem describes the nation assembled, waiting for a "miracle, the one miracle and only." To traditional Jews, when the nation assembles waiting for a miracle, it is clear that it is awaiting the giving of the Torah at Mount Sinai. Not so for Alterman, as the date of the poem (December 26, 1947) suggests. Now the miracle, the "one and only," is the creation of the state.

Alterman's poem is riddled with a subtle derision of Jewish ritual practice. In the biblical account, as the nation prepares to receive the Torah, Moses tells the men not to approach a woman. But in "The Silver Platter," the central characters, the boy and the girl, are inseparable, virtually indistinguishable. There will be no old-fashioned separation of the sexes here. In the Torah, the Israelites are commanded to wash their clothes as part of their preparation for revelation (Exodus 19:10); but in the poem, the boy and the girl are caked with dirt, and they do not wash. Saving the Jews, Alterman wants to suggest, requires that you get dirty. Cleanliness, purity, and holiness, Alterman insists, will not keep the Jews alive.

For these writers, the Zionist revolution was about more than Jews recovering the power they had once had. It was also about the new Jew shedding the burden of religiosity that had been so central to the Jews of Europe.

Because of this, it is important to note, the secularism of contemporary Israelis has roots that are very different from the secularism of their American counterparts. If American Jews drifted away from Jewish life as a result of the temptations of an inviting America (despite high-profile and fascinating reencounters with faith and religious observance in New York, Boston, Los Angeles, and elsewhere), Jews in Israel did not merely drift away. In Palestine and then Israel, they fled, disgusted by what Jewish religious life had done to their ancestors in Europe. Israeli secularism is characterized not by indifference but by ridicule. It is suffused with anger and derision, a view that has seeped through discourse in Israeli literature and politics, and even made its way into seemingly playful children's rhymes. Bialik himself wrote one such jingle, which says, in part:

> Seesaw, seesaw
> Fall and rise, rise and fall.
> What's up, and what's down? (*Mah le-ma'alah, mah le-matah?*)
> Just me, me and you.

What, on the surface, could be more innocent, more playful and wholesome? It's simply child's play, it would seem. But one should never underestimate Bialik; he had another agenda in mind, and with his genius and prodigious knowledge of Jewish tradition, he was able to transmit the antireligious rebellion even to a younger generation, or at least to their (sometimes) knowing parents.

Here one needs to be familiar with the Mishnah, an early rabbinic text that dates from the first centuries of the Common Era, to
understand what Bialik is up to. The Mishnah says, "Whoever reflects
upon four things would have been better off had he not been born:
Mah le-ma'alah, mah le-matah, What is above, what is below, what is
before, and what is beyond. And whoever has no concern for the glory
of his Maker—would have been better off had he not been born."

What is up and what is down? In the Mishnah, the reference is to
the mysteries of life, the great theological questions with which every
religious civilization wrestles. Those are the matters we are not to
contemplate, at least according to the Mishnah. But for Bialik, what
is up and what is down? Not important theological questions, but
rather, "Just me, me and you" on the see-saw. There is nothing else
worth thinking about, he seems to suggest. Religion doesn't matter.
Just you and I do.

How does Bialik respond to the Mishnah's claim that no one
should ever ponder the question of *Mah le-ma'alah, mah le-matah*,
"What is up and what is down?" With derision. As if to stress his pride
in having no "concern for the glory of his Maker," Bialik insists that
what matters is Jewish children rising and falling, smiling and laugh-
ing in the parks of their new homeland. The questions of yesteryear,
and the warnings surrounding them, are better left ignored, even
ridiculed.

On this front, too, it would seem that Zionism has been an extraordinary success. For Israel today is, indeed, populated largely by secular
Jews. But strange though it may sound, it is also possible that the
revolution has been too successful. Despite Bialik's and Alterman's
impatience—even exasperation—with the religious tradition of the
Jew, they knew that tradition well. They loved much of it. And they
used it in their speech and throughout their work. To read "The Silver
Platter" without recognizing its biblical references is like reading
contemporary American writing and not knowing that "four score
and seven" refers to a great oration, or that "nothing to fear but fear
itself" evokes, almost effortlessly, one of the great crises of faith in

American life. To read Alterman without having the biblical text in mind is a superficial reading that misses the magic of the poem, taking no note of its being part of a grand Jewish conversation. The same is true with the little child's song about the seesaw. Sing it without knowing the Mishnah with which it's locked in combat, and you miss the entire point.

By and large, the only Israeli children who can appreciate Bialik and Alterman are those kids raised in religious schools, where the texts that are the underpinning of these great Zionist works are still taught. The levels of Jewish illiteracy among Israel's youth are now legendary, but not exaggerated. If Bialik had had grandchildren, they would not be able to understand his poetry. Two generations after the "revolution," the rebellion against Jewish tradition has rendered a generation of (largely secular) Israeli children who are best described by Hillel Halkin's pained phrase "Hebrew-speaking gentiles." They speak Hebrew, but they have no access to the richness of the very texts that made the Hebrew language eternal.

Like many revolutionaries, Bialik, Alterman, and others did not appreciate what the potential costs of their revolution might be. In liberating Jews from the constraints of religious practice, they unwittingly also rid generations of Israelis of any substantive knowledge of the tradition that they ought to have inherited. They never stopped to ask themselves whether a nonobservant society could reproduce subsequent generations laden with the kind of knowledge that they took for granted. Today we know that it cannot.

Today's Israeli youth have no idea that "Hatikvah" is an ironic play on the words of Ezekiel (as we saw at the opening of chapter one). Today's typical Israelis have no inkling of what they are singing when they giggle with their children at the simple words of the seesaw song; and what is more significant, they therefore find it difficult to say anything of substance to their kids about who they are, or why the State of Israel needs, or even deserves, to exist.

Nothing brought home this sea change in Israeli life as dramatically as an incident our son, Avi, related to me a few months after he graduated from high school. Avi chose to delay his army service by a year, and in the period between high school and the army, he attended a one-year study program. Unlike many of the "gap year" programs that exist in Israel, Avi's program was composed of both religious and nonreligious students, who'd been educated in radically different school systems. They studied economics, literature, philosophy, and Jewish texts. They read Zionist thinkers, debated the tensions between demography and democracy, and hiked the land. At the end of their program, they spent three weeks hiking from the Golan Heights to Jerusalem. It was, in many ways, Zionist education at its very finest.

But when they began to study Talmud at the beginning of the year, their teacher knew he was up against a pedagogic challenge of no small proportions. The religious kids had been studying Talmud for years, and some were reasonably capable Talmud students. For the most part, the secular kids had almost never seen a page of Talmud.

So to level the playing field, the teacher began with questions, not knowledge. He distributed Hebrew translations of the very first page of the Babylonian Talmud (which was written in Aramaic), which discusses the hours of the evening and night during which the Shema (one of the cornerstones of Jewish prayer) may be recited. "Pair up," he told the students, "one student with more background and one student with less. Go sit someplace and read the passage. And what I want you to do is to come back to the group with as many questions about the passage as you possibly can. Don't worry about answering them for now. Just come back with as many questions as you can."

So off went Avi, my son, with a friend of his who'd not had exposure to Talmud before. They sat and read, at which point Avi suggested that they start listing their questions. "What's the Shema?" his partner asked.

"Well," said Avi, "I'm not sure he means that kind of question. I think he means questions about how the argument unfolds. You know, why does Rabbi X say one thing, and why does Rabbi Y disagree?"

"But what's the Shema?" his friend asked once again.

"I really don't think we should include that," Avi began to say again, when he suddenly realized that his study partner wasn't offering a question to be submitted to the group. He was simply asking. He'd grown up in Israel all his eighteen years, had gone to Israeli

schools his entire life, spoke Hebrew fluently, and had never heard of
the Jewish liturgy's most basic prayer. Most American Jewish children
with even a rudimentary Jewish education would know what the
Shema is. But this otherwise well-educated Israeli teenager did not.

Was Bialik's revolution a success or a failure? Have we won or
lost when Israel's best and brightest kids are willingly heading off to
critical positions in the army but at the same time do not know what
the Shema is?

The good news, of course, is that these pre-army programs of
the sort that my son attended are inundated with applications from
nonreligious as well as religious kids. Each has his or her reasons for
wanting to attend, but I'm actually more encouraged by the fact that
the secular kids want in. They seem to have intuited that though they
were raised in Israel, they have never learned the most basic things
that the Jewish state should have taught them. Despite the potential
embarrassment, they want to learn. They're willing to admit their
ignorance and to start hewing a path back to the tradition that they
know is theirs. It's an extraordinarily courageous thing to do.

Since we moved to Israel, I have met dozens of young people who
grew up on secular kibbutzim, who went to the army and then off
to university. When they got to university, some—out of intellectual
curiosity or perhaps a personal spiritual search—took a course in
Jewish studies. There they discovered that there was a whole world
of Jewish thought, literature, and life to which their kibbutz had chosen not to expose them. "Tanach to Palmach" is a phrase commonly
used for this attitude. "Tanach" is the Hebrew term for the Bible;
"Palmach" was the fighting force of the Hagganah, which was itself
the precursor to the IDF. (The terms rhyme, of course, which gives the
phrase its unique memorable quality.)

Between the Tanach, which the kibbutz saw not as a religious
work but as a "history" that describes the era in which the Jews were
sovereign on their own land, and the Palmach, which sought to help
them regain that sovereignty, there was nothing that needed to be
studied, nothing worthy of remembering. Jewish history essentially
stopped at exile and resumed with the attempt to recreate sovereignty.
The Talmud, which brilliantly reimagined Jewish religious life, did

not matter. The Middle Ages, with their voluminous biblical and rabbinic commentaries that created one of the greatest intellectual accomplishments of humankind, also did not matter. Nothing mattered between the end of the Bible and the restoration of the Jewish state.

But among many of the young people that I've met who grew up with those amputated libraries and rediscovered the "Jewish book-shelf" in the university library, the response is often one of resent-ment. "What gave the kibbutz the right to hide all this from me?" they ask with exasperation. "Why did I have to wait until my mid-twenties to find out that all this existed? Does Zionism have to entail censoring out hundreds of years of Jewish learning and intellectual accomplishment?"

Obviously, this makes the case too starkly. Yes, there was something Big-Brother-esque about the project of the new Jew. Ben-Gurion and others were certain that they knew what was best for the citi-zens of their emerging country and often didn't care what those citizens themselves wanted or believed. They were so consumed by the need to build the new state that they sometimes trampled indi-vidual rights and preferences in the process. And all too often, they created a society in which the religion that had kept the Jews alive for thousands of years was marginalized and, not infrequently, even ridiculed.

To be sure, some of this is beginning to change; Jewish stud-ies thrive in Israel, both in academic circles and increasingly in the population at large. A recovery is under way, at least to some extent. But sadly, the essential point is still unfortunately valid: the levels of Jewish illiteracy that the Jewish state has fostered simply preclude substantive discussions about what should be Jewish about the Jewish state. High school graduates who do not know the Shema are almost certainly going to be unable to produce a thoughtful answer to such questions as: What are some of the great Jewish ideas that the Jewish people produced over the past three thousand years that you believe should be at the core of today's Israeli society?

But if they cannot answer that question, why should they defend the state as do the young man and young woman in Alterman's poem?

Is it any surprise that the levels of draft-dodging are rising so precipitously? Why risk one's life to save the Jewish state if the word "Jewish" carries with it no significant connotations? If one knows nothing about the Bible and its legacy, does the notion of a Jewish state—one that is going to exact a high cost for as far as the eye can see—make any sense?

Bialik and Alterman were quite right. Bialik was right that the condition of the Jew in Europe was untenable (although as he died in 1934, he never got to know exactly how right he was), and Alterman was right that new boys and new girls, caked in dirt and blood, would redeem what was left of the Jewish people. But they may well have been naive about the advisability of leaving Jewish religious discourse in the dust, for they failed to predict how quickly Israelis—bereft of any substantive Jewish discourse—would find themselves unable to say, or to remember, why they needed a state in the first place.

Israelis are beginning to learn some of the painful lessons of secular Zionism's revolution. They are discovering some of the serious shortcomings of the new Jew that they created. They're learning that when this new Jew is incapable of any semblance of a Jewish conversation, it's hard to say much about what the State of Israel should become. It's impossible to say why the state matters. And there's simply no way to speak about how the high cost of living in Israel (and the issue is hardly financial) can be justified.

It's still too early to know whether Bialik's revolution ushered in a great era of Jewish flourishing, or whether the young people he helped to create will ultimately be the cause of the downfall of the very state of which he dreamed so passionately. What we do know is that when Israelis begin to ask themselves once again why the Jews need a state, they'll have to ask, no less, how much Jews—and Jewish Israelis who want to survive, in particular—need to *know* in order to preserve the Jewish state. And when they have that conversation, they are going to realize that in addition to maintaining a modern fighting force and cutting-edge technologies, they are going to have to reimagine and reinvent the Israeli Jew all over again.

That is going be a daunting task, and a painful one. But so was the creation of a world-class fighting force an overwhelming undertaking.

Israelis knew, however, that it simply had to be done, or they would not survive. Nor will Israel survive with an image of the Jew so liberated from Jewish content that he or she can say nothing of substance about what Israel is, what it should be, or why it matters. The time has come to honor the revolution that was Zionism by inventing the new Jew once again. For its newly reconceived vision of the Jew, no less than its military, is going to be key to Israel's hope for a future.

Chapter Eleven

THE WARS THAT MUST BE WAGED

A story is told of two Jewish peddlers in Eastern Europe who were making their way from one town to another. In the middle of their journey, they came upon an enormous tree that had fallen across the road, and there was no way for their horse and cart to go over it, or under. They looked for a route around it, to the right or to the left, but found nothing. So there they sat, utterly dumbfounded, unable to progress.

A short while later, two Gentile peddlers came along and found the same tree blocking the road. They looked to the right, then to the left, and realized there was no going around the tree. So, they rolled up their sleeves, grabbed the fallen tree, and with a huge grunt, slowly dragged the tree off the road. They dusted themselves off, climbed back in their cart, and continued on their way.

The two Jewish peddlers looked at each other. "Goyim," said one to the other, a look of disgust on his face, derision in his voice. "Everything they do, they use brute force."

—Jewish folk tale

Israeli prime minister Golda Meir is reputed to have said to Egyptian president Anwar Sadat on the eve of the peace talks with Egypt, "We can forgive you for killing our sons. But we will never forgive you for making us kill yours."

Assuming that she actually said it, it was a remarkable, almost poetic thing for one leader to say to another. No sane person wants to kill. No one, even in war, ought to relish the loss of life on the other side.

But still, there is something almost perverse about Golda's possibly apocryphal remark, and something even more disturbing about the fact that it has been lauded and cited thousands of times across the Jewish world. For how can Jews not understand how wrong—and how dangerous—her sentiment was? As Ruth Wisse puts it so eloquently:

> Golda expressed more concern with Israeli children's decency than with her enemies' designs on them. She would have demonstrated greater understanding of her Egyptian counterpart and greater appreciation of political reality had she asked Sadat to convey to his people the message, "We Jews are here to stay," requiring decency, tolerance, and realism of *them*.

But Golda was not alone. Jews worldwide make the mistake to which Wisse points, in large measure because they have internalized an incorrect reading of the role of war and self-defense in Jewish tradition. They have been taught, explicitly or not, that Judaism is a virtually pacifist tradition. And they thus incorrectly believe that being required to use military force has pushed Israel into an "un-Jewish" posture.

Because many Jews today, particularly those who have been raised in the comfort and security of the United States, see the world of physical might and military activity as inherently un-Jewish; more and more young Jews find themselves increasingly uncomfortable with Israel, even embarrassed by it. Many of these young people, and some who are not so young, either have intuited and internalized a Western liberal commitment to pacifism (rarely honored by governments, of course) or have come to believe that there is ultimately nothing worth fighting or killing for. To many of them, passivity is practically always preferable to violence, and they expect Israel—the world's most visible locus of Jewish behavior—to live up to that standard.

But Israel is surrounded by hostile populations on all sides (except for the coastline). The pacifist ethos that now has many Jews, including Israelis, in its grip developed in a wholly different world. It now thrives on U.S. college and university campuses, places that are inhabited almost exclusively by people who have never known real danger from genuine enemies, and who have never had to spend a single day defending their lives or their countries. That ethos might be noble; but it is tragically wholly irrelevant to Israel's condition. Were they to subscribe to that ethos, Israelis would be overrun by their enemies almost instantaneously.

Therefore, Jews in general, and some Israelis in particular, will need to rethink their visceral sense that war is thoroughly "un-Jewish." And then they will have to make a decision: they can choose to defend themselves even at the cost of occasionally using massive force, with all the ambivalence that that inevitably arouses, or they can cease to exist. They can adopt the Jewish tradition's (often neglected) awareness that force is at times a necessary condition of staying alive in a hostile world, or they can internalize values from other cultures and try to live in an increasingly pacifist and therefore passive Jewish state, for as long as it can hold out.

If American Jews have intuited that Judaism is a pacifist tradition as a result of some of the values that are often touted in their circles in the United States, their Israeli counterparts have often reached that conclusion as a result of the simple weariness that they feel following decades of unrelenting conflict. It is not difficult to understand the exhaustion that Israelis feel, or their desire to put the era of war-making behind them. For generation after generation, Israeli children have gone off to battle in the same places that their fathers captured and for which their grandfathers fought, all with no end in sight. Approximately 25,000 military dead and countless more wounded and scarred in a country of just 7 million (many of these losses suffered when the country was much smaller) is an appalling price. Israelis' fatigue, and even their sense of desperation, is thoroughly understandable.

And yet, when peace is not achievable, when enemies still seek to destroy the Jewish state and thereby to destroy the Jewish people, there is, sadly, no choice but to wage war, however long it may last. This is what Jews in Israel, the United States, and beyond must begin to understand. Of course, the tradition of ambivalence about the obligation to fight and to defend oneself is a healthy thing, and losing it would be tragic. But Jews dare not, to use Israel Zangwill's memorable formulation, imagine that they are "too sophisticated a people for so primitive and savage a function."

Today ambivalence about the legitimacy of making war in order to guarantee Jewish survival paralyzes the Jewish world. It causes rifts—in both Israeli society and portions of Diaspora Jewish leadership—so deep that Israel too often cannot or does not act. Young American Jews, convinced that because Israel is at war the Jewish state is not living up to authentic Jewish values, are increasingly walking away from commitment to Israel. Israelis, too, appalled at what war has sometimes required of them, have too often begun to claim that Judaism demands of them something different. And they, too, feel a diminished sense of obligation to the Jewish state. When this happens, the perennial Jewish yearning for peace becomes not a blessing but a point of weakness that in the face of today's political realities the Jewish people can scarcely afford. Somehow, Jews across the world today need to be re-awakened to the fact that at its most sophisticated, Jewish tradition never shied away from war, particularly when war was necessary for the preservation of the Jewish people.

In the suburban, Democrat-voting, liberal American Jewish household in which I came of age, there was an unspoken ethic that military conflict was to be avoided at virtually all cost. Thirty years after the liberation of Auschwitz, the shadow of what humankind had done earlier in the twentieth century still hung over our household. Our home was explicitly opposed to the Vietnam War, essentially convinced that war was the greatest scourge on the planet.

On one level, we *knew* that our adoption of an almost-pacifist position (though that was never articulated as an ideological commitment as such) was the result of historical weakness. We were taught Jewish history and philosophy in a way that made passivity and Judaism sound like the most natural combination. Yes, we did understand that this worldview was the result of the fact that Jews had often had no alternative to passivity. But truth be told, it was even more than that. Looking back on the community I knew growing up, it is now clear to me that something much more pernicious was at play. We would never have stated it in these terms, of course, but the Jewish community of my youth was much more at ease celebrating the manifold intellectual, religious, and literary accomplishments of the Jewish people than it was thinking about ourselves as warriors. We learned about the Maccabees, the heroics of the Warsaw Ghetto uprising, and the successes of Israel's new army in 1948, but still, there was a haze of victimhood that hovered just above everything else. In a strange way, it now seems to me, we were actually comfortable with the role of victim.

The Shoah was the most recent and the most ghastly of the examples, but it was far from the only one. The First Temple had been destroyed by the Babylonians. The Second Temple had been sacked by Rome. Even Masada, which we mentioned in the previous chapter, had another dimension to it. Yes, young prestate men and women hiked there to proclaim, "Masada will not fall again." But was our attraction to Masada also partly inspired by the fact that it was the scene not of victory but of the "heroic" suicide of a group of revolutionaries? Was it confirmation of the immutable victimhood of Jewish life?

Even the great achievements of European Jewry about which we learned were overwhelmed by the horrors of the Crusades and pogroms. We read poems like Bialik's "In the City of Slaughter" and wept at the images of what had happened to Jews before and during the twentieth century. To be sure, we also read other works by Bialik, many of them much more hopeful. And we read Agnon. And listened to recordings of the Israeli Philharmonic. And we learned about Marc Chagall. There was a definite pride in two thousand years of Jewish creativity.

Still, though, the overall message was clear: when it came to *fighting*, we were essentially told, "Jews don't fight." And if Jews *are* involved in violence, it is almost certainly violence that is done to us. Fighting was *nisht kein yiddische zach*, as the Yiddish phrase goes—it just wasn't a Jewish thing. War was ugly and barbaric and therefore it was almost preferable to remain the victim than to perpetrate the cruelties that winning might actually require.

But June 1967 suddenly and unexpectedly complicated that picture. The Israel Defense Forces of the Six Day War was not the ragtag IDF of 1948 mythology. By 1967, Israel's army was a modern, well-equipped, highly disciplined and trained fighting force, and its victory was due to the fact that it was superior to the Arab forces in virtually every conceivable way. Jews had become fighters. Nor did the Jews have to wait to be attacked before responding. The fact that Israel initiated the hostilities (though they were clearly going to break out either way) with a surprise attack on Egypt's air force changed the course of the war. The fact that the Jews struck preemptively saved the State of Israel and possibly the Jewish people. June 1967 forced us to reconsider the image that we'd had of ourselves.

The image of the Jew-as-victim was suddenly washed aside. In the days and weeks following the war, a combination of relief and pride overcame the former image of the Jew. Suddenly and unexpectedly, Jews reveled in the image of themselves as capable warriors. People spoke about Israel in ways that they never had before. The Israeli soldier became the new icon of Israel for many American Jews. People began to visit Israel in unprecedented numbers. Israel was now more than a country—it was a place where a different kind of Jew was apparently coming to life. Thousands of American Jews, including my family, set out for Israel to live there. While many, my family among them, came back after a year or two, the image of Israel—and with it, the image of the Jew—had changed. Six days of war had indelibly altered the way in which Jews thought about themselves and about the use of physical power.

Or had they? It is perhaps telling that of all the images of the Six Day War, the one that is by far the most famous is David Rubinger's celebrated photograph that we mentioned in the previous chapter. As we suggested, part of the power of the photo stemmed from the fact that the image of the Israeli fighter was so different from the image of the surrendering Jew that had come to represent the Jewish experience in twentieth-century Europe. But there is also an irony to Rubinger's photograph. For though the Six Day War was won through vicious fighting, the photograph shows soldiers at rest, almost at peace. Their helmets are off, their weapons nowhere in evidence. Why would a picture like *this* be the one that would come to symbolize the Six Day War for so many Jews?

Perhaps it was because, despite the pride that Jews the world over took in the IDF's victory and their relief that Israel would not be pushed into the sea, they were still, on some level, uncomfortable with the notion of Jews as fighters. *These* soldiers seem so young and so innocent. The angle of the shot makes the soldiers almost blend into the Western Wall, giving them an iconic aura. But at the same time, the soldiers have their backs to the Wall; they are clearly not praying, and thus, the picture does not have overtly religious overtones. The photo had something for everyone. But most important, I believe, it became so popular because its nonwarlike nature was actually a relief in the face of the country's overwhelming militarism, in the face of the fact that they'd conquered thousands of square miles, that they'd tripled the size of the Jewish state, and that hundreds of thousands of Palestinians were now living under Israeli military rule. The message that Jews read into this photograph was that yes, Israelis could win wars if they had to, but at their best, and most natural, Jews are not fighters, people of the sword. The "People of the Book" might have to win battles, but at the end of the day, the image of themselves that they sought to hone was not the military Jew but the awestruck Jew, the Jew without the helmet, the unarmed Jew who is almost one with the Western Wall.

But if that is the case, then Jews are going to have to learn to think about themselves very differently. Because the Middle East is not likely to know peace for generations to come. Treaties will come and go, *hudnas* and *tahadiyehs* will be initiated and then violated, and there will inevitably be periodic discussions of far-reaching settlements of the Israeli-Palestinian conflict. But sadly, a realistic appraisal of Jihadist Islam (recall the attacks on New York, Washington, Bali, London, and Madrid) suggests that some Muslims will not compromise in their battle to rid the world of the values now represented by the United States, Western Europe, and Israel, among others. The ongoing statements of Hamas, Hezbollah, and Iran that Israel must, and will, be destroyed suggest that the Muslim world has not even begun to accept the idea of a Jewish state in "their" region of the world. As long as that resistance persists, Israel will have to fight for its survival. Therefore, it is critical that both Israelis and Jews around the world come to understand that the image of the Jew at war is not at all in conflict with the values that Jewish tradition has long espoused.

Despite Israel's Declaration of Independence's opening statement that "[t]he land of Israel was the birthplace of the Jewish people," the biblical account makes clear that the Israelis became a people, as such, in the crucible of Egyptian slavery. It was only upon leaving Egypt that they could be described in any meaningful way as a people.

But as the Bible tells the story of the Exodus, "When the king of Egypt was told that the people had fled, Pharaoh and his courtiers had a change of heart about the people and said, 'What is this we have done, releasing Israel from our service?'"(Exodus 14:5). Pharaoh pursued them toward the Red Sea, where he apparently believed that he could trap them. His ultimate plans remain unclear. Did he plan to kill them? To restore them to slavery?

Regardless of what Pharaoh's intentions may have been, the Israelites were clearly in danger. Yet according to the biblical account, a miracle took place, the sea split, and the Israelites (later to be called the Jews) marched through the sea. Just as the Egyptians, who had followed them into the sea, were about to reach them, the waters closed in on the pursuers. The Israelites, safe on the other side, saw their former taskmasters and pursuers drowned and Pharaoh's army destroyed. They were finally free, and thus, one would think, had ample cause for celebration.

Therefore, it is no surprise that in the biblical account, the Israelites do celebrate, and sing the famous Song at the Sea (Exodus 15:1–18). But later Jewish tradition apparently was very discomfited by the notion of Jews celebrating their salvation if that escape came at the expense of other lives. The rabbis of the Talmudic period, who often amplified biblical accounts with narratives of their own, told a revealing tale about what was alleged to have happened in heaven as the Children of Israel broke into song at the side of the sea. According to this *midrash* (rabbinic legend), as the Israelites were singing, praising God for their salvation and the deaths of the Egyptians, the heavenly angels also sought to join the song and the praise. But instead of reveling in their song, God chastised them, asking, "The work of My hands is being drowned in the sea, and you would chant hymns?" (B. T. Megillah 10b). Even at the moment of victory, even if that victory had saved the people, the Jewish tradition was uncomfortable with the violence and death that victory itself necessitated.

Interestingly, there is another rendition of this rabbinic tale, which is cited much less frequently than the version just mentioned. In this rendering, the story begins much the same, but this time, as the angels try to sing to God as the chase is unfolding, God reprimands them, saying, "My troops are in distress, and you would sing to Me?" (Exodus Rabbah 23:7). In this version of the narrative, it is not the Egyptians about whom God is worried, but the Israelites themselves. And here, the people about whom God is concerned are called not "the work of My hands," but "My troops." The implications are clear: the Israelites *are* troops, there *are* battles that must be waged, victories that must be won, and critical causes that can be achieved only through the use of force. This version of the *midrash* is infinitely more comfortable with the image of Jews as warriors—but tellingly, it is also the version that is much less known and is almost never cited.

The Song at the Sea is hardly the only example of the rabbis of the Jewish tradition seeking to downplay the militarism of Jewish experience, or to raise near-pacifism to an ideal. They did the same with Hanukkah, one of the most popular holidays of the Jewish calendar year.

Hanukkah, of course, is also a military victory celebration. The Maccabees, the heroes of the holiday, were a band of Jewish fighters of the second and first centuries before the Common Era, who took to the hills and the caves outside Jerusalem to attack the Seleucid forces. Despite their small numbers, they forced the Greeks to retreat. Ultimately the Maccabees regained control of the Temple and of Jerusalem for the Jews.

But this victory could not have come about without combat, suffering, and even death, all wrought by the Jews. Sadly, if the Jews wanted their autonomy back, they were going to have to fight—and to kill—for it.

Nevertheless, despite Hanukkah's overtly militaristic origins, the focus of the holiday gradually metamorphosed from military power to the miracle of the oil. Now God, and not the Maccabee fighters, was at center stage. The accounts of the Maccabean revolt that emerge closest to the events themselves attest to the victory celebrations having lasted for eight days. The reasons for that number of days, however, are interesting. In the first account, Judah and his brothers "decreed that the days of the rededication of the altar should be observed . . . for eight days," with no reason given. The tradition of the celebration lasting eight days is found in yet another account, this one also the product of eyewitness accounts, according to some scholars. This time, the eight days are said to have been a postponed celebration of the holiday of Sukkot, which also lasts eight days, but which the fighters apparently were unable to celebrate on its original date in the fall season due to the demands of the war that they were then waging.

What is significant about these traditions is that they have been utterly forgotten. Ask any Jewish schoolchild why Hanukkah lasts eight days and they will respond that when the Maccabees recaptured the Temple, they found a sole cruse of oil for use in the Temple with enough oil only for one day. But miraculously, when the Hasmoneans lit the lamp, the oil lasted for eight days, until more oil was ready. The eight days of Hanukkah, the elementary schoolchild would relate, commemorate the miracle of the oil lasting eight days.

But the miracle of the oil is nowhere attested in the "eyewitness" accounts. Instead, it's found for the first time in the Talmud (B. T. Shabbat 21b), a text that emerged hundreds of years later. One can imagine a variety of explanations for how and why this transformation in the emphasis on Hanukkah takes place, but for our purposes, it's enough to note that in the earlier stories, the Maccabees are the absolute heroes and no God-created miracle takes place. But these various traditions fade somewhat into the background relative to the version in which God, not human beings, and a religious miracle, not a story of battle and warfare, take the spotlight. Originally, the holiday celebrated military victors; in its present form, it celebrates a miracle of oil, wrought by God. To be sure, the "new" version of Hanukkah does not in any way deny the role of the Jewish warriors, but it certainly does shift the focus. It is therefore not surprising that early Zionists, who knew that they would have to fight for their independence, insisted that the Hanukkah story be "restored" to its former version.

In an attempt to make the Hanukkah story more fitting for the challenges that Zionism faced, the poet Aharon Ze'ev (1900–1968)— among many others—rejected that passive, God-centered rabbinic reading (or rereading) of the Hanukkah narrative, and wrote a children's song that became an antireligious mainstay of the secular Zionist celebration of Hanukkah. The poem insists that "[a] miracle did not happen to us, we did not find a cruse of oil." Instead, Ze'ev insists, something else wrought the miracle: "We chiseled away the stone until we bled." Not God, but people. Not miracles, but pure physical might. Not oil, but courage. Those are what will save the Jewish people.

What was the point that Ze'ev wanted the children who would sing his song to understand? It was simple: to survive, the Jews will have to fight and be willing to bleed. There is no choice. If it proved anything at all, the history of Jews in Europe was a clear indication that the Jews dared not wait for another of God's miracles. *Zionists had uncovered the secret of Jewish survival, and they had done so by chiseling away the stone until they bled.* Miracles were necessary, to be sure, but this time, they believed, Jews would have to create those miracles on their own.

To many contemporary Jews, the Zionist desire to focus on those elements of Jewish life that did make use of power, that celebrated the Jews' ability to defend themselves, may sound like a call to edit the Jewish tradition, to make the Jews into something that they never were. But historically, Judaism has long recognized war as a sadly necessary element of what it takes to stay alive.

There are far too many examples of this in the biblical and rabbinic traditions to enumerate them all here, but a few merit mention because, as we've said, so many Jews today assume otherwise. They assume that the "default" Jewish position is a passive, non-military one, that somehow, Israel's security challenges have imposed something essentially non-Jewish on "authentic" Judaism. And thus, they struggle. What's truer to our nature: the passivity of authentic Jewish life, or the militarism that Israel's survival requires?

But such a choice is neither genuine nor necessary. Classical Jewish thinkers never abhorred necessary warfare to the extent that contemporary Jews, colored by a post–World War II culture, have assumed. Indeed, it's possible to read the Jewish tradition in a way that suggests that a willingness to wage war was actually a sine qua non for being part of the Jewish people. To be counted among that people, one had to be willing to fight—for Jewish survival, for the Jewish homeland, for Judaism's values.

This is hardly the sort of claim that falls on sympathetic ears today, particularly among American Jews who are understandably conflicted about the different sorts of contributions to Jewish survival they and their Israeli counterparts make; but it is no exaggeration. And it comes not from some peripheral Jewish text or an early modern Zionist polemic, but from the Book of Numbers, from the very story of the Jewish people as they make their way toward their homeland for the very first time.

As the Bible tells the story, the Israelites had escaped Egyptian slavery and were on their way to the Land of Israel. As the nation prepared for entry into the Promised Land, two and a half of the twelve tribes—Reuven, Gad, and half the tribe of Menasseh—decided that they preferred to stay on the far side of the Jordan River, where the land was plentiful and where they believed they could make good lives for themselves. "It would be a favor to us," they said, "if this land were given to your servants as a holding; do not move us across the Jordan" (Numbers 32:5).

Moses's first response is to remind them of their responsibility to the remainder of the tribes. "Are your brothers to go to war while you stay here?" (Numbers 32:6). Eventually a compromise is reached, when these tribes agree to join in the battle for the land:

Then they stepped up to him and said, "We will build here sheepfolds for our flocks and towns for our children. And we will hasten as shock-troops in the van of the Israelites until we have established them in their home, while our children stay in the fortified towns because of the inhabitants of the land. We will not return to our homes until every one of the Israelites is in possession of his portion. But we will not have a share with them in the territory beyond the Jordan, for we have received our share on the east side of the Jordan." Moses said to them, "If you do this, if you go to battle as shock-troops, at the instance of the LORD, and every shock-fighter among you crosses the Jordan, at the instance of the LORD, until He has dispossessed His enemies before Him, and the land has been subdued, at the instance of the LORD, and then you return—you shall be clear before the LORD and before Israel; and this land shall be your holding under the LORD." [Numbers 32:16–22]

Participating in the people's battles is not a choice, Moses insists. Being an Israelite means being willing to risk, and to fight, for the collective good. If Jewish survival was at stake, those who wished to be counted as part of that community had to defend its existence. The same could well be true today. Since the survival of the State of Israel is so central to the survival of the Jewish people, contemporary Jews could equally plausibly claim that being willing to risk one's life for the sake of the Jewish people is still a central part of what it means to be a Jew.

One can easily understand why observers from afar would look askance at the militarism that has at times come to characterize Israeli society. Who could possibly not feel the sadness of the losses that both Israelis and their enemies endure? Nor can any fair-minded defender of Israel deny that the Israeli army has occasionally abused power (though clearly at rates infinitely lower than virtually any other army that we could point to). People who have power will almost inevitably misuse it, and decent civilizations need to be on guard against that at all times.

Jews have known this for centuries. Rabbi Judah Halevi (1075–1141), in his *Kuzari*, a lengthy fictitious dialogue between a rabbi and a Gentile king, in which the rabbi seeks to convince the king of the "truth" of Judaism, acknowledges this point. Typically, throughout the book, whenever the king raises an objection to the rabbi's argument, the rabbi deftly shows him where he has erred. Indeed, throughout the hundreds of small arguments that make up the *Kuzari*, there are only two instances in the entire book when the rabbi hears the king's objection and admits that he is wrong.

In one of those two instances, the rabbi points with pride to the fact that Jews have no record of killing their enemies. He notes this "clean record" as a mark of Jewish ethical superiority. But the king retorts that the Jews have a clean record only because they have had no power. "That would only be so if your lowly state would be of your own device. But in your case it has been forced upon you; were you given the opportunity, you would kill your enemies."

In this instance, the rabbi does not point to an error in the king's logic. The rabbi admits that he has no response; "[Y]ou have discovered my shame, Khazar king," he replies.

But that does not mean that peoples that wish to survive can avoid using power. Sometimes, there are simply no alternatives. Israel's enemies—Hamas, Hezbollah, and Iran are three prime examples— are at least honest about the fact that their goal is not territorial compromise; they state openly that they are committed to the destruction of Israel. And thus, if Israel has any hope of surviving, it needs to wage battle. That was true in the past, it holds now, and it assuredly will be the case well into the future.

That is why the Torah, when it sees an existential threat to the Jewish people, demands that that threat be utterly destroyed. Again, this is no suggestion; it is a demand, plain and simple:

> Remember what Amalek did to you on your journey, after you left Egypt—how, undeterred by fear of God, he surprised you on the march, when you were famished and weary, and cut down all the stragglers in your rear. Therefore, when the Lord your God grants you safety from all your enemies around you, in the land that the Lord your God is giving you as a hereditary portion, you shall blot out the memory of Amalek from under heaven. Do not forget! [Deuteronomy 25:17–19]

The command to utterly wipe out those enemies who are sworn to the Jews' destruction is portrayed as so utterly critical that an entire Jewish royal dynasty was erased for failure to carry it out. Hundreds of years after the initial encounter with the tribe of Amalek that is described in the Torah, King Saul led his people to war. Once again, that war was against Amalek, which still survived despite the Torah's command to obliterate them. Saul went to war against Amalek as commanded, but apparently out of mercy spared Agag, their king, as well as their animals. The prophet Samuel reproached him in a much-quoted encounter, and asked, "What is this bleating of sheep in my ears, and the lowing of oxen that I hear?" (I Samuel 15:14). Saul offered an unconvincing explanation, which Samuel, of course, rejected out of hand, and the damage was done. As a punishment for not having pressed the war to its ultimate end, Saul is told, "I [Samuel] will not go back with you; for you have rejected the Lord's command, and the Lord has rejected you as king over Israel" (I Samuel 15:26).

One could easily be tempted to feel sorry for Saul; he did, after all, what many of us would want to do. He hesitated to kill, because the destruction to him seemed wanton. Why, then, does Jewish tradition depict Saul as such a colossal failure? Because, it seems, he failed to appreciate that genuine leadership entails realistically assessing one's enemies, and when necessary and possible, destroying them. In Samuel's biting words, "You may look small to yourself, but you are the head of the tribes of Israel, and the Lord sent you on a mission, saying, 'Go and proscribe the sinful Amalekites; make war on them until you have exterminated them. Why did you disobey the Lord?'"

Sadly, the history of Israel in the Middle East suggests that the Book of Samuel may have been rather perspicacious. For the refusal to take extraordinary action, we are being warned, is but the beginning of long-term ineffectiveness in combating evil. Neville Chamberlain's delusional deal with Hitler comes to mind here. So does the West's enduring refusal to take significant steps to prevent Iran from attaining a nuclear weapon. Nor can one help but recall the years of Israeli inaction after the Disengagement; thousands of *kassams* rained down on Sderot and other towns in the area, and for the most part Olmert's government, still recovering from its poor performance in the Second Lebanon War, simply refused to act.

It is precisely for this reason that Jewish law has an entire category of war called *milhemet mitzvah* ("commanded wars"), or wars that *must* be waged. In these wars, there is no requirement to receive permission from the Sanhedrin (the Jewish High Court) to conduct the war, something that was necessary in the case of other, discretionary, wars (B.T. Sanhedrin 2a). Such required wars included the campaigns to capture the land, defensive wars against marauding enemies, and continued efforts to destroy Amalek, the archetype of unadulterated evil in the Jewish tradition.

It is precisely because Amalek has come to signify evil incarnate in the Jewish tradition that the command to destroy Amalek figures so centrally in Jewish life, including in the holiday of Purim. To many observers, Purim seems mere childish fun. To be sure, with its costumes, groggers (noisemakers used to drown out the name of Haman as it's read from the Book of Esther), and merriment, Purim can indeed appear trivial. But that assessment misses the point of the Book of Esther and of the holiday in general.

A careful look at the rituals of Purim suggests that the holiday is actually about something infinitely more serious than the costumes and merry-making might suggest. On the Sabbath before Purim, the passage from Deuteronomy and the command to destroy Amalek is read. Furthermore, the villain of the Purim story, Haman, is said to have been a descendant of Amalek. Purim is introduced, then, by a reminder that evil needs to be thoroughly uprooted and destroyed.

Consider also the fact that when the Book of Esther, or the *megillah*, is read, Jewish law requires that one hear every single word. Now, on the face of it, that may not seem strange; serious reading should require hearing every word, should it not? Interestingly enough, though, Jewish tradition usually does not make that claim. If on a regular Sabbath morning one misses some of the reading of the Torah, Judaism's most sacred text, no religious obligation has been failed. The same is true with the recitation of the Haggadah on Passover, or with a myriad of other examples. By and large, Jewish tradition commands its members to read those texts, but does not penalize them for missing a word here and there.

Not so with Purim. On that Shabbat before Purim, as the command to destroy Amalek is read in synagogue, Jews are obliged to hear every single word. And similarly, on Purim itself, the entire Book of Esther is read, and here, too, Jewish tradition insists that each and every adult Jew make sure not to miss a word. Why?

Clearly, Jewish tradition wants Jews to read the Megillah with an intensity and with attention to the story that is required for virtually no other Jewish text. And why might that be? Perhaps the answer lies in Mordecai's warning to Esther when she seeks to avoid taking personal risk in order to intervene on behalf of her people:

> Do not imagine that you, of all the Jews, will escape with your life by being in the king's palace. On the contrary, if you keep silent in this crisis, relief and deliverance will come to the Jews from another quarter, while you and your father's house will perish. And who knows, perhaps you have attained to royal position for just such a crisis. [Esther 4:13–15]

Mordecai's words are a warning. If the Jews are endangered, *all* the Jews are endangered. No one ought to imagine that he or she will be spared. (Sadly, the history of the twentieth century validated his point with horrific clarity.) But his words are also a demand. What it means to be part of this people, he suggests, is to be willing to defend it, even at personal risk. Just as Moses told Reuben, Gad, and half the tribe of Menasseh that they could have their land across the Jordan only if they fought with their brothers, so, too, Mordecai tells Esther that what it means to be a Jew is to risk for them, to fight for them, to join with them. That the Jews at the end of the Book of Esther take up arms and thoroughly destroy their enemies makes the point ever more clear.

Whatever misgivings Jews may rightly have about the horrors of war, the image of the Jew as risk-taker and as warrior is not foreign to Jewish tradition. Jews have long heard the call to become warriors in order to guarantee Jewish, or Israeli, security. That call is neither new nor a bastardization of classic Jewish values. If anything, Israeli life is forcing Jews to confront their tradition's long-standing views about the legitimate use of power—views we have ignored too long, much to our own detriment.

Our claim should not be misunderstood; nothing here is meant to suggest that the Jewish tradition celebrates violence or war, or that it should. There are infinitely more sources that could be cited about Judaism and peace than there are about Judaism and war, and it is well that it is so. What is problematic is the fact that many contemporary Jews have internalized a message about the centrality of peace in Judaism to the point that they have come to believe that there is something profoundly "un-Jewish" about war.

But there is something "un-Jewish" about being a warrior only if there is something "un-Jewish" about surviving. No thinking person could deny the horrific nature of war. But that does not make the conduct of war contrary to Jewish principles. Indeed, it is the unwillingness to fight for survival that is actually a departure from what the Jewish tradition has always advocated. Yes, being appalled at the suffering of others, even of our enemies, is a central tenet of Jewish life. "If your enemy falls, do not exult," urges Proverbs 24:17, and the Jewish tradition has taken that seriously. But Jews are still permitted, indeed commanded, to defeat their enemies.

Western society recognized the unfortunate indispensability of war long ago. Plato, in *The Republic*, places soldiers immediately below rulers in the hierarchy of his idealized society. For without the capacity for self-defense, there is no value in a society honing its worldview; that worldview would have no chance of surviving, much less of flourishing. It is time that Jews began to understand that this is true of their own survival, as well.

None of this means that Israel ought to conduct its wars wantonly. I still recall the day in July 2002 when Israel sent an F-16 to drop a one-ton bomb on the home of Salah Shehadeh, then the military chief of Hamas in Gaza. The air strike was successful, and Shehadeh was killed. But so were fourteen other people, including nine children. Pleased though Israelis were about the fact that Shehadeh, a long-wanted terrorist, was dead, they were despondent about the collateral deaths. The fact that they hadn't been intended did nothing to mollify an Israeli population that was beside itself, and mortified.

Shehadeh deserved to die. About that, Israelis were not terribly divided. But that was not the way to kill him, people said, both on the left and on the right. Israelis wanted the prerogative to defend themselves, but they insisted on a standard perhaps higher than what other powers might invoke.

Eventually the government apologized. And the IDF changed its policy. So in September 2003, when the IDF decided to assassinate Sheikh Ahmed Yassin, the founder and "spiritual head" of Hamas, it again sent an F-16, but this time with a quarter-ton bomb. The bomb worked perfectly, and the pilot hit his target. But the building was only damaged, and Yassin was scarcely wounded.

Interestingly, the typical Israeli was satisfied. True, the attack had failed, and one of Israel's most dangerous enemies was still at large. But Israelis were pleased with the fact that care for civilians had trumped killing Yassin. They knew that the Israeli Air Force would eventually kill Yassin (which it did, with a helicopter strike on his car), but in the meantime, Israelis preferred to be different.

This is a terribly difficult balance, but that is both the challenge and the gift of statehood for the Jews. Jewish statehood is not merely about having a flag, or running the bureaucratic institutions of government. It is also about Jews assuming responsibility for their own safety and learning how to balance that responsibility with the obligation to be decent. But it is balance that is key. When the commitment to decency is so overwhelming that Jews grow fearful of defending themselves, Jews have actually abandoned the tenets of their tradition and have created a weak, almost pathetic, version of what Jewish life ought to be. As Ahad Ha-am (Asher Ginsburg), the great ideologue of cultural Zionism, once said, "It is a disgrace for five million human souls to unload themselves on others, to stretch their necks to slaughter and cry for help, without as much as attempting to defend their own property, honor and lives." For Israel to survive, Israelis and Israel's supporters are going to have to internalize that perspective. The very possibility of a Jewish future demands nothing less.

Israel would not deserve anyone's support were it not regularly extending an olive branch, seeking ways to end the grueling conflict that has been forced on it for almost a century. But even so, Israel cannot afford to lose its defensive edge. Israel and Jewish sovereignty create an opportunity for a radically different kind of Jewish existence than was possible when there was no Jewish state. Ahad Ha-am was right. Allowing that gift to slip away, while the Jews simply hope that their enemies will not attack, would be nothing short of a disgrace.

Israel affords Jews much more than statehood. It affords them the opportunity to take responsibility for their own survival, and in so doing to recapture a dimension of traditional Jewish life that two thousand years of forced passivity had forced them to forget. That is an opportunity we dare not squander.

Chapter Twelve

THE JEWISH STATE AND THE STATE OF THE JEWS

Almost all our great men . . . whose education and social position have prepared them to be at the head of a Jewish State—are spiritually far removed from Judaism and have no true conception of its nature and its value. Such men, however loyal to their State and devoted to its interests, will necessarily envisage those interests by the standards of the foreign culture which they themselves have imbibed. . . . In the end, the Jewish State will be a State of [Jewish] Germans or Frenchmen.

—Ahad Ha-Am, "The Jewish State and the Jewish Problem" (1897)

It is almost as if there are two Israels, two countries so utterly different one from the other that it would have been hard to imagine them as part of the same project of national regeneration. In Jerusalem, Israel seems cut out of the lithographs that Jews have been hanging in their homes for centuries. There's the outer wall of the Old City, the Western Wall, the El Aksa Mosque, and the Temple Mount. Though a modern city in many ways, it's still filled with narrow alleyways and old Arab houses, and with religious Jews of all stripes walking the streets alongside Arabs in traditional clothing. Jerusalem is much more than that, of course, but from a tourist's perspective, the city seems a veritable Disneyland of Jewish history and identity.

In Tel Aviv, however, matters are entirely different. Though Tel Aviv was the first Hebrew-speaking city, it feels very much like any cosmopolitan European metropolis. Tel Aviv has very few ultra-Orthodox Jews. It is home to virtually no Arabs. Unlike in Jerusalem, in Tel Aviv one hears almost no Yiddish or Arabic. The architecture is European; the cafés and promenades could have been lifted from any one of a number of continental cities. Were it not for the sights and sounds of Hebrew, it might be difficult to know that one was in the Jewish state. When residents of Tel Aviv "have to" go to Jerusalem, they often say that they feel as if they have entered a different country.

These stereotypes are highly oversimplified, but they are still important. They allude to the radically different senses that Israelis have about what ought to be Jewish about the Jewish state. They reflect the absence of a shared center in Israeli life, the need for a common discourse about what should be unique about the Jewish state that Israel desperately needs to engender. If Israel wishes to save itself, it will have to address this, too.

It will not suffice to distinguish Israel from America, to address the demographic challenge posed by Israel's indigenous Arab population, to restore a Jewish willingness to fight for survival as long as that is required, and even to create a new Jew for the twenty-first century. All of those are necessary, but they are not sufficient. Israelis are also going to have to ask themselves if Israel is the "Jewish state" because a plurality of its populace is Jewish, or whether, alternatively, what is Jewish about the state is the content of its citizens' worldviews, the fingerprints on its culture, and the "conversation" that unfolds daily in the news, in politics, and across communities and neighborhoods.

The suggestion that Israel has to address its Jewish content may sound surprising, for on the surface, Judaism seems to be thriving in the Jewish state. Much of the world's most serious Jewish scholarship emanates from Israeli academe. Israel produces countless journals and books devoted to Jewish religion and culture. *Yeshivot* (institutions of traditional Jewish learning) abound. Jewish (not just Hebrew, but *Jewish*) art and theater thrive in secular Israel as they do nowhere else. There is even some religious creativity emerging from Jewish *religious* circles, particularly in the area of women's roles.

Even in terms of personal practice, Judaism seems secure in the Jewish state. No less than 98% of Israelis have a mezuzah on the front door of their homes; 85% participate in a Passover seder, and 71% *always* light Hanukkah candles. Clearly, a wide array of highly public, religious rituals (especially those that are about identity and do not limit personal behavior) are alive and well.

But the same study that published these statistics also noted a soft underbelly of Jewish identity in Israel. "The sense of intra-Israeli and pan-Jewish unity is eroding," it opined. Among well-educated, secular Israelis, "the intensity of Jewish identity is gradually declining, and there is confusion regarding the meaning of the term 'Jew' and the definition of the character and attributes that the Jewish State should possess." Even the "modern-Orthodox" community, that segment of the religious community that is both Zionist and open to the Western world, is having trouble holding its own. What seem to be growing are the groups on the edges of the spectrum: "there are more haredim [ultra-Orthodox] among second generation Ashkenazim . . . but the proportion who are non-religious/non-observant has also risen."

What the secular left and the religious right share, ironically, is a move away from Zionist commitment. The ultrareligious right, whose children do not serve in the army, often advocates theocracy instead of democracy. Many ultra-Orthodox Jews speak Yiddish rather than Hebrew, refuse to stand for the siren on Yom Ha-Shoah or Yom Ha-Zikaron, and do not participate in many of the other defining elements of Israeli culture. In all, they are far removed from the fabric of Israeli life, and increasingly, their way of life is arousing the ire of other segments of society. Many Israelis take umbrage at a community that does not serve in the military or that uses Israel's highly fractured political system to wrest governmental financial support for families who have more than ten children when husbands and fathers do not work, all the while showing disdain for mainstream Israel.

On the left, draft-dodging is on the rise, embarrassment about Israel's policies leads many to think about leaving the country, and many more have long since succumbed to the moral self-flagellation and the loss of Zionist commitment that we have described throughout this book. Many of these people embrace the modern Western world with enthusiasm and hold overtly dismissive views toward anything ancient. For them Israel is about autonomy, modernity, education, the pursuit of economic well-being, and participation in Israel's music and arts culture. What is increasingly absent from their picture is a coherent and articulate commitment to what was once the Jewish part of the mix.

This is less strange than it sounds. Recall where many Israelis came from. Given the ideological moves toward secularization that were under way in the Europe that produced their parents, grandparents, or great-grandparents (among the Bund, socialists, and others), it should not surprise us that contemporary Israelis of European extraction have been the inheritors of much of that ethos. The constant struggle to survive in Europe, which led to a desire not to be different anymore, continues to color secular Israeli life. Those Israelis whose families hailed from Europe, who still set much of the tone for the media and who therefore have great influence over the thinking of the elites, come by their secularist tendencies quite honestly. North African Jewish culture is different, but it, too, is increasingly imbibing the values of the European community it often (justifiably) resents.

Given Israel's relentless struggle to stay alive (a struggle that, tragically, shows no sign of abating), it is easy to understand why many Israelis want to be left alone to live an uncomplicated, nonideological life. Exhausted by decades of fighting with no end in sight, their primary goal in life is not necessarily to stand for anything in particular. They see countries that are not at war, societies in which people simply go about their business, building lives, charting careers, and raising children, and they decide that they want that, too. Zionist success, they believe, can be achieved through living lives of normalcy.

Add to that the factor we mentioned earlier, that the processes of Jewish secularization in the United States and in Israel have been very different one from the other, and the picture becomes even more understandable. In America, what led many American Jews to abandon or to modify tradition was the lure of America, the desire not to be different. American Jews hoped that if they just accommodated themselves to the prevailing ethos of America, they would finally have found a home and would at long last share in the riches of their host society.

The United States provided precisely that opportunity. Thus, the move away from Jewish life in America was more often than not a matter of *seeking* success rather than rebelling *against* something. When individual American Jews find themselves yearning for tradition or meaning or a return to Jewish life, there is no ideology that they have to transcend in order to make their way "back." Indeed, in a nation like the United States with so palpable a religious pulse at its core, the return to Jewish life often feels authentically American, even if it is not Christian.

Not so in Israeli life. Israel is heir to a very different ethos of assimilation. It is certainly true that some Israelis have simply sought more personal autonomy, fewer antiquated mores, and perhaps even a more "rational" foundation to their lives. But Israeli society as a whole did not merely drift away from Jewish life; it rejected Jewish tradition as a matter of principle and ideology.

We've seen that already, in Bialik's critique of traditional Judaism and in Alterman's insistence that the state would replace the Torah as the "true miracle." But their revolution, as we've seen, was more successful than they might have imagined possible. The descendants of the labor Zionists of the 1930s and 1940s do not know the Shema, do not recognize the biblical references in Israel's classic poems, and are wholly incapable of having conversations with Jewish content. This creeping trend toward wholesale Jewish illiteracy is no less a threat to Israel's future than many of the other challenges we've discussed in this book, and it, too, demands attention.

The suggestion that Israel must address this loss of Jewish content in Israeli life does not mean that Israel should abandon everything that it has accomplished thus far, of course. Quite the contrary. It is a plea for something much more nuanced, a return to the sort of era when such poets as Bialik, Alterman, and Rachel the Poetess, such men of letters as Yosef Brenner and A. D. Gordon, such political figures as Ben-Gurion and Jabotinsky, and such religious figures as Rabbi Abraham Isaac Kook all competed in the public square with radically different conceptions of Zionism. They were all Zionists, and they all sought a society with a profoundly Jewish kernel. What they disagreed about was how to create that. It is *that* sort of public discourse, that sort of competition over ideas, which once character-ized prestate Zionist society. It urgently needs to be restored.

Restoring Judaism to the heart of Israel's national debate will not be easy, but neither is it impossible. There is even good news in that slightly harrowing story about the Shema, my son, and his friend. Part of the good news, as we've suggested, is that many young people are seeking a way back to the world of Jewish tradition. But beyond that, there is cause for optimism in the fact that programs like those, for religious kids, secular kids, mixed populations, and virtually every social characteristic one can imagine, are cropping up all over Israel. A renaissance of sorts, particularly among the young, is beginning to develop.

Listen carefully, and you hear the yearning for Jewish substance, or at least for some sort of Jewish engagement, everywhere. I still recall my visit to an Israeli high school near Sederot, some of whose students had just returned from a trip to the United States. As the students were debriefing with the principal, one extremely articulate young woman told him that the trip had made her angry. When he asked her why, she said, "Because as an Israeli, who's grown up in Israel my entire life, I shouldn't have had to go to the San Bernardino Mountains to see *havdalah* for the first time in my life."

Havdalah, the ceremony with which Jews traditionally conclude the Sabbath, was something that many, many American Jewish kids know something about, even if they don't do it regularly. This Israeli student had never seen it before she went to California. She felt cheated and deprived by what Israel, her school, her community, and her family had not offered her.

Growing up in the United States, I don't believe that I ever met a single Jew who'd never set foot in a synagogue. I met people who hardly ever went, who went occasionally and only did so kicking and screaming, but I don't believe that I met a single Jewish person who'd never seen the inside of a synagogue.

But my children, who've grown up in Israel, have countless friends—Israeli Jews, born and raised in Israel—who've never been in a synagogue. In the United States, many Jews feel no reason to go; but in Israel, many believe they have good reason *not* to go. In America, where Jewish identification without some religious veneer is not impossible but is difficult, most American Jews do *something* to express that identification. In Israel, however, no one could possibly claim that the only expression of Jewish connectedness or commitment is religious practice. Israeli life is suffused with Jewish content, as we've seen. That fact, combined with the antipathy to religious ritual that many Israelis have inherited from that early generation of founding Zionists, leads many of them to search for spiritual fulfillment in Nepal or India, or in a variety of other religious and non-religious traditions. For too many, though, it leads nowhere near Jewish learning or the institutions of Jewish life.

For Israel, however, this is much more than a matter of personal preference. It is actually a matter of national security. For what is disappearing from these people's lives is not only ritual. What is also gone is the capacity for Jewish conversations; these people have lost the ability to say anything coherent or substantive about who the Jews are, what the Jewish state is trying to save, or what it ought to become. This impoverishes everyone, not just those who have drifted away. It weakens the glue that binds Israeli society together, depletes the discourse that ought to be at the heart of Israel's public life, and eradicates the motivation that Israelis need to continue defending their still vulnerable state.

The bitter truth that secular Zionism's revolutionaries did not face was that disdain for Jewish tradition would inevitably, and relatively quickly, produce utter Jewish ignorance. Nor did they imagine that their secular revolution, conceived in the throes of their work to create a Jewish state, could someday represent one of the greatest threats to that state. But that is precisely what has happened. The Israeli experiment has shown the significant investment of time and education that Jewish literacy requires; it has illuminated the rapidity with which the People of the Book can lose any capacity for reading the books that have long made it distinct and it has shown how quickly passion for Jewish sovereignty can subside when Jewish literacy is a vestige of the past. The question that Israel must now ask is whether it has the fortitude to try to turn that tide.

Ignoring the accomplishments of Jewish communities from the Bible to the advent of political Zionism was much more than an act of sloppy pedagogy. It was a willful, strategic, and highly ideological course of action. Reversing this mind-set is going to require a concerted national effort, and it will take at least a generation. It will need to be a national campaign, for the campaign *toward* secularization was also a national one.

Few have said it better, or with more anguish, than Professor Aaron Ciechanover, Israel's 2004 winner of the Nobel Prize in Chemistry. Writing to the journal *Azure* in early 2008, Ciechanover laments:

> In a relatively short period of sixty years, then, we have succeeded in building something magnificent—namely, a Jewish state—and then destroying it with our own hands. We have turned our backs on everything that contributed to that extraordinary creation, including the culture of learning in all the Jewish Diasporas, and have attempted to copy, unsuccessfully, the developed countries of the West in an effort to be just like every other nation. We have hacked away at the rich and varied Jewish cultures of the world in an attempt to create an "Israeli" culture that lacks substance and meaning. The result is a superficial amalgam that is slowly dissolving in a swamp of corruption and cynicism.
>
> The era of Israel's founder, David Ben-Gurion—who, in even darker days for our country, started a Jewish Bible study group in his own home, and authored the book *Ben-Gurion Looks at the Bible*—ended all too soon, and certainly before it managed to put down strong roots. Indeed, the idea that one

of this country's leaders would study and teach the Bible in his home seems quite absurd today.

Not only is the normalcy that Israelis have long sought impossible; it is not even desirable. For normalcy as a goal will not breed the kind of distinctiveness that Israeli survival will require. If Israelis cannot articulate anything profound about Jewish civilization, or say anything about the grandest ideas that have long been at the core of Jewish life, what possible reason could there be to continue to defend a Jewish country? Why should those who are mobile and who have the resources they'd need if they wanted to leave still decide to stick it out? Is it possible to articulate a raison d'être for the Jewish state without at least some Jewish content? If Israel's young people do not have palpably Jewish souls and dreams, is there any good reason to expect them to fight "the first war, all over again," especially when that war is unlikely to end?

It would be a grave error, however, to assume that it is only secularists who are responsible for this dangerous divide between Israelis and their heritage. Indeed, just as Israel's secular culture will have to rethink its purposeful abandonment of tradition if Israel is to regain purpose, so, too, will Israel's religious establishment have to earn the respect of an enormous swath of society that now holds it in disregard, if not in contempt.

Unlike America, which has no chief rabbi, or England, in which chief rabbis have long been held in high esteem, Israel's Chief Rabbinate is seen as politicized, often corrupt, and perhaps most important, horribly out of touch with the spiritual issues that Israelis face. In the United States, rabbinic leaders have learned that they are the heads of a purely voluntary community, and that to be successful, they need to make a persuasive case for Jewish life. In Europe, that is also largely the case. Yet Israel's rabbinate lives as if rabbinic hegemony over Jewish communities continues unchanged from the Middle Ages, as if the Enlightenment and Emancipation had not yet arrived.

But times have changed. Israelis do not need the Chief Rabbinate for anything on a day-to-day basis. They do not seek the rabbinate's blessing or sanction for how they live, and to their minds, the rabbinate has nothing to say that might enrich them. Since the Chief Rabbinate cannot force itself into the lives of everyday Israelis, the challenge of Israel's contemporary religious leadership is precisely like that of America's Jewish community: it needs to learn to make a compelling case for Jewish life.

Were the rabbinate doing its job, it would recognize that the critical issues in Israel's religious life are not which vegetables can be consumed during the sabbatical year or whether certain chains of stores may be open on Shabbat. Those issues matter, of course, especially to the religious community. But in the larger scheme of Israeli life, they are far from the only issues that make a difference for society as a whole.

Other, non-ritual questions matter no less. What will ultimately determine the character of the Jewish society that develops in Israel is the question of *why* anyone interested in the Western world, anyone exposed to Western philosophy and European culture, and anyone interested in humankind's millennia of grappling with powerful ideas about the human condition ought to care one whit about the role of Jewish tradition in their lives. That is the question that Israelis are asking, both consciously and not.

But nothing that the rabbinate says or does even intimates that Judaism has something to say about what constitutes a life of worth. The rabbinate says nothing about a society grappling with both unprecedented wealth and a growing gap between rich and poor. It is silent on the question of how to raise children who revere Jewish tradition, but who also respect and appreciate the contributions of other cultures and religions. It does not even address the question of how a society can be at war for generation after generation and still resist the temptation to hate. Those are the sorts of questions that matter for Israelis, and those are the issues about which most of Israel's religious leadership says absolutely nothing.

In June of 2008, as Israel prepared to celebrate the holiday of Shavu'ot (which marks the revelation of the Torah at Sinai), posters began to crop up all over cities advertising the various classes that would be offered all night long, as there is a tradition among religious Jews, and increasingly, among some secular Jews, to study until dawn. In Jerusalem, the variety of lectures being offered was simply stunning. There were lectures by men, and some by women. Some were in synagogues, others were in community centers. Most were in Hebrew, some were in other languages. Among the young, the topics of interest had to do with things like balancing the quest for peace and the quest for justice, or the simmering controversies regarding conversion and the rabbinate.

And then, walking down one of Jerusalem's main streets one Shabbat afternoon, I saw the huge posters advertising the lecture that one of the chief rabbis would be offering at Jerusalem's Great Synagogue. The topic? "The view of halakic experts regarding the custom of praying at the graves of righteous men."

For a moment, I wasn't sure that I'd read the poster correctly. But I had. And I found it stunning. Of all the topics that one might choose to address in a country facing the issues that Israel faces, *that* was the topic the chief rabbi chose? When secular Israelis see that kind of poster, they decide that the rabbinate has nothing interesting to say about the critical issues of our day; therefore, they assume, Judaism must not either. Thus one more nail is driven into the coffin of Israeli Jewish discourse.

Israelis do not hear the Chief Rabbinate discuss ethics or moral issues. If anything, all too often the rabbinate's responses to questions of modernity are knee-jerk, small-minded legalistic reactions that avoid serious engagement with the questions of the day. When the chief rabbi of Israel joins with Muslim and Christian leaders in pleading with gay and lesbian organizers to cancel their gay pride parade rather than "damage the holiness of Jerusalem" but says nothing about the complex etiology of sexual orientation or about the pain that gays and lesbians feel in a society that is not sufficiently open to them, Israelis decide that the rabbinate is out of touch with people's most compelling questions. It's not that the rabbinate would have to sanction homosexuality; most Israelis understand that that is not going to happen at any time in the foreseeable future. But by refusing to address these moral and individual issues, the rabbinate fails in its

responsibility to make a case for Judaism in the marketplace of Israel's
ideas. It is worse than irrelevant; it is an affront to the intellectual richness that has long characterized Jewish life, and it convinces more and
more Israelis to seek profundity elsewhere.

Some Orthodox young men and women are today marrying at a
later age than they used to. That creates a whole array of social and
moral questions for modern-religious Jews, questions that deserve
serious discussion. But when the rabbinate issues a ruling that bans
unmarried women from using *mikva'ot* (pools for ritual immersion)
with the expectation that this will limit the phenomenon of premarital sex among the faithful, Israelis shake their heads in bewilderment
and disbelief. They are almost amused to think that the rabbis believe
that by closing *mikva'ot* to unmarried women, they will prevent those
unmarried women from sleeping with the people they love. They
are disappointed that the rabbinate sees nothing positive in the fact
that unmarried women, even if they *are* violating a traditional standard about premarital sex, still wish to make classic Jewish rituals part
of their lives, rather than bolting entirely. When they see this, many
Israelis decide that the tradition those rabbis represent must surely not
be for them.

Thus, with every passing year, Israeli cynicism about, resentment
of, and disdain for the rabbinate—and for the tradition it represents—
continues to grow and to deepen. Some hope that other branches of
Judaism, such as Reform or Conservative Judaism, which still struggle
to gain a foothold in Israel, might offer an alternative. But then they
see that the unholy alliance of politicians and rabbis blocks that progress,
too, and they give up. They simply decide that Judaism is not for them.

Sadly and ironically, it is the rabbinate's behavior, no less than
anyone else's, that makes the restoration of a serious Jewish element
to Israel's civil discourse even more difficult.

But imagine a rabbinate that spoke compellingly to Jews about
a more profound role for Judaism in their lives. Imagine a rabbinate
that spoke of the Talmud not as a twenty-volume law code but as an
ongoing debate with the Greco-Roman world regarding the nature of
the life well lived, the composition and structure of the ideal society,
and the means for introducing sanctity into human life. What would

happen if Israelis were introduced to the fact that the Talmud—the volumes that have been the backbone of religious Jewish communities for a thousand years—is a book about competing ideas? Might Israelis not be won back by a book in which even those opinions that do not win are preserved—because Judaism has long insisted that there is much to learn from them, too?

There is an enormous amount that a sophisticated religious establishment might have to say to Israeli society. How should newly financially comfortable Israelis balance their desire for material goods with the desire to improve their world? Who should be the beneficiaries of their newfound resources—the poor in Israel, or those who are much poorer but live outside of the Jewish state?

National ethical questions abound as well. We've pointed to some of these examples already. There was the question of whether parts of Jerusalem should be traded for peace. Or how to retain both Israel's democracy and its Jewish character. Or what to do with refugees from Darfur.

What matters for our purposes is not what Israel ultimately decides on each of these issues. What matters is that if the discussion of that issue in Israel seems almost identical to the conversations that Americans might have had—for example, about making a trade for captured soldiers who were in the hands of Iraqi insurgents—then the conversation might be sophisticated, even moral, but it would not be *Jewish*. And if these pivotal decisions in Israeli life are not *Jewish* in some profound way, what is the point of the enormous costs that having a state exacts?

Recall the case of Gilad Shalit, the captured Israeli soldier. Is there any way to give meaning to the horrific, years-long suffering that Gilad Shalit's parents endured if living in Israel, and serving in the army, is not about trying to create something *different*? About this, the rabbinate has been silent. And because of that, most Israelis do not think that the world of Jewish life has anything to do with making meaning of the Shalit tragedy. It's more than an enormous missed opportunity; it's one further step toward confirming Israelis' belief that Judaism has no value. And that, in turn, prompts them to wonder whether Israel's survival makes any difference at all.

Or consider, for example, Israel's relationship with Turkey. Israeli leaders have long considered Turkey a prime strategic ally because it is both Muslim and democratic. Turkey has ties to the West, which also makes it an attractive ally for Israel. Its shared border with Syria is an added strategic advantage. In times of drought, there has even been talk of Israel purchasing water from Turkey.

But all relationships come with their price, and the Israeli-Turkish relationship has been no exception. Most noteworthy has been the Turkish demand that Israel stay silent on the international discussion of the Armenian genocide, which Turkey continues to deny. Israeli history textbooks, as a result, avoid discussion of the Armenian genocide. Turkey has even insisted that Israel pressure American Jewish groups, such as the Anti-Defamation League, to avoid references to genocide in Turkey.

One can certainly understand Israel's desperate desire to have an ally in the Muslim world, and to do everything possible (especially if all that is asked, essentially, is silence) to foster that alliance. But Israel would understandably show no understanding if another country denied the Shoah. A country born out of the ashes of Auschwitz has unique responsibilities, both to its own national memory and to the memory of others who have suffered genocide. There is no defensible way for Israel to insist on the sanctity of Jewish memory while denying the sacred memories of other communities, no matter how different the case of the Shoah may have been from the massacre of the Armenians.

One could take the argument further. Maybe the Jewish state, knowing what it does about Jewish history and human suffering, ought to do more than refuse to ignore the Armenian genocide. Perhaps it ought also be on the front lines of advocating for the Kurds and their quest for independence, regardless of what Turkey might think about that. Ought Israel save its neck and risk its soul by capitulating to Turkey's demands? I think not.

At stake here is much more than what Israel puts in its textbooks, or how it nurtures an alliance with a potentially significant ally. The real question has to do with whether Israel has created a society that pulses with Jewish sentiment and insight, a country in which people cannot discuss strategic questions without recognition of the unique perspectives that Jewish history and Jewish culture might bring to bear. The issue is not Gilad Shalit, Sudanese refugees, or Israel's relationship with Turkey. The issue is whether Israel will remain qualitatively Jewish—Jewish enough to justify its existence, and Jewish enough to make the horrific price that Israelis will have to continue to pay for many years into the future worth enduring.

Let the central issue not be misunderstood. Israeli society at large does not necessarily need to become more religious. There are those who believe that it should. So let them compete in the Israeli marketplace of ideas. Some will make their case theologically, claiming that ritual observance is what God demands. Others will sidestep theological arguments, claiming instead that it is Judaism's way of life that has preserved the Jewish people, and to abandon those practices endangers the Jewish future. Secularists will insist that their choices do not do damage to the possibility of Jewish continuity. Some of them believe that the era of Bialik and Brenner, and Ben-Gurion and Kook, *can* be revived. One cannot help but pray that they are right. But others disagree.

So let the serious debate begin. The problem is that there is no Israeli marketplace of ideas; instead, those who seek a more religious society often try to create it through legislation rather than persuasion.

But legislating religious society is the worst thing that one could do for the long-term vitality of a Jewish Israel. Some observers of the explosion of New York Jewish intellectuals in the 1940s, a generation that included Alfred Kazin, Irving Howe, Sidney Hook, Mary McCarthy, Lionel Trilling, and many others, have suggested that what made that generation of New York Jews so intellectually prolific and creative was their pride in "being at once outsiders and insiders." Torn between the European immigrant Jewish experience and their simultaneous exposure to the wider world of New York, they created America's most vital and creative Jewish generation. A similar cultural, intellectual, and religious burst of creativity could take place in Israel, too, if only religious and secular leaders alike embraced Israel's Jewishness as well as the allure of the West and the world beyond.

Israel needs to celebrate the tension between insularity and open-ness, between the particular and the universal, between the uniquely Jewish and the more cosmopolitan. For this is the crucible that has always produced Judaism's greatness. Such was the world of the rabbis of the Talmud. It was the intellectual world that produced Maimonides, who was also deeply influenced by Muslim thought and literature. It was the kind of world from which Bialik and Ben-Gurion came. Many of Zionism's early leaders were deeply grounded in Jewish life, but they were worried about the looming anti-Jewish crisis they knew was coming to Europe, and they had been tempted beyond return by the intellectual richness of late-nineteenth- and early-twentieth-century Europe. The Land of Israel was the place where they imagined they might create some synthesis.

The challenge facing Israel, the threshold for saving Israel, is to see if a society predicated on profound and creative debate can be re-created. Israel needs to renew the Zionist public square with its often vitriolic exchange of ideas. For it is in the intensity of those interchanges that Judaism has always shined brightest. And it is in the intensity of those debates that the Jewish state might attain true Jewish greatness.

The word "Israel" means something. It is the biblical name that God gave Jacob after he wrestled with the angel. "Your name shall no longer be Jacob, but Israel, for you have striven with beings divine and human and have prevailed" (Genesis 32:29). The very name "Israel" connotes wrestling, struggling, grappling, the interaction of the human with what is beyond human.

The real challenge facing Israel is to produce a society worthy of its name.

BECAUSE ISRAEL IS NOT
JUST A STATE

The Jews huddling around their radios on November 29, 1947, holding their breath and listening to the General Assembly vote, needed no explanation for why the Jews needed a state. The horrors of twentieth-century Europe had made that abundantly clear. For their generation, statehood meant a new lease on life, the possibility of a future after their people had narrowly avoided extinction.

In the decades that have passed since the Shoah, though, many Jews have grown uncertain about the need for Jewish sovereignty. To them, Israel is the story not of recovery and healing, but of roadblocks and occupation. For them, Israel is a source not of pride, but more often, of shame.

The most urgent task facing the Jewish people at the beginning of the twenty-first century is countering this trend. For that to happen, Jews need to speak about Israel not in terms of the Shoah or even of enduring anti-Semitism (for those are images of which young Jews have long since tired), but about the purpose of the Jewish state, about what sovereignty enables the Jews to do and to become.

Without the sense that the Jewish people is actually trying to accomplish something in Israel, there is no way to see the Jewish state as anything other than a problem. Absent the claim that Israel has a purpose, that something transformative is taking place in their relatively new country, Israelis and Jews in the Diaspora will continue to see themselves as nothing more than a cause of conflict, a creator of checkpoints, the obstacle blocking the road to Palestinian statehood.

This book has sought to articulate what it is that the Jewish state does for the Jewish people. After the world conspired to allow the Nazis to eradicate Jews, Israel proclaimed that it would afford any Jew a home at any moment. In so doing, it brought security and restored hope to Jewish life. It has enabled the Jews to believe once again in the possibility of a future.

Israel was also to be the setting in which Jews could imagine what they should become after two thousand years of exile. "Why did these things happen to us?" was not what Israel would ask. What mattered would be a different question: "Given that these things did happen to us, who and what do we need to be?" Israel would allow the Jews to reclaim their role as actors in history. Only in Israel, as full-fledged participants engaged in constant dialogue with the variety of voices of the tradition that had shaped their conversations for millennia, might they begin to imagine what twenty-first century Jewishness should look like.

The purpose of the Jewish state is to transform the Jews.

But statehood has exacted a high price from Jews around the world. Enemies still seek Israel's destruction. In the international community, Israel is now reviled. Israelis have tired of fighting and of sending their children to war, but they have no idea how to settle the conflicts that consume them.

Nor has the transformation of the Jews been complete. In many ways, in light of what existed in Palestine in 1947, what has been built in Israel is nothing short of miraculous. The ingathering of Jews has created a dynamic and heterogeneous society. But this, too, has been a dream only partially realized. For with the massive waves of immigration have come poverty, discrimination, and racism. Crime is on the rise. Trafficking in women continues, with little intervention by the authorities. Israeli schools, which have long since lost their erstwhile high international ranking, have become increasingly segregated. As Israel has moved from socialism to a free-market economy, some people have fallen behind. Too many children live below the poverty line, while in northern Tel Aviv, "yuppie" suburbs continue their sprawl.

Many of these problems are not unique to Israel, of course, but coupled with a loss of faith in the purpose of the state, they often feel overwhelming. Israelis and Jews across the world *could* tackle these challenges, but in order to do so, they would need to be able to say why saving the enterprise called Israel matters in the first place. Enabling them to do so is the great challenge the Jewish people now faces.

Were Israel just a state, the high cost it exacts might not be justified. But as we have seen throughout this book, Israel is not just a state. It breathed life into the Jewish people at precisely the moment when the Jews might have given up. It gives possibility and meaning to a Jewish future. It enables the Jews to reenter the stage of history.

That is why the calls for Israel's demise must be resisted. For what is at stake is not just the Jewish state but the Jewish people as well. Statehood has revitalized the Jewish people, but the Jews are very unlikely to get another state should this one fail. Whether the calls are for the outright destruction of Israel, or for the gradual erosion of Jewish sovereignty through ideas like a shared binational state between the Jordan River and the Mediterranean Sea, the result would be the same. Jewish life as we know it would be lost. The regained optimism, vitality, and confidence of the Jewish world would disappear, probably within a generation.

Israel's enemies understand that. It is time that the Jews did, too.

Therefore, Israeli Jews and Jews in the Diaspora have a decision to make. They can capitulate before their enemies and give up the battle to stay alive, or they can decide that the Jewish people has not come this far to fail now. If they want to survive, Jews will need to prepare themselves for a conflict that may not subside for generations.

But facing its enemies is not the primary battle that Israel must wage. Rather, Israelis have to decide if they believe in the Jewish state deeply enough to undertake the difficult and painful challenges that another century of thriving will require. Herzl was right: what matters most is will. What matters is that Zionist discourse—a conversation about why the Jews need a state, what kind of state they need, and how they are going to build and sustain it—be rekindled.

No longer can ostrich-like avoidance of the painful questions suffice. Israelis need to wrestle with the question of how the Jewish state should be Jewish. They will have to ask themselves how they can re-create a Jewish public square, and how much their children will need to know in order to participate in it. They will need to convince those who do not wish to be part of the future of the Jewish state not to live in it. They must ask how they want Israel to be unique, different from other countries that they nonetheless admire. They must learn to admit what they do not like about their own country, without giving up on Zionism altogether.

This task will not be simple. For too long, those who care about Israel have assumed that Israel's necessity, and its character, were beyond debate. They are not. But it is not yet too late to recover. For thousands of years, Jews have thrived on intense debate, on the cultivation of ideas, on disagreements that, though painful, often have led to greatness. They must do so once again.

Now is the time to reinvent Zionism, to re-create the conversation about why the Jews need a state and to ask what they are willing to do to preserve it. Nothing more ambitious is possible. And nothing less ambitious will suffice.

Acknowledgments

During the years that I was writing this book, I was privileged to work in two extraordinary institutions and to receive thoughtful assistance and feedback from numerous friends and colleagues. It is a pleasure to have an opportunity to thank them, however inadequately, for all they contributed to this project.

I began writing this book while working at the Mandel Foundation, Jerusalem and at the Mandel Leadership Institute. I am grateful, in particular, to Morton L. Mandel, whose vision created the Mandel Foundation and whose generosity continues to sustain it. One of the Jewish world's great philanthropists and institutional leaders, Mort is an inveterate optimist who has actually helped build the future he believes Israel deserves. Working with him for almost a decade was both an honor and an extraordinary learning experience; not a day goes by when I am not still influenced by all that I learned from him. Annette Hochstein, president of the Mandel Foundation in Israel, was much more than a colleague and a teacher. She was, and remains, a cherished friend. Beyond all that she did for me during the years of our collaboration, I would like to note, with particular thanks, the two mini-sabbaticals that she made possible in order for me to undertake this project.

In 2007, I was invited to join the leadership of the Shalem Center in Jerusalem and to help continue the work of its extraordinary founders, Yoram Hazony and Daniel Polisar. Though I did not fully appreciate it then, this was an invitation to join a unique intellectual

environment and to work with some of the Jewish world's most interesting and creative scholars, committed to Zionism and to an Israeli
future even more extraordinary than its present. Dan and Yoram have
been profoundly supportive of this project in many ways, and I'm
grateful for both their friendship and their wisdom. In conversations
both formal and impromptu, my colleagues and friends at Shalem
have done much to enrich my thinking on many of the issues raised in
these pages. Beyond Yoram and Dan, I would like to thank the friends
and colleagues with whom I've had numerous conversations that have
influenced some of the ideas in this book in ways large and small.
To Ofir Haivri, Yossi Klein Halevi, Yosef Yitzhak Lifshitz, Michael
Oren, and Rona Yona, my thanks. Sharon Ben Hamo, my extraordinarily capable assistant at Shalem, not only manages our office with
grace and equanimity, but also contributed to research and literature
searches for this book with wisdom and efficiency. I am very grateful.
Thanks also go to Moshe Behar, a student at the Hebrew University
and a member of the staff of our Student Programs Department, who
assisted with library searches at the Hebrew University.

A number of friends and colleagues outside the worlds of Mandel
and Shalem read portions of the manuscript. Others enriched these
pages with their comments on the issues raised herein or referred
me to sources of which I was not aware. To Scott Copeland, David
Ellenson, Gil Graff, Yosef Kanefsky, Avi Katzman, Amos Lehman,
Yaakov Lozowick, Monty Noam Penkower, Stuart Schoffman, Dan
Senor, Saul Singer, Wendy Singer, and David Wolpe, my thanks.
And my thanks go, as well, to Lili Adar of the Ben-Gurion Research
Institute for the Study of Israel and Zionism, for her assistance with
searches on David Ben-Gurion. Tzvikah Stendler, on the staff of Ben-
Gurion's house in Tel Aviv, and Hani Hermolin, the librarian there,
provided valuable assistance in searching Ben-Gurion's writings.

I was fortunate to have the assistance of a number of superb
interns while writing this book. Yael Weinstock, a very talented gradu-
ate student at the Hebrew University, worked with me at the Mandel
Foundation and did many of the literature searches as this project
first took form. The Shalem Center has several programs that bring
outstanding students from among the most prestigious institutions

in the United States to study, work, and do research. I was fortunate to benefit from the assistance of several. During the 2007–2008 academic year, Samuel Eckstein (Johns Hopkins University) completed research on areas of the manuscript that were still in formation and did the bulk of the work on the notes at the end of this volume. I doubt that I would have finished this book when I did without his wise and thorough contributions to the project. During the summer of 2008, I was fortunate to work with three outstanding students who came to Shalem as part of its Summer Internship Program. David Denker (Georgetown University), Davida Shiff (University of Pennsylvania), and Zahava Stadler (Princeton University) read the manuscript, word by word, several times, with extraordinary care and often astonishing insight. Between them, they suggested several hundred significant changes and improvements. Discerning readers and capable writers all, they have improved almost every page of this book, and saved me from some potentially embarrassing gaffes. This book is infinitely better than it would have been without the work and diligence of these four exceptional students. In addition, my nephew, Benjamin Bardin (Columbia University), was the first person other than me to read a late version of the entire manuscript from start to finish. I'm grateful for his many valuable suggestions and corrections.

It goes without saying that the views expressed in this volume are mine alone, and they do not necessarily represent those of either the Shalem Center or any of those individuals who lent me assistance on the project. I alone am responsible for any remaining errors or omissions.

Several segments of this book were published as brief articles as the manuscript took form. I'm grateful to Gerald Burstyn of the *World Jewish Digest* for publishing the discussion of hope as a critical dimension of Israel in "A Country Called Hope" (March 2007), part of the discussion of Bialik as "Forgetting Our Faith" (April 2008), and the notion of Israel as restorer of the Jewish future in a series of articles titled "Israel at 60" (May 2008). The passage on the failure of Israel to speak about itself as a story first appeared in *Sh'ma* (May 2008). The chapter on Jews as warriors was commissioned as a monograph by the Steinhardt

Foundation for Jewish Life in 2006. I am grateful to David Gedzelman, Yitz Greenberg, and Bill Robinson for their thoughtful feedback on several drafts of the paper, and to Donniel Hartman for an invitation to present that paper at a conference of the Hartman Institute and the Steinhardt Foundation in the summer of 2006.

Though I know that it is unusual to thank the person who took the author photo, Zion Ozeri is more than a world-class photographer. He is a cherished friend. A former tank commander in the IDF, he has now become one of the Jewish people's most accomplished photographers, and of late, an insightful Jewish educator, as well. Zion and I have spent many early mornings in his family's kitchen talking about this book, with him asking about its contents, prodding me to make progress, and ultimately, congratulating me when it was done. I'm honored that his work, too, appears as part of this volume.

To Stephen Kippur, executive vice president at John Wiley & Sons, I am profoundly grateful for the initial invitation to write for Wiley, and for his support and encouragement throughout. Eric Nelson, my editor on both this and my previous book, is an exceptional professional who did much more than edit this book. He guided the concept as it matured, spent many months encouraging me to rethink parts of the book, and recrafted its form several times until we thought we had it right. I learned a great deal from him in the process, and remain profoundly grateful for his wisdom and his partnership.

Richard Pine, the consummate literary agent with whom I've had the privilege of working since my first book almost fifteen years ago, has become a trusted advisor and friend. I'm grateful for all that he has done on behalf of the books that I've written, and look forward to our working together for many years to come.

Translations from the Hebrew Bible are taken from *Tanakh: The Holy Scriptures, The New JPS Translation According to the Traditional Hebrew Text*, often with minor emendations on my part.

This book is dedicated to my teacher, mentor, and cherished friend, Professor Seymour Fox. I first met Seymour in July 1996, at a conference sponsored by the Mandel Foundation to which he had invited me. During that summer, he encouraged me to bring my family to Jerusalem for a sabbatical year at Mandel. Thanks to him, we came to Israel in July 1998, and we never left.

Our lives as we know them simply would not be were it not for Professor Fox's friendship and generosity of spirit. Seymour not only brought us to Israel, but afforded me a set of professional challenges and opportunities that were unlike anything I'd ever known. He introduced me to new fields of academic endeavor, encouraged and cajoled me, and lent our family advice and support in every conceivable way when we needed it. A larger-than-life figure to all who knew him, he came to be someone whom we all loved.

Though by no means Pollyannaish about Israel, Seymour had a profound and abiding love for the Jewish state and for what it had accomplished. Though often critical of Israel's leaders, its people, its mistakes, and its shortsightedness, he didn't have a cynical bone in his body. He loved this country, and he loved it unabashedly. He also taught me to love it—perhaps the greatest gift he could have given me.

I still remember the day that Seymour and I went to visit an Israeli general about a program we were inaugurating at the Mandel Foundation. We were in a conference room on an army base with the general and a few of his subordinates, when suddenly, they all had to leave. Seymour and I were left alone in the conference room, the walls of which were adorned with an Israeli flag, a copy of "*Hatikvah*," and an assortment of military paraphernalia and posters. It was quiet in the room. Seymour turned to me and said, with his imitable booming voice that intimidated most of the people who met him until they came to love him, "Tell me, Gordis. Why is it that every time I'm in a room like this, I feel like crying?"

He felt like crying, I'm convinced, because amid all the worries, he never lost sight of the extraordinary accomplishment that Israel is. Not a particularly theological person, Seymour simply knew that Israel was miraculous.

Seymour Fox died suddenly, early in the morning on July 10, 2006, two days before the beginning of the Second Lebanon War, and almost precisely ten years to the day after I'd met him. I feel extraordinarily blessed to have had his friendship for those ten short years. I can't fathom how different my life would have been had he not invited me to Jerusalem in 1996, and there are moments when I'm still unable to imagine living the rest of my life without his counsel and friendship. I hope that this book, which reflects some of his optimism sobered by realism, is the beginning of a fitting tribute to his memory. Somewhere up there, I'd like to believe, he knows how grateful I am for all that he gave me, and how much Elisheva, our children, and I loved him.

Elisheva and I arrived in Israel ten years ago with three small children who were not terribly thrilled about being here. Now, a decade later, one has finished the army, one is about to be drafted, and one is in high school. Our children, Talia, Aviel, and Micha, have made this country their own in ways that Elisheva and I will never be able to. We are deeply grateful to each of them for showing us the ropes no less than we've helped them make a life here. The views expressed in this book have been honed and have gained much nuance thanks to many hours of conversation with our children around the Shabbat table, in the car on family trips, and on many other occasions. For their profound love of Israel, their deep moral instincts, their keen intelligence and articulateness, and their devotion to causes far beyond themselves, Elisheva and I are enormously proud of each of them and adore them, perhaps more than they can know.

I doubt that it would ever have occurred to me to write a book about Israel and purposefulness were it not for Elisheva. Since the moment I met her, thirty years ago this summer, she has modeled— first for me and now for our children as well—what it is to live a life of purpose. She knew decades before I did that living in Israel would fill our lives with meaning in a way that no other place could. She has taught our children to focus their lives on the "big questions," and they are the extraordinary people they are thanks to what she has modeled for them. It was Elisheva who wanted to accept Seymour Fox's invitation to come here for a year more than any of us did, and it was she who announced in the middle of that year that she had no intention of leaving.

Thankfully, our children are now sufficiently mature to know what an extraordinary woman they have for a mother. If they are fortunate enough to find partners as challenging, nurturing, and loving as I did, they will be truly blessed.

When I was finishing my previous book, *Coming Together, Coming Apart,* three years ago, our daughter was just being drafted. Now, as I conclude this volume, Talia has just left the army and her younger brother, Avi, is about to be drafted. With Israel no closer to peace than it was when we arrived here, but with our lives about to change dramatically once again with Avi in the army, I conclude—on behalf of Elisheva and myself—with the words of the Psalmist (Psalms 121:4, 7–8):

> See, the guardian of Israel
> neither slumbers nor sleeps. . . .
> The Lord will guard you from all harm,
> He will guard your life.
> The Lord will guard your going and coming
> now and forever.

Jerusalem
July 2008
Tammuz 5768
60 years since Israeli Independence

Notes

The abbreviation "B. T." refers to the Babylonian Talmud.

Israel, Post Euphoria

The chapter epigraph is taken from B. T. Tamid 32b.

1 Victory Over Hitler (Tel Aviv, Israel: Yedioth Ahronoth Books and Chemed Books, 2007).

1 *"to define the state of Israel"* Ari Shavit, "Burg: Defining Israel as a Jewish State is the key to its end," *Haaretz*, Sunday, June 15, 2008, at www.haaretz.com/hasen/spages/868215.html.

1 *In a postpublication interview* Ibid.

2 *"Throughout the country"* Michael Oren, *Six Days of War: June 1967 and the Making of the Modern Middle East* (New York: Oxford, 2002), pp. 135–136.

4 *Barak made far-reaching concessions* Dennis Ross, *The Missing Peace: The Inside Story of the Fight for Middle East Peace* (New York: Farrar, Straus and Giroux, 2004).

4 *"Al Aksa Intifada"* This term is meant to imply that the war on Israel's citizens—riding public buses, sitting in cafes, and driving in their own private cars—was justified because of some attack on the Al Aksa Mosque. But Al Aksa, of course, was never attacked; the most that can be said is that Ariel Sharon's visit to the Temple Mount was ill-advised or provocative. Yet one could also argue (more convincingly, I believe) that in making an unarmed, nonthreatening walking tour of the area, Sharon was simply, and perhaps knowingly, triggering Arafat's long-planned response before Israel made a cataclysmic and perhaps irreversible mistake by giving Arafat more territory before the Palestinians had proved beyond any shadow of a doubt that they had no intention of letting Israel live in peace.

7   *"no chance of peace"*   Yossi Verter, "Peres—No Chance of Peace with the Palestinians," *Haaretz*, July 6, 2008, at www.haaretz.com/hasen/spages/998836.html.

8   *some excellent books*   By far the best of these is Alan Dershowitz, *The Case for Israel* (Hoboken, NJ: Wiley, 2003).

8   *Others have asked*   Mitchell G. Bard, *Will Israel Survive?* (New York: Palgrave Macmillan, 2007).

9   *fools and children*   B. T. Bava Batra 12b: Rabbi Yohanan said, "From the day that the Temple was destroyed, the role of prophecy was taken from the prophets and was given to fools and children."

1. The State That Reinvented Hope

11   *A recent study*   Steven Cohen and Ari Kelman, "Beyond Distancing: Young American Jews and Their Alienation from Israel," The Identity Project of Reboot, Andrea and Charles Bronfman Philanthropies, 2007 at www.acbp.net/pub/BeyondDistancing.pdf (last accessed on November 7, 2007).

14   *"At that the voice suddenly stopped"*   Amos Oz, *A Tale of Love and Darkness*, trans. Nicholas de Lange (Orlando: Harcourt, 2005), pp. 356–57.

15   *"My father told me"*   Ibid., p. 359.

16   *Hitler had not won*   It would be an exaggeration to say that everyone in Israel is conscious of this notion at every turn. Sephardic Jews, who came mostly from Northern Africa, constitute a large portion of Israel's society. And because they did not live in Europe, they experienced the years of 1938 to 1945 very differently. The Shoah does not have the hold on their memory that it has on that of European Jews.

19   *an echo of* "Hatikvah"   There is an irony to this anthem that most people today sadly miss, for to fully understand *"Hatikvah,"* one has to appreciate the biblical references that are at its core. At the beginning of the second stanza is a phrase that seems innocuous enough: "Our hope is not yet lost." But the phrase isn't as simple as it seems; it is actually a play on a famous biblical image, or more precisely, a principled rejection of that biblical image. In the passage from the Book of Ezekiel known as the Vision of the Dry Bones, there appears a vision of hope, of a divine promise that the nation, languishing in exile, will be brought back to life. But the Vision of the Dry Bones begins with desperation, not with hope. And in expressing that desperation, the prophet conveys God's message, saying, "And He said to me, 'O mortal, these bones are the whole House of Israel. They say, "Our bones are dried up, *avedah tikvateinu*, our hope is lost; we are doomed."'" The key point, for our purposes, is the brief phrase "our hope is lost." *"Hatikvah"* quotes it, and

misquotes it. It takes the phrase that says "our hope is lost" and renders it as *od lo avedah tikvateinu*: "our hope is not yet lost." Because many of the Jews who heard "*Hatikvah*" when it was first written knew the biblical verse and understood that the author of the poem had rejected the Bible's claim that our hope was lost, they also understood that the anthem was claiming that Israel was about more than mere life.

20   *Come, Hebrew Song*   The informal translation is mine. Original Hebrew lyrics taken from the insert supplied with the two-CD set by Dalit Ofer and Yoram Rotem, eds., *Four in the Afternoon: The Best Songs from the Radio Program* [in Hebrew], p. 16.

26   *The purpose of the trip*   Yossi Beilin, *The Death of the American Uncle: Jews in the 21st Century* (Tel Aviv: Yedioth Aharonoth-Chemed, 1999).

26   *Jewish college students suddenly pledged*   For a thorough discussion of the educational principles underlying the Birthright Program, see Leonard Saxe, Charles Kadushin, et al., eds., "Birthright Israel Launch Evaluation: Preliminary Findings" (Brandeis University: Cohen Center for Modern Jewish Studies, August 2000).

27   *posthumous victory*   Fackenheim's notion that there is a 614th commandment (a command added to the traditional 613 commandments) not to give Hitler a posthumous victory is found in his *The Jewish Return Into History* (New York: Schocken Books, 1988).

28   *And in thousands of cases*   The Birthright experience has been analyzed by several scholars, and what I've sketched here is my informal take on what is powerful about the experience. More detailed analysis can be found, for example, in Leonard Saxe and Barry Chazan, *Ten Days of Birthright Israel: A Journey in Young Adult Identity* (Hanover, NH, and London: Brandeis University Press and University Press of New England, 2008).

28   *to settle every Jew*   Between 1882 and 1947, in successive waves of immigration, some 543,000 Jews immigrated to Palestine, joining the mere 24,000 who already lived there. During the first three years of Israeli statehood (1948 to 1950), the average annual growth rate of the Jewish population was about 24%; from 1948 to 1952, massive immigration added 711,000 Jews to a population of 630,000. Many of these immigrants were Jews who had fled the Nazi death machine in Europe or Jews who had been evicted from Arab lands when the Jewish state was created. More recently, Israel absorbed a massive influx of Soviet immigrants. From 1990 to 1998, when the Israeli population was approximately 4.56 million, Israel took in 879,486 Russian immigrants, which created a growth rate of 19.3%. In 1991, 15,000 Jews were airlifted in one single day in "Operation Solomon," and smaller waves of Ethiopian immigration have continued.

29 *unfazed and unrepentant* Rebecca Spence, "Longtime Leader Breaks Glass Ceiling at Reform Seminary," February 9, 2007, at www.forward .com/articles/10045. In this interview, Ellenson, always the consummate gentleman and institutional leader, gives credit to his lay leadership, but those familiar with him and the challenges of American Jews coming to Israel at the time are well aware that it was Ellenson's leadership that single-handedly preserved the Hebrew Union College year-in-Israel experience.

29 *"Jewish national rebirth"* David Ellenson, "Solidarity Breeds Responsibility," in *Contact: The Journal of the Jewish Life Network* (a publication of the Steinhardt Foundation), vol. 5, no. 2, Winter 2003, p. 8.

31 *a 2008 report suggested* The report claimed that only 52% of men were drafted. The 48% who are not drafted include Israeli Arabs and ultra-Orthodox Jews. Among those who would be expected to serve, about seven thousand avoid the draft annually, the report said. Coverage of the report (in Hebrew) is available online on the Ynet site at www.ynet .co.il/articles/0,7340,L-3562509,00.html.

2. Jews Making Jewish Decisions

The chapter epigraph is taken from Shlomo Sand, *When and How Was the Jewish People Created?* (Tel Aviv: Resling Press, 2008), p. 30. The loose translation from the Hebrew is mine.

33 *the British did not use the word* Significantly, when the British undid this policy with the White Paper of May 1939, they did employ the word "state," writing that "His Majesty's government now declares unequivocally that it is not part of their policy that Palestine should become a Jewish State."

34 *Israel's greatest accomplishment* Michael Ignatieff, *Isaiah Berlin: A Life* (New York: Vintage Press, 2000), p. 182.

34 The Jewish State (Tel Aviv: M. Newman Publishing House, 1954), p. 38.

34 *The phrase "Jewish people"* Mordecai Kaplan, the father of Reconstructionist Judaism, did more than perhaps anyone else to stress the centrality of peoplehood in Jewish life. His magnum opus, *Judaism as a Civilization* (Philadelphia: Jewish Publication Society, 1981), first published in 1934, uses the term "civilization" instead of "peoplehood." But in *The Future of the American Jew* (New York: The Macmillan Company, 1948), Kaplan speaks extensively about peoplehood. See especially chapters 3 and 4.

35 *"We have honestly endeavored"* Herzl, *The Jewish State,* pp. 38–39.

39 *Department for Bequeathing the Language* See Rona Yona, "Zionist Terminology and the Jewish Sources: Berl Katznelson and the Creation of the Term 'Hanhalat Halashon (Bequeathing the Language)'" in *Hebraic Political Studies*, vol. 2, no. 4, Fall 2007, p. 448.

40   *whose Hebrew writing played a central role*   Monty Noam Penkower, "The Kishinev Pogrom of 1903," in *Modern Judaism*, vol. 24, no. 3, 2004, pp. 195, 211.

42   *the secularization of Zionism*   Hillel Halkin, *Letters to an American Jewish Friend: A Zionist's Polemic* (Philadelphia: Jewish Publication Society, 1977), pp. 199–200.

43   *"Jewish return to history"*   Emile Fackenheim, *The Jewish Return into History: Reflections in the Age of Auschwitz and a New Jerusalem* (New York: Schocken Press, 1978).

43   Humboldt's Gift   (Baltimore: Penguin Books, 1976), p. 7.

44   *"I shall never believe"*   Jean-Jacques Rousseau, *Émile*, trans. Allan Bloom (New York: Basic Books, 1979), pp. 303–304, as cited in Yoram Hazony, "Beyond Survival," *Azure*, no. 13, Summer 2002, p. 153.

45   *redemption of captives*   See the Talmudic discussion in B. T. Hullin, 7a, among others.

47   *"poor of your city"*   See, for example, B. T. Bava Metzia, 31a and 71a.

47   *deny entry and refuge*   Matthew Wagner, "Israel Not Obligated to Aid Refugees," in *The Jerusalem Post Online Edition* on June 6, 2007, at www.jpost.com/servlet/Satellite?cid=1180960626685& pagename=JPost%2FJPArticle%2FPrinter.

48   *vehemently disagreed*   "Professor Daniel Friedmann sworn in as new Justice Minister," in *Haaretz* (February 7, 2007), at www .haaretz.com/hasen/spages/822972.html.

48   *refugees must be admitted*   Yuval Yoaz, "Justice Minister, citing Torah: We must take in Darfur refugees," in *Haaretz* on May 29, 2007, at www .haaretz.com/hasen/spages/864566.html.

48   *what should constitute Jewishness*   The American Reform movement accepts patrilineal descent, i.e., claims that a child is Jewish if *either* the father *or* the mother is Jewish. The Israeli Chief Rabbinate and Israeli law do not, however.

3. The First War, All Over Again

The chapter epigraphs are taken from (1) Ali Waked, "Haniyeh After the Fire": Ynet on June 12, 2008, at www.ynet.co.il/Ext/Comp/ArticleLayout/ CdaArticlePrintPreview/1,2506,L-3554958,00.html (last viewed on June 13, 2008). The free translation is mine. (2) Yossi Beilin, "We've Already Had Cease Fires," on Ynet, June 12, 2008, at www.ynet.co.il/Ext/Comp/ArticleLayout/ CdaArticlePrintPreview/1,2506,L-3554712,00.html (last viewed June 13, 2008). The free translation is mine.

58   *Had we returned to the late 1940s*   The Fedayeen were paramilitary terrorists groups that conducted cross-border raids against Israel's civilian

population between 1949 and 1956. Approximately 1,300 Israelis were killed and wounded by these groups, who operated from bases located in Egypt, Jordan, and Lebanon.

62 *"In the midst of the battles"* Yonatan Bassi, "The Blessings of Jacob, or the Prophecies of Jacob," *Shabbat Shalom*, no. 479; *Parashat Ve-hechi* 5767, January 6, 2007.

4. A Nation That Dwells Alone

The chapter epigraphs are taken from (1) John Mearsheimer and Stephen M. Walt, "The Israel Lobby and U.S. Foreign Policy," at http://ksgnotes1.harvard.edu/Research/wpaper.nsf/rwp/RWP06–011, pp. 5–6. (2) Joshua Teitelbaum, "Analysis: Iran's Talk of Destroying Israel Must Not Get Lost in Translation," *Jerusalem Post*, June 22, 2008, at www.jpost.com/servlet/Satellite?apage=2&cid =1213794295236&pagename=JPost%2FJPArticle%2FShowFull.

66 *American Israel "lobby" had a "stranglehold"* Mearsheimer and Walt, "The Israel Lobby and U.S. Foreign Policy," p. 18.

66 *a function of Jewish power* Orit Nir, "Professor Says American Publisher Turned Him Down," *The Forward*, March 24, 2006, at www.forward.com/articles/6806/.

66 *"The Israel Lobby and U.S. Foreign Policy"* (Farrar, Straus and Giroux, 2007).

67 *"The general tone of hostility"* William Grimes, "A Prosecutorial Brief Against Israel and Its Supporters," *New York Times*, September 6, 2007, at www.nytimes.com/2007/09/06/books/06grim.html.

67 *"Anyone familiar with the tortured history"* Tim Rutten, "Israel's Lobby as Scapegoat," *Los Angeles Times*, September 12, 2007, at http://articles.latimes.com/2007/09/12/calendar/et-rutten12.

67 *"it's a narrative that recounts"* David Remnick, "The Lobby," *New Yorker*, September 3, 2007, at www.newyorker.com/talk/comment/2007/09/03/070903taco_talk_remnick.

68 *from* Commentary *on the right* An assortment of the reviews includes Christopher Hitchens, "Overstating Jewish Power," *Slate*, March 27, 2006, at www.slate.com/id/2138741; Eliot A. Cohen, "Yes, It's Anti-Semitic," *Washington Post*, April 5, 2006, p. A23, at www.washingtonpost.com/wp-dyn/content/article/2006/04/04/AR2006040401282.html; Tony Judt, "A Lobby, Not a Conspiracy," *New York Times*, April 19, 2006, at www.nytimes.com/2006/04/19/opinion/19judt.html; Gabriel Schoenfeld, "Dual Loyalty and the 'Israel Lobby,'" *Commentary*, November 2006, at www.commentarymagazine.com/viewarticle.cfm/Dual-Loyalty-and-the—Israel-Lobby—10136?search=1; and, slightly more positive than the others, Philip Weiss, "Ferment Over

'The Israel Lobby,'" *The Nation*, April 27, 2006, at www.thenation
.com/doc/20060515/weiss.

68   *a* New York Times *best-seller*   According to the Amazon.com Web site
viewed on August 31, 2007.

69   *"a people that dwells alone"*   I have emended the JPS translation slightly.
Balaam, the seer engaged by the Moabite king, Balak, to curse Israel, saw
"a people that dwells alone" as one of Israel's great strengths. To many
Israelis, however, matters feel very different.

69   *"Today I have come"*   The transcript of Yassir Arafat's speech is widely
available, including at http://select.nytimes.com/mem/archive/pdf?res=
F50E15FA3F5D12738DDDAD0994D9415B848BF1D3.

70   *"the United States will not abide"*   Martin Gilbert, *Israel: A History* (New
York: William Morrow, 1998), p. 467.

70   *"Since my people entrusted me"*   Remarks by Yassir Arafat on receiving
the Nobel Prize for Peace in Oslo, December 10, 1994.

71   *"The World Conference recognizes"*   The draft resolution is on the
New York Times Web site at http://query.nytimes.com/gst/fullpage
.html?res=980CE4D91639F937A3575AC0A9679C8B63.

72   *"Palestinians accuse Israel"*   Suzanne Goldenberg, "The Lunar
Landscape That Was the Jenin Refugee Camp," *Guardian*, April 16,
2002, at www.guardian.co.uk/israel/Story/0,2763,685133,00.html.

72   *"Blasted to Rubble"*   David Blair, "Blasted to Rubble by the Israelis,"
Telegraph (London), April 17, 2002, at www.telegraph.co.uk/news/.

72   *cartoon showing two identical scenes*   The cartoon is no longer available
on the *Le Monde* Web site, but it can be viewed at www.honestreporting
.com/graphics/lemonde.jpg.

73   *the ultimate outrage*   Annan is quoted in "Activities of Secretary-General
in Spain, 6–10 April", on April 10, 2002, at www.un.org/News/Press/
docs/2002/sgt2319.doc.htm.

73   *"the separation fence"*   The quote may be found in the November 15, 2007,
report of the Intelligence and Terrorism Information Center at the Center
for Special Studies. The Intelligence and Terrorism Information Center,
which opened in 2001, is part of the Israel Intelligence Heritage and
Commemoration Center (IICC), a nongovernmental organization dedicated to the memory of the fallen of the Israeli Intelligence Community.

74   *"wiped off the map"*   "Iran Hosts 'The World without Zionism,"
Jerusalem Post, October 26, 2005, at www.jpost.com/servlet/Satellite?pa
gename=JPost%2FJPArticle%2FShowFull&cid=1129540603434.

74   *"fairy tale"*   Alvin H. Rosenfeld, "'Progressive' Jewish Thought and
the New Anti-Semitism," American Jewish Committee, December
2006, at www.ajc.org/atf/cf/%7B42D75369-D582–4380–8395-
D25925B85EAF%7D/PROGRESSIVE_JEWISH_THOUGHT.PDF,

p. 1. The following discussion of anti-Zionism among "progressive Jews" is deeply indebted to Rosenfeld's essay.

74   *"if one day"*   Joshua Teitelbaum, "Analysis: Iran's Talk of Destroying Israel Must Not Get Lost in Translation," *Jerusalem Post*, June 22, 2008, at www.jpost.com/servlet/Satellite?apage=2&cid=1213794295236&pagename=JPost%2FJPArticle%2FShowFull. See also Joshua Teitelbaum, "What Iranian Leaders Really Say About Doing Away with Israel," published by the Jerusalem Center for Public Affairs, 2008, at www.jcpa.org/text/ahmadinejad2-words.pdf.

75   *The anti-Israel tenor*   Rosenfeld, "'Progressive' Jewish Thought and the New Anti-Semitism," p. 6.

75   *"we believe Zionism"*   Jacqueline Rose, *The Question of Zion* (Princeton, NJ: Princeton University Press, 2005), p. 72. Cited in Rosenfeld, p. 9. Rose is professor of English at Queen Mary University of London, UK. Her other books include *Sexuality in the Field of Vision*, the novel *Albertine*, and *On Not Being Able to Sleep*. She contributes regularly to the *London Review of Books*, and wrote and presented the documentary "Dangerous Liaison—Israel and America."

75   *same performance of Wagner*   Rose, *The Question of Zion*, pp. 64–65. Alvin Rosenfeld discusses Rose's claim and its manifest absurdity.

75   *boycott of Israeli academics*   Rosenfeld, "'Progressive' Jewish Thought and the New Anti-Semitism," p. 6.

76   *British academics said nothing*   These examples appeared as a series of advertisements in the *New York Times*, June 4, 2007, page A15, and were referenced at www.adl.org/boycott on that date. I'm grateful to my father for bringing these ads to my attention.

76   *"You are imposing standards on Israel"*   Asaf Uni, "Israeli, U.K. Academics Meet to Discuss Proposed Academic Boycott," at http://haaretz.com/hasen/spages/860902.html.

77   *"that shitty little country"*   "'Anti-Semitic' French Envoy Under Fire," December 20, 2001, at http://news.bbc.co.uk/2/hi/europe/1721172.stm.

77   *"We no longer recognize the State of Israel"*   Jostein Gaarder, "God's Chosen People,"*Aftenposten*, August 5, 2006, in English at http://informationclearinghouse.info/article14532.htm.

77   *European Commission survey*   Ambrose Evans-Pritchard, "Israel Is No. 1 Threat to Peace, Says EU Poll," *Daily Telegraph*, November 13, 2003, at www.telegraph.co.uk/news/worldnews/middleeast/israel/1445904/Israel-is-No-1-threat-to-peace,-says-EU-poll.html.

78   *"problem without a solution"*   Benjamin Schwarz, "Will Israel Live to 100?" *Atlantic Monthly*, August 2005, at www.theatlantic.com/doc/200505/schwarz.

78   *"Is Israel Finished?"*   *Atlantic Monthly*, May 2008.

79   *"The problem with Israel"*   Tony Judt, "Israel: The Alternative," *New York Review of Books*, vol. 50, no. 16, October 23, 2003.

79   *"[W]hat if there were no place"*   Ibid.

80   *Zionism is "so incendiary"*   Adrienne Rich and Jacqueline Rose are discussed at greater length in Rosenfeld, "'Progressive' Jewish Thought and the New Anti-Semitism," pp. 16–17.

80   *Joel Kovel   Overcoming Zionism: Creating a Single Democratic State in Israel/Palestine* (London: Pluto Press, 2007).

80   *"to be a true Jew"*   Rosenfeld, "'Progressive' Jewish Thought and the New Anti-Semitism," p. vi.

80   *Jimmy Carter   Palestine: Peace, Not Apartheid* (New York: Simon and Schuster, 2006).

81–82 *"not about their own existence"*   Cited in Ruth Wisse, *Jews and Power* (New York: Schocken, 2007), p. 184.

5. The Next Six Million

The chapter epigraph is taken from Benny Morris, "This Holocaust Will Be Different," *Jerusalem Post, UpFront Magazine*, January 18, 2007, p. 8.

87   *"Should the Reich become involved"*   *Encyclopedia Judaica*, vol. 8, pp. 853 854.

88   *"What you have today"*   "Cotler: 'Try Ahmadinejad for Genocide Calls,'" *Jerusalem Post*, March 18, 2008, at www.jpost.com/servlet/Satellite?cid=1205420721615&pagename=JPost%2FJPArticle%2FShowFull.

88   *"Ahmadinejad did not say"*   Joshua Teitelbaum, "What Iranian Leaders Really Say about Doing Away With Israel," Jerusalem Center for Public Affairs, at www.jcpa.org/text/ahmadinejad2-words.pdf, p. 6.

88   *"I don't think he is inciting to genocide"*   Stephen Walt was quoted in "'Israel Lobby' Authors in Jerusalem: Ahmadinejad Not Inciting to Genocide," *Haaretz*, June 13, 2008, at www.haaretz.com/hasen/spages/992363.html. Also cited in Teitelbaum, "What Iranian Leaders Really Say about Doing Away With Israel."

88   *"portrayed Jews as parasites"*   This comment, and the subsequent quotes in this paragraph, are taken from Teitelbaum, "What Iranian Leaders Really Say about Doing Away With Israel."

92   *they are virtually limitless*   Larry Collins and Dominique Lapierre proposed something similar in their novel *The Fifth Horseman* (New York: Avon Books, 1987).

6. Israeli Arabs in a Jewish State

The chapter epigraph is taken from "The Future Vision of Palestinian Arabs in Israel," published by the National Committee for the Heads of the Arab Local.

Authorities in Israel, at www.mossawacenter.org/files/files/File/Reports/2006/Future%20Vision%20(English).pdf.

96 *"Solidarity with these heroes"* Al-Hayat Al-Jadida, July 16, 2006, cited in Palestinian Media Watch at www.pmw.org.il/Bulletins_Aug2006.htm.

97 *"resistance is not terror"* Al-Hayat Al-Jadida, August 6, 2006, cited at www.pmw.org.il/Bulletins_Aug2006.htm.

97 *"What happened in Nazi Germany"* Ibid.

97 *the divide between Jewish and Arab Israelis* Gideon Alon, "Poll: 18% of Israeli Arabs Backed Hezbollah in War," Haaretz, August 24, 2006.

98 *Arabs are "the indigenous people"* "The Future Vision of Palestinian Arabs in Israel," published by the National Committee for the Heads of the Arab Local. Authorities in Israel, at www.mossawacenter.org/files/files/File/Reports/2006/Future%20Vision%20(English).pdf, p. 9.

98 *"Israel is the outcome of a settlement process"* Ibid., p. 5.

99 *even early Zionist leaders* Ze'ev Jabotinsky, "The Iron Wall," at www.informationclearinghouse.info/article14801.htm. Originally published in Russian under the title "*O Zheleznoi Stene in Rassvyet*" on November 4, 1923, and in English in *The Jewish Herald* (South Africa) on November 26, 1937.

99 *proposed a constitution for Israel* "The Democratic Constitution," published by Adalah: The Legal Center for Arab Minority Rights in Israel, at www.adalah.org/eng/democratic_constitution-e.pdf.

99 *"The State of Israel must recognize"* "The Democratic Constitution," pp. 4–9.

100 *A third document* Yousef T. Jabareen, "An Equal Constitution for All? On a Constitution and Collective Rights for Arab Citizens in Israel," at www.mossawacenter.org/files/files/File/An%20Equal%20Constitution%20For%20All.pdf.

100 *"The Jewish majority must remember"* "An Equal Constitution for All?" p. 21.

100 *declaring that Israel* Ibid., p. 33.

100 *"This is an exclusive Jewish-Zionist anthem"* Ibid., p. 35.

100 *"allocating immigration and citizenship"* Ibid., p. 77.

100 *politically left-leaning Israeli author-activists* David Grossman and Amos Oz, quoted by Ari Shavit, "Elective Affinities / Reality Bites," Haaretz, January 10, 2003, at www.haaretz.com/hasen/pages/ShArt.jhtml?itemNo=250055&contrassID=2&subContrassID=14&sbSubContrassID=0&listSrc=Y.

100 *a fourth document* "The Haifa Declaration," at www.mada-research.org/archive/haifaenglish.pdf. The English version of the document online is not dated or given page numbers, but the date of publication is mentioned by al-Tayb 'Anim in his article "Four Documents, One Position" [in Hebrew] in *Eretz Acheret*, April-May 2007, p. 19.

102   *"is not the Arab minority itself"*   Richard Boudreaux, "Arabs Say Israel Is Not Just For Jews," *Los Angeles Times*, February 22, 2007, at www .latimes.com/news/printedition/la-fg-arabs22feb22,1,4741929,full.story.

102   *"equality is not the issue"*   Ibid.

102   *"We pushed the Arab citizens"*   Avi Sagi and Yedidyah Stern, "We Are Not Strangers in Our Homeland," *Haaretz,* March 24, 2007, at www.haaretz .com/hasen/objects/pages/PrintArticleEn.jhtml?itemNo=841287.

103   *"Accordingly, they launch"*   Ibid.

103   *"The Arab elite"*   Ibid.

104   *"You lost me"*   See, for example, Galit Nadav, "You Lost Me," in *Eretz Acheret* issue on the Vision for Israeli Arabs, April–May 2007, pp. 20–22.

104   *Some Israeli Arab leaders were not willing*   Azmi Bishara, "We Arabs Are the Original Owners of This Land," *Jerusalem Post,* April 13, 2007, at www.jpost.com/servlet/Satellite?cid=1176152787106&pagename=JPos t%2FJPArticle%2FshowFull.

105   *"Just as the Moslems liberated Jerusalem"*   Ali Waked, "MK Tsartsur: If We Organize Correctly, We Will Liberate Jerusalem," at www.ynet.co.il/ articles/0,7340,L-3377822,00.html. The translation from the Hebrew is mine. The quotation of Barakesh is from the same Ynet article; the translation from the Hebrew is also mine.

105   *expressed what many were feeling*   Amnon Miranda, "MK Schenler: Tsartsur's Comments Are Proof of the Hypocrisy of Arab MK's" at www .ynet.co.il/articles/0,7340,L-3377947,00.html. The translation from the Hebrew is mine.

105   *He was not alone in his worry*   Fadi Eyadat, "New Poll Shows 68.4% of Israeli Jews Fear Israeli Arab Uprising," *Haaretz,* March 12, 2007, at www.haaretz.com/hasen/spages/836427.html.

106   *In another incident*   Interview with attorney Ali Haider by Eatta Prince Gibson, "The Back Page" *The Jerusalem Report*, February 18, 2008, p. 48.

106   *American Jews on the political left began to worry*   Shmuel Rosner, "Jewish Money and the Arab Question," *Haaretz*, April 6, 2007, at www .haaretz.com/hasen/spages/845106.html.

107   *"womb of the Palestinian woman"*   Arafat's comments to this effect have been cited in countless locations. See, as one example, Bennett Zimmerman, Roberta Seid, and Michael Wise, "Voodoo Demographics," in *Azure*, no. 25, Summer 2006, p. 63.

107   *"Above all hovers the cloud"*   Nahum Barnea, "Olmert Calls for Unilateral Disengagement from Majority of Territories," *Yedi'ot Aharonot*, December 5, 2003, cited in Zimmerman, Seid, and Wise, "Voodoo Demographics," p. 62. Population statistics about the Arab populations in the territory captured by Israel are a highly contentious

issue, for they are often used to argue for or against Israeli withdrawal from these territories. To oversimplify, the basic argument is that the more Arabs there are in the territories, the more important it is for Israel not to hold on to them, because if it does, Jews will be rendered a minority in the State of Israel.

107   *In a much-discussed article*   Sergio DellaPergola, "Demographic Trends in Israel and Palestine: Prospects and Policy Implications," in *The American Jewish Yearbook 2003* (New York and Philadelphia: The American Jewish Committee and the Jewish Publication Society, 2003), p. 3. This article is also available at http://ajcarchives.org/ AJC_DATA/Files/2003_3_SpecialArticles.pdf. For a very different set of prognoses, particularly regarding the demographics of the territories, see Zimmerman, Seid, and Wise, "Voodoo Demographics," and DellaPergola's response in "Correspondence" in *Azure*, no. 27, Winter 2007, pp. 3–21.

107   *"An emerging Israeli Arab minority"*   Ibid, p. 43.

108   *"new historians"*   This group is eloquently described in the *New York Times* in the following way: "[T]he Israeli scholar Benny Morris coined the term 'new historians' to describe a handful of young Israeli writers who were recasting the standard Zionist narrative. Rather than a David-and-Goliath tale of outnumbered idealists miraculously outlasting invading hordes, they said, the story of Israel's triumphs was both more explicable and less heroic. Morris and his colleagues shifted the focus of historical inquiry away from the wonder of Jewish national rebirth to military and diplomatic maneuverings on the one hand and Palestinian suffering on the other." Ethan Bronner, "The New Historians," *New York Times*, November 9, 2003, at http://query.nytimes.com/gst/fullpage .html?res=9804EFDB1430F93AA35752C1A9659C8B63.

108   *debunked the Israeli myth*   Benny Morris, *The Birth of the Palestinian Refugee Problem, 1947–1949* (Cambridge, UK: Cambridge University Press, 1989).

109   *"I think he made a serious historical mistake"*   Ari Shavit, "Survival of the Fittest (an interview with Benny Morris)," *Haaretz,* January 9, 2004, at www.haaretz.com/hasen/pages/ShArt.jhtml?itemNo= 380986&contrassID=2.

110   *"We dispossessed no Arabs"*   Golda Meir, "On the Palestinians," *New York Times,* January 14, 1976, p. 35, also at http://select.nytimes.com/gst/ abstract.html?res=FA0F15FE355C107B93C6A8178AD85F428785F9.

110   *"We hear the constant repetition of the claim"*   Ruth Gavison, "The Jewish State: A Justification," in *New Essays on Zionism*, p. 13, reprinted from *Azure*, no. 15, Summer 2003.

7. The Withering of Zionist Passion

The second chapter epigraph is taken from Aumann's comments at the Seventh Herzliya Conference of the Institute for Policy and Stragegy of the IDC Herzliya, and can be found at www.herzliyaconference.org/Eng/_Articles/Article.asp?Art icleID=1842&CategoryID=223 (last viewed on August 23, 2007).

115   *technically at war with Israel*   These facts are well attested. For one arti-
cle of many, see Reuters, "Sudanese Refugees in Israel Face Uncertainty," *Ynet*, May 30, 2006, at www.ynetnews.com/articles/0,7340,L-3256713,00 .html.

117   *Israel's moral fiber*   Yeshayahu Leibowitz and John P. Egan, "Yeshayahu Leibowitz: Liberating Israel from the Occupied Territories," *Journal of Palestine Studies*, vol. 15, no. 2, Winter 1986, pp. 102–108.

117   *For complicated reasons*   For the most complete treatment of how Israel lurched into a long-term occupation of the West Bank and Gaza strip, see Gershom Gorenberg, *The Accidental Empire: Israel and the Birth of the Settlements, 1967–1977* (New York: Holt Publishing Company, 2007).

118   *"no recognition of Israel"*   The oft-quoted phrase is cited by Michael Oren, *Six Days of War: June 1967 and the Making of the Modern Middle East* (New York: Oxford University Press, 2002), p. 321. A lengthy set of references to Arabic language declarations is listed in Oren's notes; see note 21 on p. 399.

118   *"accidental empire"*   The phrase is taken from the title of Gershom Gorenberg's book *The Accidental Empire: Israel and the Birth of the Settlements, 1967–1977* (New York: Holt Publishing Company, 2007).

119   *"lethal to Israel's moral credibility"*   Tony Judt, "The Country That Wouldn't Grow Up," *Haaretz*, May 4, 2006, at www.haaretz.com/hasen/ spages/711997.html.

120   *the post-Zionist ethos of Israeli universities*   Yoram Hazony, *The Jewish State: The Struggle for Israel's Soul* (New York: Basic Books, 2001).

120   *"What we see"*   Interview with Yisrael Aumann and Aaron Ciechanover by Sever Plocker, "Israel's Downfall?" October 29, 2006, at www .ynetnews.com/articles/0,7340,L-3320959,00.html, first published in the weekend section of Israel's daily *Yediot Ahronot*.

121   *What most astonished him*   Amnon Rubinstein, "Home-Made Israel Bashers," *Jerusalem Post,* February 27, 2008, at www.jpost.com/servlet/ Satellite?cid=1204127193588&pagename=JPost/JPArticle/ShowFull.

121   *Israel was a "failed state"*   David Landau, quoted in Gary Rosenblatt, "Haaretz Editor Urged Rice to 'Rape' Israel," *The Jewish Week,* December 26, 2007, www.thejewishweek.com/viewArticle/c41_a1531/News/Short_ Takes.html.

121 *"If you will it, it is no dream"* The German *"Märchen"* does not actually mean "dream." Though there is no perfect English equivalent, it is also sometimes translated as "fairy tale," i.e., that which cannot be achieved.

122 *50% of Israeli schoolchildren* Danielle Singer, "Survey Shows 50% of Israeli Kids Don't Know Who Herzl Was," *Jerusalem Post*, June 30, 2008, at www.jpost.com/servlet/Satellite?cid=1214726166236&pagename=JP ost%2FJPArticle%2FShowFull.

122 *of all the peoples of the Western world* Barbara Tuchman's comment is in "Israel: Land of Unlimited Impossibilities," in her book of essays, *Practicing History* (New York: Ballantine Books, 1981), p. 134.

8. More than Just a Hebrew-Speaking America

The chapter epigraph is taken from Louis D. Brandeis, "Zionism Is Consistent with American Patriotism," in Paul Mendes-Flohr and Jehuda Reinharz, eds., *The Jew in the Modern World: A Documentary History* (New York and Oxford: Oxford University Press), 1995, p. 496.

125 *eleven minutes after* Benny Morris, *1948: The First Arab-Israeli War* (New Haven: Yale University Press, 2008), p. 178.

126 *"the Negev represented for the Jews"* Ibid., p. 53.

126 *Chaim Weizmann's plea* For a fascinating account of the conversation between Truman and Eddie Jacobson that led to Weizmann's visit to the White House, see Merle Miller, *Plain Speaking: An Oral Biography of Harry S. Truman* (New York: Berkley, 1973), pp. 213–218.

126 *"the greatest living democracy"* Morris, *1948: The First Arab-Israeli War,* p. 178.

126 *"It carries the shield of democracy"* See the speech by Senator John F. Kennedy at the Zionists of America Convention at the Statler Hilton Hotel in New York City, August 26, 1960, discussed in John T. Woolley and Gerhard Peters, *The American Presidency Project*, University of California at Santa Barbara, Gerhard Peters (database), at www.presidency .ucsb.edu/ws/?pid=74217.

126 *"Israel also has a large stake"* Speech by President George W. Bush, "President Calls for New Palestinian Leadership," in the White House Rose Garden, June 24, 2002, at www.whitehouse.gov/news/releases/ 2002/06/20020624–3.html.

127 *"Both nations were founded"* AIPAC, "The US-Israel Relationship," at www.aipac.org/Publications/AIPACAnalysesIssueBriefs/The_U.S.-Israel_Relationship.pdf.

130 *despite what Pat Robertson may believe* Pat Robertson, during an address to the American Center for Law and Justice in November 1993, called America a "Christian nation," and said that "there is no such thing as

separation of church and state in the Constitution. It is a lie of the Left and we are not going to take it anymore." His speech can be found at www.beliefnet.com/story/220/story_22001_1.html (last viewed on October 23, 2007).

130 *"May it be to the world"* Cited in William Kristol, "The Choice They Made," *New York Times*, June 30, 2008, at www.nytimes.com/2008/06/30/opinion/30kristol.html?_r=1&hp&oref=slogin.

131 *"the real tension"* The quotations in this paragraph are from Ruth Gavison, "The Jewish State: A Justification," in David Hazony, Yoram Hazony, and Michael Oren, eds., *New Essays on Zionism* (Jerusalem and New York: Shalem Press, 2006), pp. 23–24.

131 *"The idea of national self-determination"* Ruth Gavison's remarks at a meeting of the Burkle Center for International Relations at UCLA were reported on the Burkle Center Web site in a February 19, 2004, article titled "Ruth Gavison Offers a Vision of a Democratic, Jewish Israel," at www.international.ucla.edu/burkle/news/article.asp?parentid=7876.

132 *"combines the extension of civil and political rights"* The quotations in this paragraph are from Sammy Smooha, "The Model of Ethnic Democracy," Flensburg, Germany: European Centre for Minority Issues, Working Paper No. 13, October 13, 2001, pp. 24–25.

132 *"find themselves being used as fig leaves"* Nadim Rouhana, "'Constitution by Consensus': By Whose Consensus?" *Adalah Newsletter*, vol. 7, November 2004, p. 2, at www.adalah.org/newsletter/eng/nov04/ar1.pdf.

133 *"bundle of rights"* The phrase is Yoav Peled's, from "Ethnic Democracy and the Legal Construction of Citizenship: Arab Citizens of the Jewish State," *The American Political Science Review*, vol. 86, no. 2, June 1992, p. 434.

133 *"owe more than Justice requires"* Michael Sandel, *Liberalism and the Limits of Justice* (Cambridge, UK: Cambridge University Press, 1982), p. 179; cited in Peled, "Ethnic Democracy and the Legal Construction of Citizenship," p. 433.

133 *"of the Jews"* The phrase beginning "of the people" is commonly attributed to the U.S. Constitution, but that is an error. Its source is Abraham Lincoln's Gettysburg Address.

134 *"Jewish and Democratic State"* The "Human Dignity and Liberty" Basic Law was passed by the Twelfth Knesset on March 17, 1992.

135 *There were those who wished to see* Interestingly, a poll conducted in October 2007 by Keevoon, an Israeli poll and population study group, suggested that even voters who had cast their ballot for the most liberal of the major Israeli parties (Meretz) supported the proposal to continue

selling JNF lands only to Jews (45% in favor to 44% against). In the more centrist parties, the rate was closer to 75% and above, and among the right-wing parties, it actually hit 100% in some cases. See "Poll: 81% of Israelis Want JNF Land for Jews Only" at Ynetnews, October 11, 2007, at www.ynetnews.com/articles/0,7340,L-3458945,00.html.

135 *On the basis of that law* A third party, Moledet ("Homeland") was close to Kach's positions, but it was not disqualified, because the transfer that it advocated was limited to the Arab noncitizens of the territories and not to Israeli Arab citizens themselves.

136 *But the court insisted* For a much more complete discussion, see Peled, "Ethnic Democracy and the Legal Construction of Citizenship," p. 437; and Ruth Gavison, "20 Years to the Yardor Decision—The Right to Be Elected and the Lessons of History," in *Eighty to Shimon Agranat* (eds. Ruth Gavison and Mordecai Kremnitzer), Jerusalem: Graph-Press Publishers, 1986, pp. 145–213 (Hebrew).

136 *an ethnic democracy cannot sustain the rights of minorities* For a defense of ethnic democracy as legitimate democratic rule, see, among others, Ruth Gavison, "Jewish and Democratic? A Rejoinder to the 'Ethnic Democracy' Debate," in *Israel Studies*, vol. 4, no. 1, 1999, pp. 44–72.

136 *the civil and democratic rights of the Arab population* Peled, "Ethnic Democracy and the Legal Construction of Citizenship," p. 439.

137 *the Israeli Declaration of Independence* This translation of Israel's Declaration of Independence is taken from the Web site of the Jewish Agency for Israel—The Department for Jewish-Zionist Education, at www.jafi.org.il/education/50/act/bg/indep-MFA.html. For another excellent translation, see the Avalon Project of the Yale University Law School, at www.yale.edu/lawweb/avalon/mideast/israel.htm.

137 *"to trust people to know their own minds"* "The American Idea," *Atlantic Monthly*, vol. 300, no. 4, November 2007, p. 14.

137 *"the sublime notion"* Ibid., p. 20.

138 *"the American idea"* Ibid., p. 20.

138 *"If any one idea"* Ibid., p. 33.

140 *According to one study* Fact Sheet No. 2, Carsey Institute's Reports on Rural America, Fall 2006, at www.carseyinstitute.unh.edu/documents/RuralDead_11–8final.pdf. See also a discussion of this report at www.cbsnews.com/stories/2007/03/16/opinion/main2578529.shtml.

141 *A 2008 report* For a summary of the main findings of the IDF report on Ynet (in Hebrew), see the online article at www.ynet.co.il/articles/0,7340,L-3562509,00.html.

143 *"Rock of Israel"* See, for example, II Samuel 23:3 and Isaiah 30:29. Interestingly, some translations, such as that of the Avalon Project at Yale University (www.yale.edu/lawweb/avalon/mideast/israel.htm), render

this phrase as "the Almighty," or even "God," missing the point of the subterfuge.

144   *"social contract"*   Ruth Gavison and Yakov Medan, "Foundation for a New Social Contract: Between Observant Jews and Freethinkers in Israel" (Jerusalem: Avichai Foundation and Israeli Institute for Democracy, 2003).

145   *"the ban on the public display or sale of bread"*   Tzipi Livni was quoted in Ethan Bronner, "On the Eve of Passover, Bread Stirs Deep Thoughts in Israel," *New York Times*, April 18, 2008, at www.nytimes.com/2008/04/18/world/middleeast/18israel.htm.

145   *"still trying to define itself"*   Ibid.

146   *sixty years have passed*   For an interesting discussion of some of the challenges scholars face in writing Israel's constitution, and about the importance of their succeeding, see Daniel Polisar, "Israel's Constitutional Moment," *Azure*, no. 20, Spring 2005, pp. 15–26.

9. Israel's Arabs, Israel's Conundrum

The chapter epigraph is taken from Charles de Secondat Montesquieu, *The Spirit of the Laws*, ed. and trans. Anne M. Cohler et al. (Cambridge, UK: Cambridge University Press, 1989), p. 156. Cited in Yoram Hazony, "The Guardian of the Jews," in *New Essays on Zionism* (Jerusalem: Shalem Press, 2006), p. 38.

151   *"Our young state"*   Eliezer Kaplan is quoted in Benny Morris, *1948: The First Arab-Israeli War* (New Haven: Yale University Press, 2008), p. 52.

151   *"In my heart"*   Ibid., pp. 75–76.

151   *the British Peel Commission*   Ibid., p. 18.

151   *"[t]he only just and permanent solution"*   Ibid., p. 19.

151   *"From your entry to Jerusalem"*   Ibid., p. 197.

152   *"Even though he understood"*   Ari Shavit "Survival of the Fittest (an interview with Benny Morris)," *Haaretz*, January 9, 2004, at www.haaretz.com/hasen/pages/ShArt.jhtml?itemNo=380986&contrassID=2.

154   *"would a country be found for this people"*   David Ben-Gurion, *Like Stars and Dust: Essays from Israel's Government Year Book* (Ramat Gan, Israel: Masada Press, 1976), p. 147. The translation from the Hebrew is mine.

154   *That's a kind of real faith*   Yossi Klein Halevi, "Faith Hill," *New Republic*, July 31, 2006.

155   *Approximately 15% of Israel's Arabs*   The Central Bureau of Statistics of the State of Israel Prime Minister's Office published a report titled "The Arab Population in Israel" in 2001 that showed that 21% of Israel's Arab live in the Haifa District, of which Wadi Ara is the most significant part. The document is available at www.cbs.gov.il/statistical/arabju.pdf. Because of the obvious political implications of these demographic

statistics, the numbers themselves are highly contested. Estimates such as this 15% figure vary, often wildly.

155 *While they cannot permit themselves*   See Nachman Tal in "Strategic Assessment," published by the Jaffe Center for Strategic Studies at Tel-Aviv University, vol. 2, no. 4, February 2002, at http://www.tau.ac.il/jcss/sa/v2n4p5.html.

156 *their inhabitants would retain their rights to Israeli citizenship*   Yoav Rabin and Roy Peled, "Transfer of Sovereignty over Populated Territories from Israel to a Palestinian State: The International Law Perspective," *Minnesota Journal of International Law*, vol. 17, no. 59, 2008, p. 98.

158 *strategic reasons not to move the border*   See David Newman, "Demarcating an Israeli-Palestinian Border: Geographic Considerations," published by the Jerusalem Center for Public Affairs, Jerusalem, under the heading "Jerusalem Letters of Lasting Interest," Jerusalem Viewpoints No. 362, July 15, 1997, at www.jcpa.org/jl/hit10.htm.

159 *Jordanian forces attacked Palestinians*   Judith Miller, "Yasir Arafat, Palestinian Leader and Mideast Provocateur, Is Dead at 75," *New York Times*, November 12, 2004, at http://query.nytimes.com/gst/fullpage.html?res=9B02E7D61F3CF931A25752C1A9629C8B63.

160 *A recent Harvard University study*   Todd Pittinsky, Jennifer Ratcliff, and Laura Maruskin, "Coexistence in Israel: A National Study," published by the Harvard Kennedy School Center for Public Leadership, at http://content.ksg.harvard.edu/leadership/images/CPLpdf/coexistence%20in%20israel.pdf, p. 3.

160 *there was a transfer of populations*   As is true in the case of Israel, demographic statistics in the Cyprus conflict are highly contended and disputed. The figures provided here represent the standard ranges cited. Chaim Kaufmann uses the figures 200,000 and 60,000, respectively, in "When All Else Fails: Ethnic Population Transfers and Partitions in the Twentieth Century," *International Security*, vol. 23, no. 2, Autumn 1998, p. 151.

162 *Chaim Kaufmann, for example*   Chaim D. Kaufmann, ibid., p. 124.

10. Creating the New Jew

The chapter epigraph is taken from "Jewish Massacre Denounced," *New York Times*, April 28, 1903, p. 6., at http://select.nytimes.com/gst/abstract.html?res=F10713FC345412738DDDA10A94DC405B838CF1D3. Actual casualty figures ended up being lower than this initial description.

165 *Hayim Nachman Bialik*   For a brief description of Bialik's work in Kishinev, see Monty Noam Penkower, "The Kishinev Pogrom of 1903" in *Modern Judaism*, vol. 24, no. 3, 2004, pp. 196–197 and 210–211.

165   *"Is my wife"*   David G. Roskies, ed., *The Literature of Destruction: Jewish Responses to Catastrophe* (Philadelphia: The Jewish Publication Society, 1988), p. 162. According to Jewish law, if the wife of a *kohen* (a member of the priestly class) has intercourse with another man while she is married to him, he must cease sexual contact with her.

166   *"For too long"*   Max Nordau, "Jewry of Muscle," in *The Jew in the Modern World: A Documentary History*, Paul Mendes-Flohr and Joshua Reinharz, eds., 2nd ed. (New York and Oxford: Oxford University Press, 1995), pp. 547–548.

167   *"The Bible tells a heroic story"*   Moshe Halbertal, *People of the Book: Canon, Meaning, and Authority* (Cambridge, MA: Harvard University Press, 1997), p. 132.

167   *one of the earliest Zionist projects*   For a superb study of this phenomenon, see Meron Benvenisti, *Sacred Landscape: The Buried History of the Holy Land since 1948* (Los Angeles: University of California Press, 2002).

167   *photograph of a Jewish boy*   The photograph can be seen at www.shoah.dk/Pics/new_page_11.htm. Amazingly, the child did not die. His name is Tzvi Nussbaum; he is the child of parents who had previously moved to Palestine, but who found life there too difficult and returned to Europe. This photo is the subject of Richard Raskin's *A Child at Gunpoint: A Case Study in the Life of a Photo* (Aarhus, Denmark: Aarhus University Press, 2004), which posits four possible identities (including Nussbaum) for the boy in the picture. Excerpts from this book can be seen at www.deathcamps.org/occupation/gunpoint.html. The photograph was also the subject of an article in the *New York Times* entitled "Rockland Physican Thinks He Is the Boy in Holocaust Photo Taken in Warsaw," by David Margolick, May 28, 1982, at http://select.nytimes.com/search/restricted/article?res=F70A1FF63B5C0C7B8EDDAC089 4DA484D81.

168   *looking away from the wall*   I'm grateful to my friend and colleague Yossi Klein Halevi for pointing this out to me. See Halevi's account of the photograph, "The Photograph: A Search for June 1967,"*Azure*, no. 29, Summer 2007.

170   *Moses tells the men*   Exodus 19:15. Interestingly, by the way, that is not what God tells Moses to say to the people. This gender distinction is Moses's addition, a point explored compellingly by Judith Plaskow, *Standing Again at Sinai: Judaism from a Feminist Perspective* (New York: HarperOne, 1991).

171   *"Seesaw, seesaw"*   Daniella Gardosh and Talmah Alyagon, eds., *My 100 Songs: Best Loved Israeli Nursery Rhymes* (book accompaniment to a two-cassette package) in Hebrew; (Tel Aviv, Israel: Kinneret Publishing House, 1970), p. 10. The translation is mine.

172   *"Whoever reflects upon four things"*   Mishnah Hagigah 2:1. Translation from Jacob Neusner, *The Mishnah: A New Translation* (New Haven and London: Yale University Press, 1988), p. 330.

11. The Wars That Must Be Waged

180   *"Golda expressed more concern"*   Ruth Wisse, *Jews and Power* (New York: Schocken, 2007), p. 156.

182   *"too sophisticated a people"*   Cited in Wisse, *Jews and Power*, p. 112. Israel Zangwill (1864–1926) was a well-known political activist and Jewish writer, associated with the Zionist pacifist movement for part of his life.

184   *David Rubinger's celebrated photograph*   For a very insightful discussion of this photograph and its place in Israeli consciousness, see Yossi Klein Halevi, "The Photograph: A Search for June 1967," *Azure*, no. 29, Summer 2007.

188   *Judah and his brothers*   I Maccabees 4:59, in Edgar J. Goodspeed, *The Apocrypha* (New York: Vintage Books, 1959), p. 391.

188   *the celebration lasting eight days*   See, for example, Goodspeed's introduction to the Second Book of Maccabees, *The Apocrypha*, p. 443.

189   *"[a] miracle did not happen to us"*   The translation from the Hebrew song, which was written in the 1930s and is entitled "We Bear Torches" (*Anu Nos'im Lapidim*), is mine.

191   *Rabbi Judah Halevi, in his* Kuzari   From Kuzari 1:114–115, in Rabbi Yehudah Halevi, *The Kuzari: In Defense of the Despised Faith*, N. Daniel Korobkin, trans. (Northvale, NJ: Jason Aronson, 1998), p. 51.

193   *encounter with the tribe of Amalek*   For the best discussion of the treatment of Amalek in the Jewish tradition, see Avi Sagi, "The Punishment of Amalek in Jewish Tradition: Coping with the Moral Problem," in *Harvard Theological Review*, vol. 87, no. 3, July 1994, pp. 323 ff. Sagi is most interesting when he points to the changes in the attitude to Amalek wrought not by literary treatments of that people but by the need to engage with specific halakic and legal challenges to the injunction to destroy Amalek.

193   *"You may look small to yourself"*   I Samuel 15:17–19, with sections omitted for brevity.

194   *wars that* must *be waged*   See, for example, the Talmudic discussion in B. T. Sotah 44b. For a contemporary overview and analysis of the rabbinic discussion, see Reuven Kimelman, "War," in *Frontiers of Jewish Thought*, Steven Katz, ed. (Washington, DC: B'nai B'rith Books, 1992), pp. 309–332.

195   *the entire Book of Esther is read*   For a masterful treatment of the Book of Esther as a work of political philosophy, see Yoram Hazony,

The Dawn: Political Teachings of the Book of Esther (Jerusalem: Shalem Press, 1995). For a radically different, and not uncontroversial, treatment of the images of the Jews' use of power, see Elliot Horowitz, *Reckless Rites: Purim and the Legacy of Jewish Violence (Jews, Christians, and Muslims from the Ancient to the Modern World)* (Princeton: Princeton University Press, 2006). For an excellent discussion of what many consider Horowitz's errors, see Hillel Halkin, "Bloody Jews?" in *Commentary*, June 2006, pp. 40–48.

196 *the legitimate use of power* For an important book-length essay on this subject, see Wisse, *Jews and Power*.

196 *Jewish tradition has taken that seriously* For excellent discussions of the roles of war and peace in Jewish thought, generally, see Michael Graetz, "War and Peace," in *Etz Hayim: Torah and Commentary* (New York: The Rabbinical Assembly, 2001), pp. 1382–1389; and a response to that essay by Benjamin Edidin Scolnic, "War and the Possibilities for Peace," in *Conservative Judaism*, vol. 57, no. 3, Spring 2005, pp. 33–48.

196 *places soldiers immediately below rulers* See *Republic* 486b, 500c; *Apology* 29b.

197 *"It is a disgrace"* Ahad Ha-am is quoted by Monty Noam Penkower in "The Kishinev Pogrom of 1903," in *Modern Judaism*, vol. 24, no. 3, 2004, p. 194.

12. The Jewish State and the State of the Jews

The chapter epigraph is taken from Ahad Ha-am, "The Jewish State and the Jewish Problem," Arthur Herzberg, ed., *The Zionist Idea* (Philadelphia: The Jewish Publication Society, 1959), p. 268.

201 *Even in terms of personal practice* The following statistics are taken from "A Portrait of Israeli Jewry: Beliefs, Observances, and Values among Israeli Jews 2000," highlights of a study conducted by the Guttman Center of the Israel Democracy Institute for the Avi Chai Foundation, at www.avi-chai.org/Static/Binaries/Publications/EnglishGuttman_0.pdf, on page 7.

201 *"The sense of intra-Israeli"* Ibid., p. 4.

201 *Even the "modern-Orthodox" community* Ibid., p. 17.

206 *"In a relatively short period of sixty years"* Aaron Ciechanover, Letter to the Editor, *Azure*, no. 31, Winter 2008, p. 4.

210 *But when the rabbinate issues a ruling* Matthew Wagner, "Chief Rabbi Prohibits Single Women from Going to Mikve," *Jerusalem Post*, February 10, 2008, at www.jpost.com/servlet/Satellite?cid=1202246357590&pagename=JPost/JPArticle/ShowFull. In Jewish tradition, married Jewish women are expected to cease sexual activity from the onset of their period until several days after it concludes. Before resuming marital relations,

they immerse themselves in the waters of the *mikve*, seen by many as a symbol of the renewal of life that is possible as the woman prepares to ovulate once again. In this particular case, the rabbinate assumed that if the *mikve* were off-limits to unmarried women, these women would cease engaging in sexual activity prior to getting married.

212   *Israeli history textbooks*   Israeli treatment of the genocide in its education system is discussed by, among others, Yair Auron, head of the Sociology Department of the Open University of Israel (see his personal page at www.openu.ac.il/Personal_sites/yair-auronE.html). Of particular interest are his 2005 book *The Pain of Knowledge: Holocaust and Genocide Issues in Education*, and his 2004 book *The Banality of Denial: Israel and the Armenian Genocide*. See also his chapter entitled "Who Is Afraid of Genocide" in the reference book *Knowledge and Silence: On Mechanisms of Denial and Repression in Israeli Society*. It is also worth noting that when MK Haim Oron tried in 2007 to get the Knesset to discuss formal recognition of the Armenian genocide, he wanted the discussions to be held in the Knesset Education Committee. See *Haaretz* articles, "Knesset Panel to Consider Recognition of Armenian Genocide" at www.haaretz.com/hasen/spages/968844.html and "Knesset Opts Not to Discuss Armenian Genocide at PM's Request," at www.haaretz.com/hasen/spages/838167.html.

212   *Turkey has even insisted*   Marc Perelman, "Armenian Genocide Crisis Tests Tight Ties Between Turkey and Israel," *The Forward*, August 29, 2007, at www.forward.com/articles/11509/.

212   *no matter how different the case of the Shoah*   My point here is that Israel should not be party to denying genocide. But this in no way implies that the Shoah and the Armenian genocide are analogous. Indeed, Professor Bernard Lewis has stressed that the massacre of the Armenians followed a revolt by Armenians against Turkey, which was not the case, obviously, with the Jews and Germany. Furthermore, Lewis argues that while the Turks planned to relocate large Armenian populations, there was no intent to murder them, and that the Turkish government actually tried, but failed, to prevent the massacre. Why Israeli textbooks could not at least mention this is not clear. Regarding Lewis's views, see www.armenian--genocide.com/2007/10/professor-bernard-lewis-condemns.html and Yves Ternon, "Freedom and Responsibility of the Historian: The 'Lewis Affair,'" in Richard G. Hovannisian, ed., *Remembrance and Denial: The Case of the Armenian Genocide* (Detroit: Wayne State University Press, 1999), pp. 243–246.

213   *"being at once outsiders"*   Jed Perl, "The Troubadour Intellectual," *New Republic*, March 26, 2008, p. 44.

Index